DEVIL'S JUKEBOX

NEIL NIXON & OWEN WILSON

Typeset by Jonathan Downes,
Cover and Layout by SPiderKaT for CFZ Communications
Using Microsoft Word 2000, Microsoft Publisher 2000, Adobe Photoshop CS.

First published in Great Britain by Gonzo Multimedia

c/o Brooks City,
6th Floor New Baltic House
65 Fenchurch Street,
London EC3M 4BE
Fax: +44 (0)191 5121104
Tel: +44 (0) 191 5849144
International Numbers:
Germany: Freephone 08000 825 699
USA: Freephone 18666 747 289

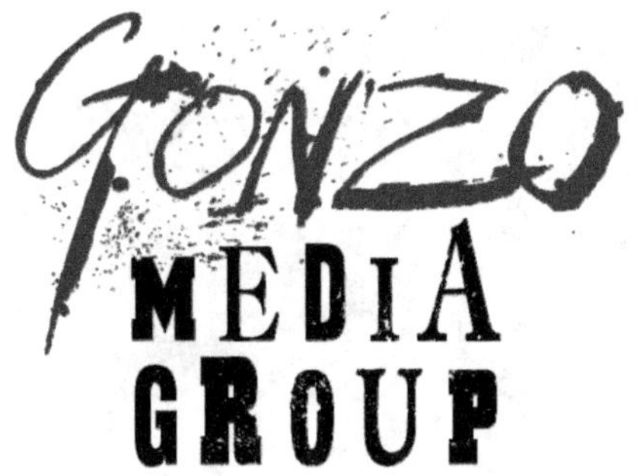

ISBN: 978-1-908728-56-2

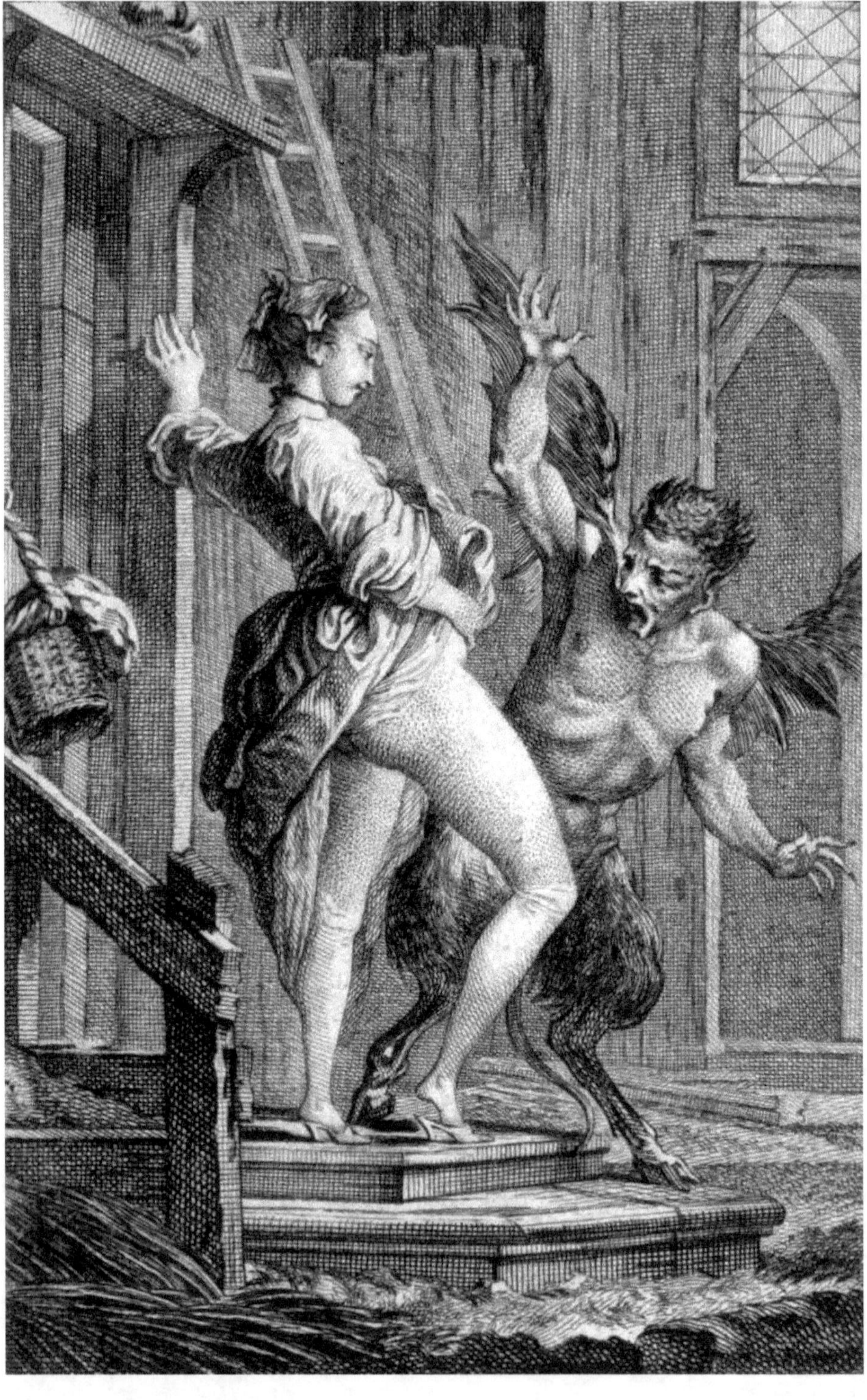

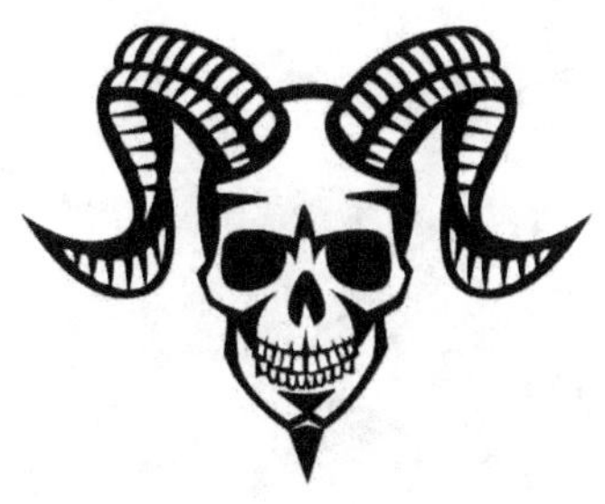

Thanks

There are a few people who responded to general queries from the authors for help to whom we owe a debt of thanks. Either the suggestions from these people ended up as choices for the book, or led to the authors finding other recordings chosen for inclusion. So, in no particular order, thank you: Matthew Watkins, Richard Clarke, Nik Hurwood, Stephen Potts, Les Wilson, Bradley Andrews, Ciaran McWilliams and Neil (Tribal Scream) Waters. Special thanks to Miss Kitty Grimm for original photography and cover design assistance. Thanks also to everyone who provided copyright permission for their artwork, website images and other pictures to be included in this book.

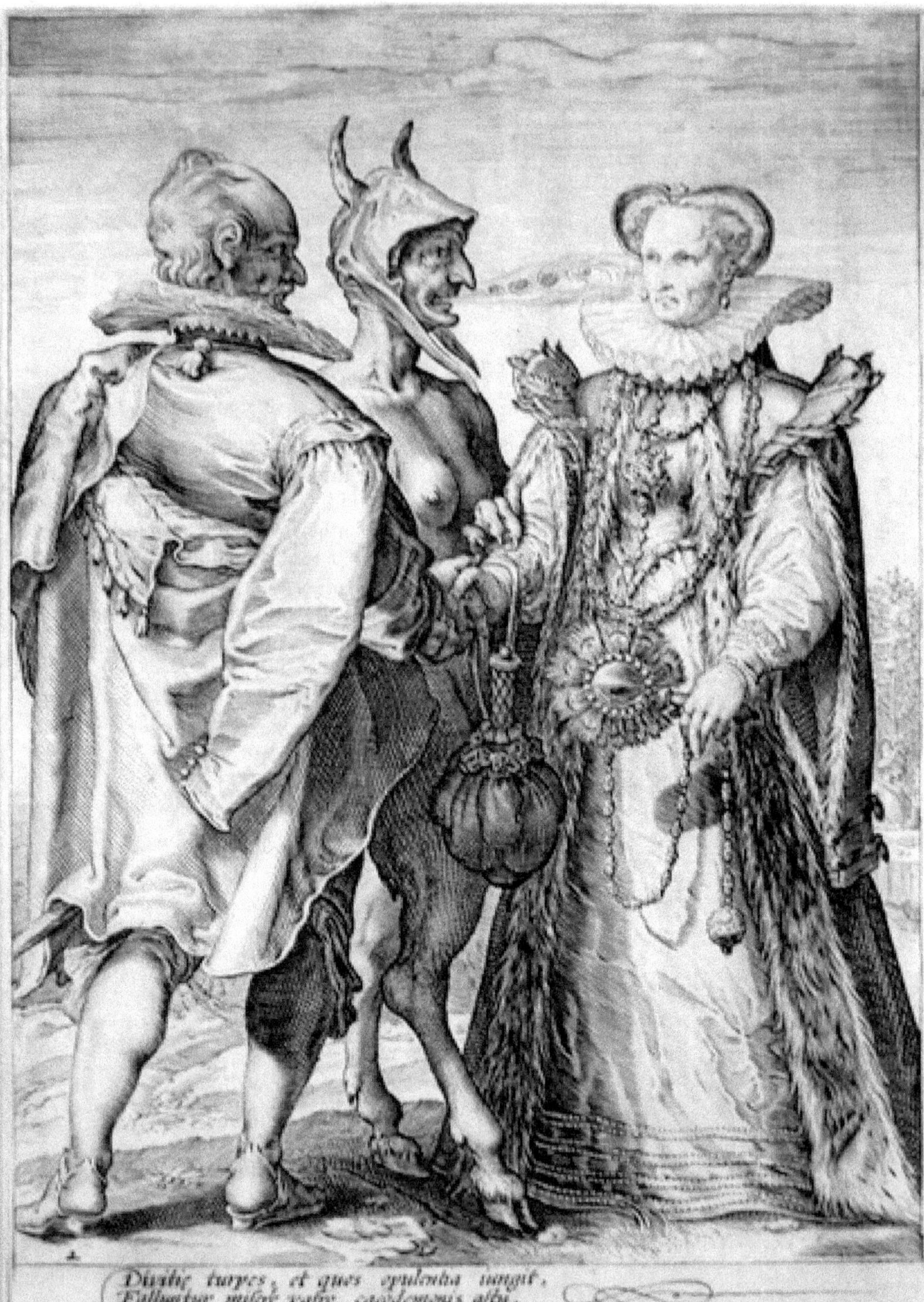
Divitię turpes, et quos opulentia iungit,
Falluntur miserè vafri cacodęmonis astu.

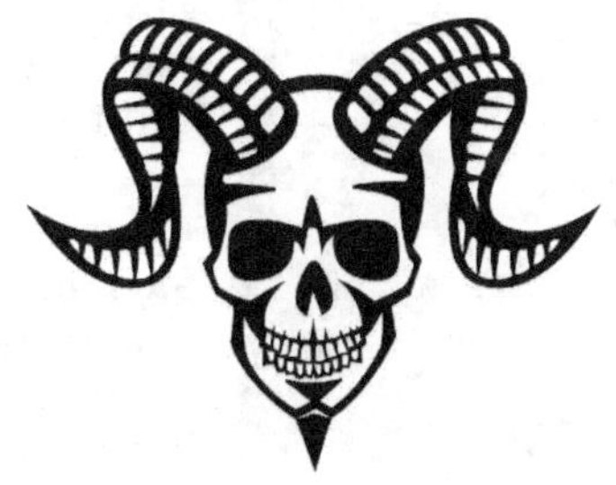

The Authors

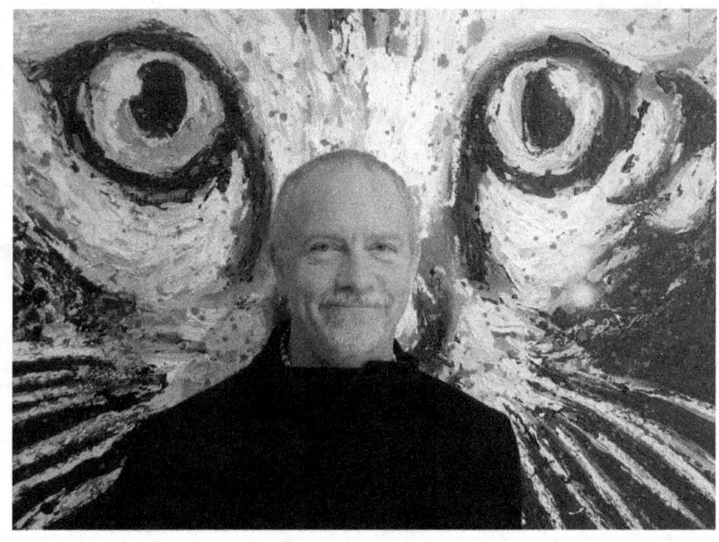

Neil Nixon: Thought up the idea for the book 500 Albums You Won't Believe Until you Hear Them which was published by Gonzo (just thought we'd mention it here). A while later he was trying to convince Gonzo to go with another idea when Jon Downes from their end said he had a title - The Devil's Jukebox – and wondered if Neil might want to give it a go. This was so much like the last project the decision was something of a no brainer. Once again the writing was mainly a case of downloading the sort of things that have been going round in his head since he could first process a thought. You could regard the knowledge displayed here as an impressive achievement or a cry for help. Either way, he's unlikely to change his behaviour now. When not writing books he juggles a range of jobs, one of which involves managing an undergraduate course in Professional Writing. A useful sideline of this course is the involvement with a community radio station – Miskin Radio – and the chance to present their alternative show, *Strange Fruit,* on which much of the music and many of the artists discussed in this book have been played. For those unwilling to chain themselves down for an online listening experience in a graveyard slot on radio *Strange Fruit* is also available on the web radio pages of Gonzo Multimedia (the people who publish this book). Neil has a website at www.neilnixon.com.

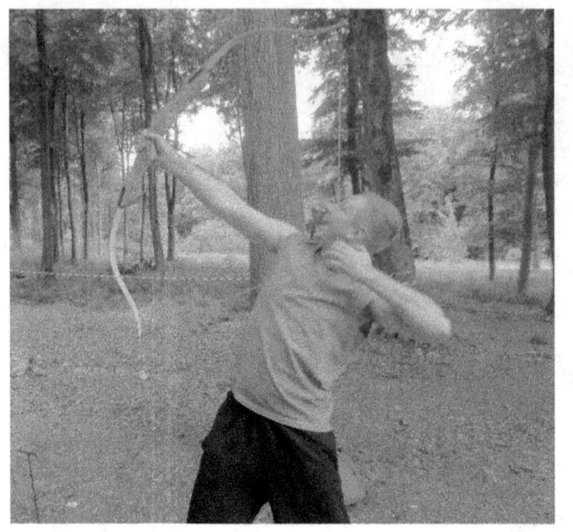

Owen Wilson: Grew up with his dad's music collection but has never been short of his own opinions. He had the good sense to make it to a respectable university (St Andrews) at the first attempt and study a subject (International Relations) with the potential to give him a decent professional living. Since when Owen has taken International Relations literally by living and working in more countries than many people visit in a lifetime.

After a few years hedge fund trading Owen now spends most of his working life in Universities encouraging people of other countries to speak English so well they can understand his books. It helps that some of these people have read the cult classic (well he thinks so) English to Go.

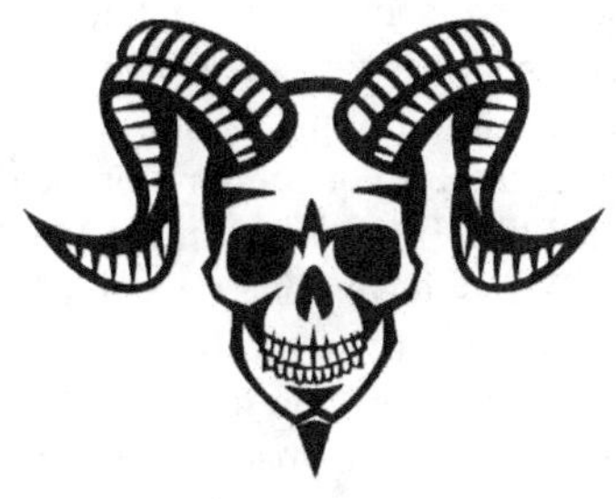

INTRODUCTION

"Please allow me to introduce myself, I'm a man of wealth and taste."

And what man of wealth and taste could bear to be without his own jukebox, in his own residence, showcasing a selection of the inspired, insane, eclectic and cultish; the totality of which demonstrates our man's wealth and taste to anyone who should happen to peruse the contents? Presumably the whole concept of this book needs no more introduction than this, so we'll go beyond the idea and make a few comments that might help you understand these contents more fully.

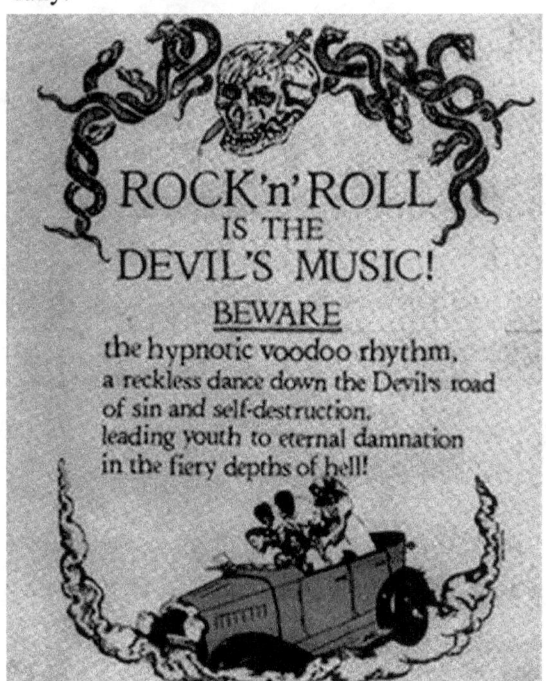

Firstly, this is NOT A BOOK ABOUT SATANISM. Granted, we've read up enough on the subject to be able to make some comments on it, and on figures like Anton LaVey and Aleister Crowley who have helped define Satanism and strengthen its links with the music industry, but the purpose of doing that was to provide more detail for the various entries. So, Satanism and Satan as covered in this book is a general idea more than any one image or concept. Indeed, some of the entries test our understanding of the Lord of Darkness and his evil deeds. Elsewhere we've included works highlighted by campaigners against all things satanic even if we, personally, think the arguments about the evil content of these works to be misguided. The purpose of doing this is to show that the understanding of what is evil in music has been shaped by people with agendas of their own, often agendas of only marginal relevance to music. One or two such figures, notably Jacob Aranza, have earned a degree of celebrity that they haven't necessarily sought or welcomed. In the case of Aranza, who wrote two books on the evils of backward masking in the eighties, his appearance in the online Encyclopedia of American Loons and the frequent derision heaped on his arguments and research (which often makes farcical claims; like Jim Steinman and Meatloaf being the same person or that Dr Hook were a "hard rock band") may have done good for both sides of the satanic debate. His outspokenness drew people to his argument suggesting that popular rock stars, often of the soft rock and high selling variety, were corrupting the minds of the young, especially in the USA. By contrast, the claims made in his books often made established fans of the music laugh at the clanging errors and some of his arguments, confirming them in their belief that their music belonged in their lives and those arguing otherwise hadn't a clue.

To put it succinctly, the Satan who owns the collection of sounds described in this book is a composite of everything people claim him to be. He's at times a decidedly old testament figure. At other times, vain; vaguely reminiscent of a general rotter rather than being some all-pervading Lord of Darkness and not above the simple twisted pleasure of remembering and collecting fuck ups from those who set out to wrong him (which is why he has Sir Cliff's greatest calamity on 45 rpm vinyl in the collection.) All of which makes him so inconsistent he can't possibly satisfy everyone's idea of how God's nemesis might operate. We're making no apologies for this because we've always seen this book project as a journey and exploration rather than a definitive trawl of Satan's favourite slammers. If anything here – like maybe Satan's guilty pleasures where Culture Club and James Last are concerned – really riles you, you might consider making your own list and publishing your own book. We'd probably buy it.

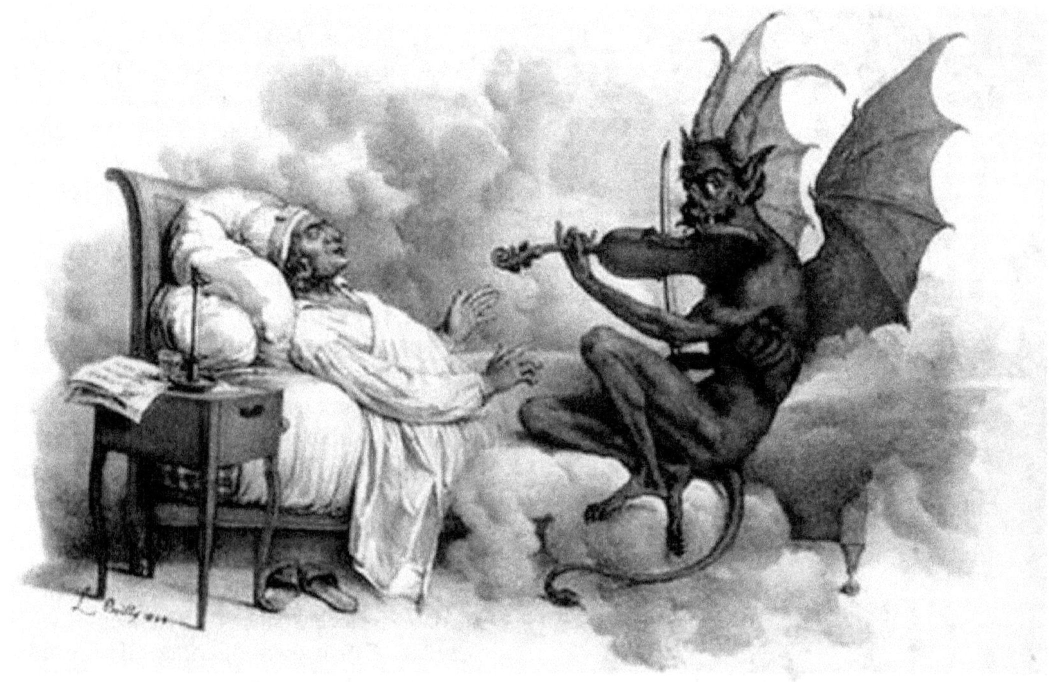

A few of the entries in this book draw words from an earlier book co-written by Neil – 500 Albums You Won't Believe Until You Hear Them – this has occurred because the information in the original entries is so relevant to the present book it seemed pointless to reword the odd paragraph. Apologies if you bought the earlier book and get occasional bouts of déjà vu reading about Burzum or the Louvin Brothers.

The purpose of this book isn't to offend, though there are works in here that were clearly intended to be offensive when released. Indeed, those of a gentler disposition, and – perhaps – anyone using this book for research rather than personal interest, might be genuinely appalled when they encounter works like Peter Sotos' "Buyer's Market." We didn't set out to make your life worse by including these. We did feel that ignoring them would be dishonest to the aims of the project and we reckoned that most of those motivated to buy this book could stand such discoveries if they were previously unfamiliar with them.

Similarly, we are not coming at this from any standpoint other than exploring the idea of how a being opposed to the main beliefs of the world's leading religions might view of the problem of stocking a jukebox with 100 tracks to offer suitable sounds for all his moods. Our arguments are included, briefly, along with enough details about the various recordings to allow you to find out more if you choose. We've assumed along the way that our typical readers are likely to be open minded music obsessives, i.e. the people our publishers identify as the most frequent visitors to their website and buyers of their DVDs, CDs and books. So there are occasions when we skip basic introductions to a particular musical act, or discussion of an album. On these occasions we do make enough of a general comment to allow those unaware of what we're going on about but interested to know more the chance to investigate the facts for themselves.

We've put in enough research to satisfy ourselves we know what we're on about, but we also apologise for any mistakes. Please be clear, this is a factually based book, drawn from research, but – from the descriptions of the musical sounds to the reasons these cuts make Hell's Hot 100 - the entries should be treated as opinions. These sound recordings exist, and we say enough about them to allow you to find all those that want to be found; though you'll struggle beyond all reason when it comes to obscurities like "Teenybopper Death (He Loves you Bernadette.)" But the discussions should be treated – for legal purposes and to avoid your blood pressure rising unnaturally – as just discussions.

Beyond that, we genuinely hope to enjoy it, get surprised, get amused and begin to think about which 100 records you reckon belong in the lair of the Lord of Darkness.

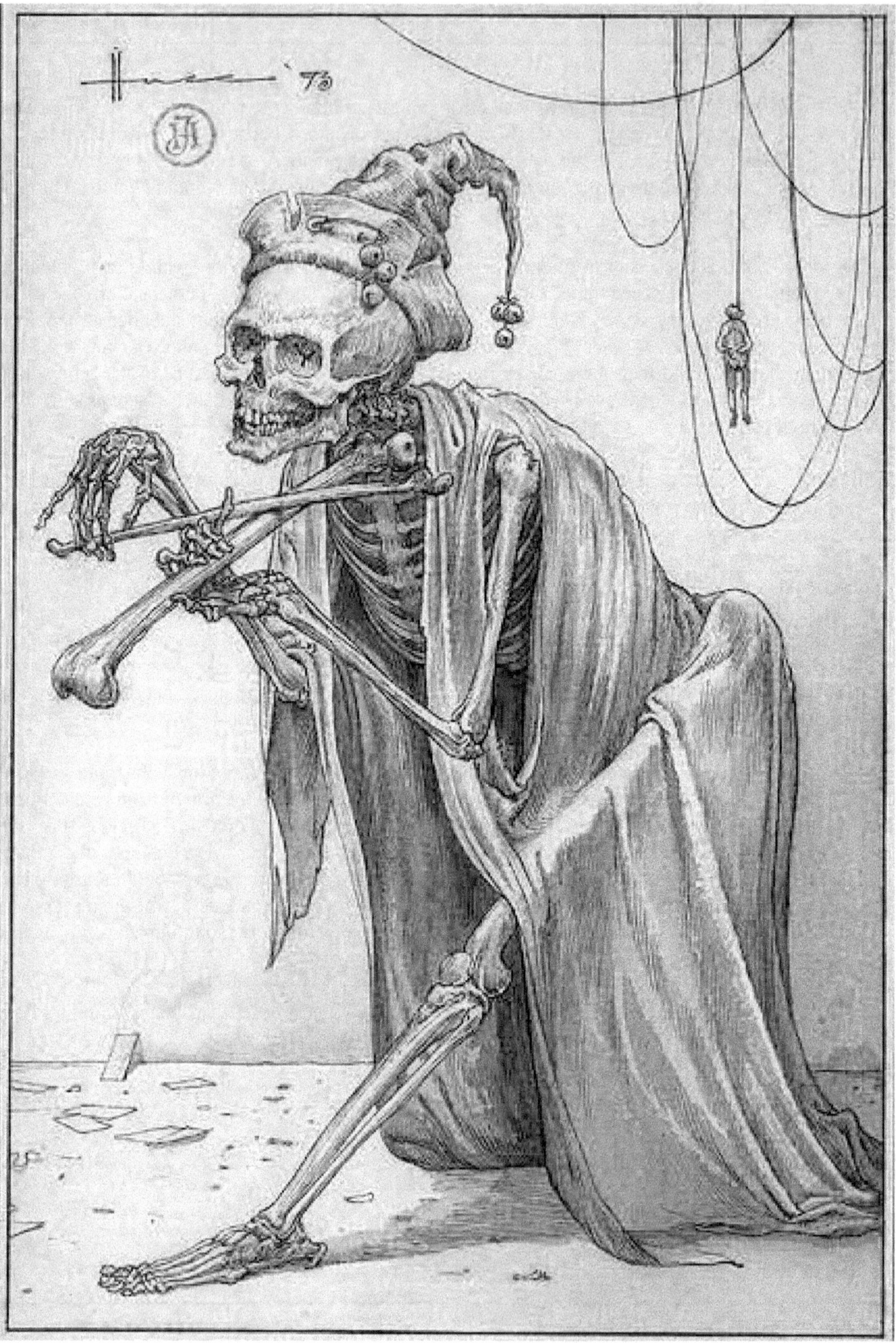

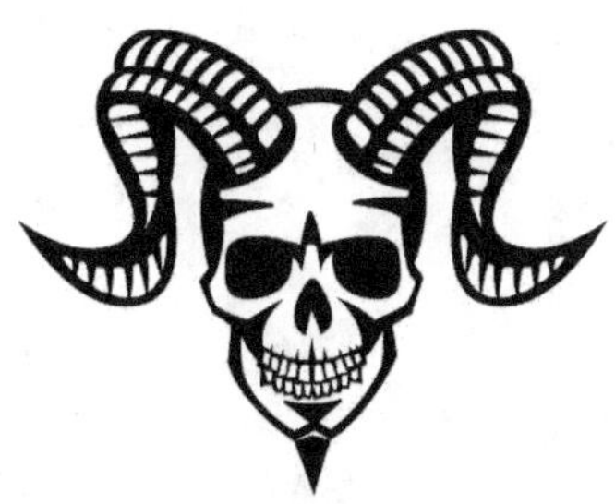

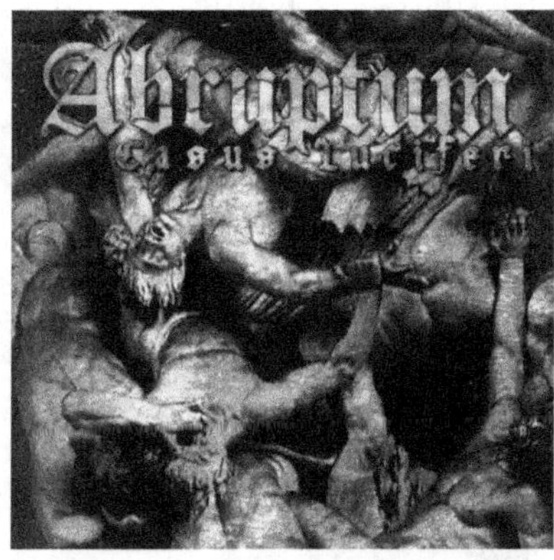

Abrumptum: ***Casus Luciferi***

Satan sez: Ooh, I'm going all déjà vu.

Abruptum started life in the late eighties, since when a stop start career and die-hard adherence to the extreme end of dark metal has kept them cultish and bred as much rumour and legend as hard fact where their career is concerned. The band's "demented dwarf vocalist" is featured on the first album "screaming as he mutilates himself in the studio" (according to Gavin Baddely's highly authoritative Lucifer Rising.) The similarly authoritative All Music Guide locates Abruptum in a bizarre middle ground between Throbbing Gristle and Darkthrone, a musical landscape seldom imagined, let alone explored. All Music...goes on to state the band are: "Responsible for what is quite simply among the most extreme heavy metal ever attempted, the group's 'music' has stumped many an experienced metal head with its brutal devotion to sheer noise."

The present authors concur and reckon any Abruptum would find favour amongst the Dark Lord's Desert Island Discs, so it'd be a shoo in for his jukebox. By 2004's Casus Luciferi (a four track work of relentless darkness exploring the original fall of Satan), the trademark style had hardened into a lengthy and unremitting exploration of sonic textures. Less blatantly extreme, more an exercise in the consummate mastery of audio disturbance in general. The title track from this album runs within touching distance of nineteen minutes, builds layers of guitar over unyielding funereal drums and suggests both a grim ceremony and lurking evil with its periodic explosions of screams or tortured guitar flurries. Speaking of evil; the band's current creative force is Morgan Steinmeyer Håkansson, a man who – for professional purposes – rejoices in the name of Evil. The self-mutilating dwarf (known as It during his time with the band, and perhaps better described as "diminutive") departed on their first hiatus in 1997.

In a world of wilful darkness and extremes, where every quiet Nordic hamlet appears to be home to some wilful bunch of church burning Satanists with their own recording studio, Abruptum (who started life in Finspång, Sweden) can claim some credit for both staying power and an adherence to their craft that continues to achieve respect.

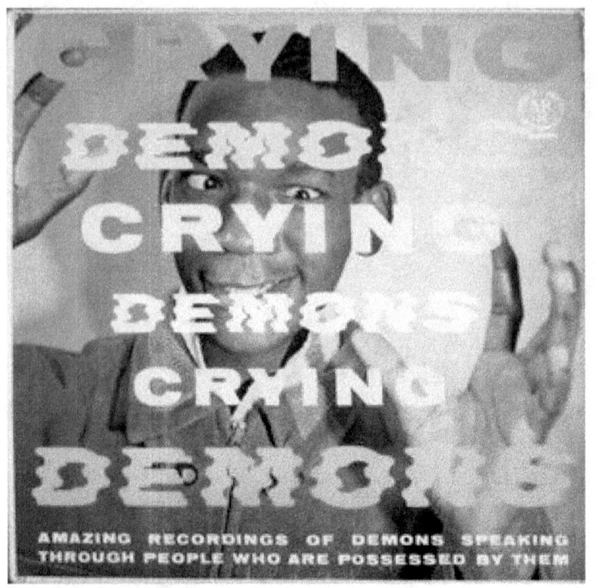

A A Allen: *Crying Demons*

Satan sez: Out demons out? (no chance baby!!)

Asa Alonso Allen (1911-1970) was a religious pioneer who played a leading role in the vanguard of evangelical preachers embracing the media. One of the first notable television evangelists, he also enjoyed a prolific recording career and had the sense to vary the content of his releases. This long player features Allen in full flow, literally casting out demons. His melodious, slightly rough-edged, invocations gradually beat incarnate demons to a standstill. The preacher is a showman with an inventive and articulate turn to match every development in the action. He anchors his work with biblical readings but retorts to the demonic interjections with the skill of a top comedian taking on a determined heckler.

An online appreciation of Allen notes: “Brother Allen's style was bold and outgoing. He sometimes wore lavender suits with white patent leather boots. His television commercials declared, "See! Hear! Actual miracles happening before your very eyes! Cancer, tumours, goiters disappear. Crutches, braces, wheelchairs, stretchers discarded. Crossed eyes straightened. Caught by the camera as they actually occur in the healing line before thousands of witnesses.”

Demons, then, were all in day’s work, and an album’s worth of material. Side one sees Allen cast out a particularly truculent spirit. The early exchanges have a parent/naughty child vibe:

“Go back to Hell from whence you came!”

“No I like it here.”

But, as the possessed woman moans and suffers Allen ramps up the rhetoric with some sterling one-liners: “Thou stubborn devil of lust, I rebuke your foul voice.” The moans and suffering get louder, someone in the congregation announces the departure of the demon and our previously possessed subject is able to talk to us after 18 minutes of Allen’s close attention. Whether Satan quakes with horror at this result, or roars with laughter at the cod theatrics and co-incidence of the whole malarkey lasting exactly long enough to fill one side of the original vinyl is the real question. We’re punting the track in here because we’re opting for the second possibility and imagining the Lord of Darkness enjoying this cut the way some clever criminals admire their own work when news reporters stand outside a recently ransacked bank vault and the police appeal for "any information."

The second side, incidentally, is a rousing sermon with interviews and a range of demonic intonations. All Hell doesn't break loose, but we do get a slight glimpse into how such an event might sound. So that probably sounds tame when your personal jukebox is located close to the real thing.

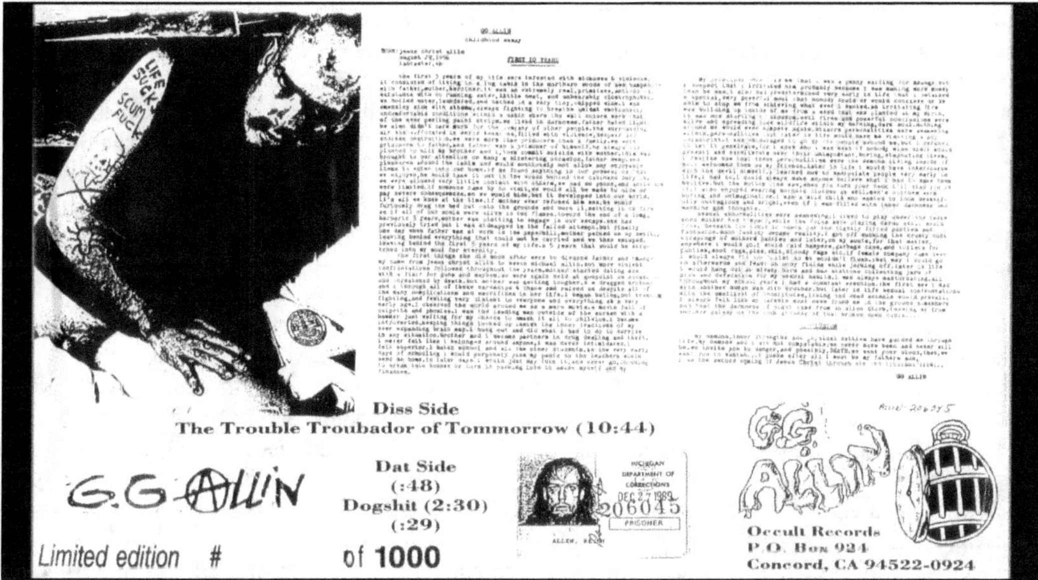

GG Allin: The Troubled Troubadour of Tomorrow

Satan sez: "Everybody wants to suck me off!"

Allin's demons pushed him through one of the most brutal and unrepentant trails of destruction in rock. Punk and extreme hard rock were his styles of choice though his work also took in spoken word recordings. Prolific beyond all reason and typically recorded with a rotation of backing musicians and minimal budgets, Allin polarised almost every audience he encountered. Any defence of his work starts by taking his claim to be the last true rock 'n' roller at face value, and seeing every element of danger and destruction in his work as art. Allin polarised the most libertine fan. It's one thing to support extreme acts, another thing to pay ticket money when the things thrown from the stage include fresh shit and the performer's naked body. Allin gigs often ended after a few numbers. Acts of destruction aimed at the venue were a regular feature. He treated fans and acquaintances in a similar way and regularly threatened suicide live on stage. A running annual event in the Allin calendar was a planned Halloween suicide at a live gig, he started these plans in 1989 but spent successive Halloweens in jail, unable to perform. He eventually died in front of fans, in June 1993, after a live gig ended in chaos and he wandered down local streets to a party, where he OD'd on heroin. Fans posed with his comatose body, unaware the ultimate monster was expiring in front of them.

His catalogue includes much work with varied backing bands – the Scumfucs, Shitkickers, Southern Baptists, AIDS Brigade and Cedar Street Sluts – most of it low-fi. "Classic" Allin albums like Brutality and Bloodshed for All are mainly full on punk, with Allin growling like a bear, there are nods to hard rock with grinding riffs and thumping drums. Tracks like "Anal Cunt," "I Kill Everything I Fuck," "Legalise Murder" (wherein he wants the right to kill a girl who chucked him) and "I Will not Act Civilized" are core Allin works, and not that far from the truth. Allin avoided one scheduled onstage suicide through being arrested for extreme violence to a girlfriend. The psychiatric report presented in his defence noted alcohol dependence and a fermenting mix of personality disorder traits linking narcissism, masochism and borderline elements. On that basis, the endless variations on brutality, sex, threats and anti-authoritarian rants in his lyrics can be taken as sincere and we can usefully assume the Lord of Darkness was acquainted with his career from the first to last note Allin ever performed. We might also usefully assume that Allin's prodigious output means there's another favoured cut awaiting upload to the jukebox every time the tracks are changed and that Satan always keeps one slot free for GG.

"The Troubled Troubadour of Tomorrow" is practically prog rock in comparison to most of Allin's outpourings. It's considered here because it's as much an insight into Allin the man as a song. "The Troubled Troubadour of Tomorrow" is over ten minutes of low-fi, live rant with screechy punk backing and improvised asides, pretty much a channelling of darkness and depravity that teeters on the edge of identity crisis throughout and makes clear the mental health issues and genuine demons that informed Allin's career. In this context, frankly, the ironic one-liner "everybody wants to suck me off" is the high-spot of this musical work both in terms of clarity and moral purpose. Seriously, it is that dark! The man was one of Satan's for sure and likely drops by, with a few others mentioned in this book, after a hard day in Hell to hang with the Lord of Darkness and listen to their own sounds.

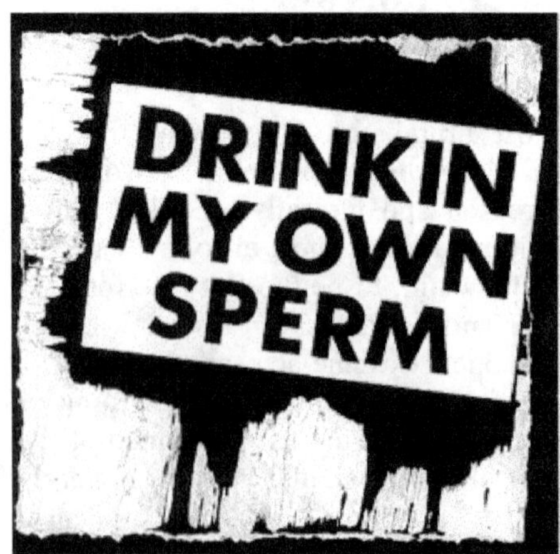

Alvaro: Drinking my own Sperm

Satan sez: Cheers!

Gloriously tasteless (the song, not the act described, which is full of flavour) and also a much-craved curio amongst cult records. This is the title track from a 1977 album by Alvaro Peña-Rojas "the Chilean with the Singing Nose." It's a joyous little meander with a backing track that collides basic pop structures and Chilean flutes, so it's both a standard catchy song and an ethnic diversion. Alvaro's accent stays strong but his phrasing and choice of words, "I drink my own bloody sperm" show an affinity with slang English, as spoken in the UK, and make the man sound all the more characterful. His main employment – as an advertising executive – also informs the lunacy.

The collision of eccentric music never veers into complete chaos. We get the sense of a character telling the story who is both out there and empathic enough to snag our sympathy. So the whole thing works like effective advertising and we're stuck with the notion of a lonely bloke, drinking his own semen. Alvaro claimed the whole thing as a revelatory story about his lonely life in late seventies London. But when his close friends and co-habitants included a pre-Clash Joe Strummer, you have to wonder how much of this song, and its parent album, is genuine craziness and how much a pose aimed at earning him attention in a competitive rock market.

Either way, like the encounter between the singer's mouth and "an old man's cock" that makes the Anti-Nowhere League's track on the Devil's jukebox a shock to the system, "Drinking my own Sperm" has the kind of vivid presence that makes it an unforgettable, and highly accessible gross out. Good for grim laughs, great for shocking any casual visitors, and good for providing some variety on those nights when the Lord of Darkness would rather not slam to the sound of mass suicide and Jim Jones' final, demented, sermon.

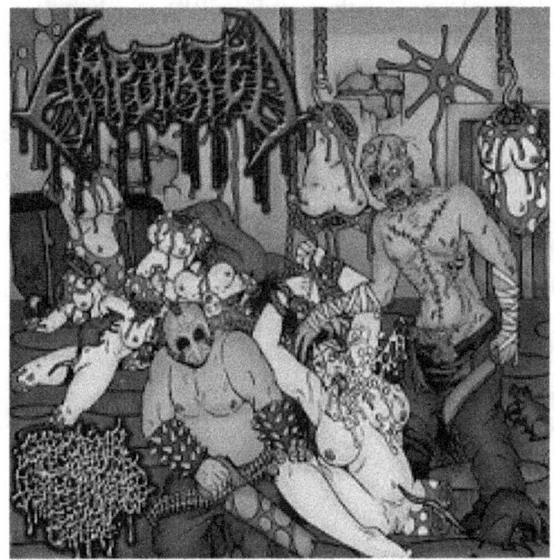

Amputated: Gargling with Infected Semen

Satan sez: Too many syllables in that title, it's a bit of a mouthful... ARF!!

If, by any chance, you're reading this tome cover to cover we'd point out early on that there's more to Satan's favoured listening than references to reproductive fluids packed into punk and goregrind songs. This track sitting between Alvaro and Anal Cunt is an alphabetical accident. Surprisingly listenable goregrinders, Amputated slow the tempos and match the sounds to the point that the slabs of guitar rise and fall without completely assaulting your ears and the drums have just enough cap on the crashing sounds to make the mix quite agreeable. Vocally you can't hear a damn thing they're singing, just the predictable growl and rasping interjections. Googling the lyrics for the whole Gargling with Infected Semen album delivers exactly what you'd expect. With regard to this title track the comedy pairing of a young female willing to drink it down (as in the sampled porn clip that opens the track) and the goregrind onslaught that follows her appearance are also part of the appeal. In a crowded market of competing atrocities Amputated's album – freely available on Bandcamp as of this writing – offers some of the best gross out laughs around. If "Gargling with Infected Semen" isn't exactly to your taste, there are other catchy comedic corkers like "Raped with a Jackhammer," "Menstrual Cunt Fart," "Projectile Beer Vomit" and "Uterus Swollen with Festering Putrescence." Face it, Amputated are renaissance men in a miasma of the mentally deranged and worthy purveyors of sounds to Satan's jukebox.

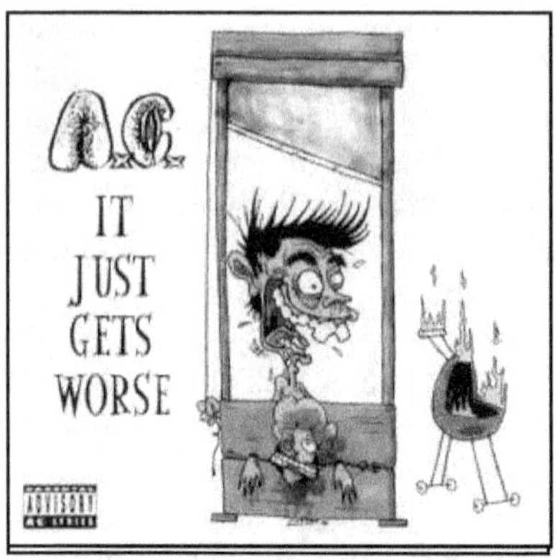

Anal Cunt: *I Snuck a Retard into a Sperm Bank*

Satan sez: One of my favourite bands; they just got worse!

If we ever get round to *The Devil's iPod* there'll doubtless be space for the entire canon of Anal Cunt (1988-2011), grindcore goliaths and general scourges of society. As for Lucifer's little jukebox; it's likely one Anal Cunt tune would make the top 100, probably on a revolving roster of favourites. We'll give this toe-tapper the honour. 29 seconds of total hysteria, blasted through at breakneck speed but offering up lyrics on the insert of the parent album – It Just Gets Worse – railing against a well-meaning "dyke" hoping to conceive with the sperm of a sensitive gay poet, and likely to find her liberal principles taxed to destruction because of the event that gives the song its title. It touches on enough taboos; misogyny, blatant offence, mocking the afflicted, homophobia etc. to be a touchstone work of an unrepentant crew.

Seth Putnam, guitarist, song-writer and chief deathgrowler with the Cunt died of a heart attack in 2011, since when the band have stayed true to their promise of not reforming, so, sadly for Satan, It Just Gets Worse may stand for all time as their definitive work. The parent album marked their sonic and critical high-point and offered up 39 audio atrocities in 33 minutes, though it also marked a head-on collision with a brick wall with regard to some of their ideas. Even the highly tolerant Earache label drew the line. One track; "Your Kid Committed Suicide Because you Suck" started life under the title of: "Connor Clapton Committed Suicide Because His Father Sucks". Cunt's macho, unapologetic and ultra-sick humour meant their parent label thought it expedient to censor some of the lyrics. Songs like "Body by Auschwitz" offer up lines like "You fat slob…here's the final solution to your flab" before the next thought is obscured by a massive sticker-print reading ANAL CUNT FUCKING OFFENSIVE.

The Lord of Darkness is likely to love every singular second of their output.

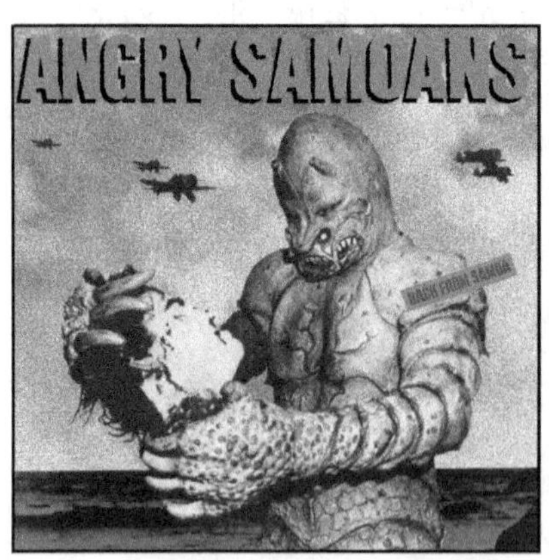

Angry Samoans: They Saved Hitler's Cock

Satan sez: Yeah, but the rest of him hangs out in Hell!

A gross out gem from the band's second album; Back from Samoa (1982). "They Saved Hitler's Cock" starts with yer man himself giving it large and loud in front of an adoring Nazi audience, stumbles into some scratchy pops and clicks as if from really old vinyl and then revs up in a punk style with really clear vocals in a grim fest of furtive fun. "They" saved the Fuhrer's manhood and it has been found under a rock, but it seems to have supernatural powers, including wanting to talk. It's debateable if the high/low point is the couplet that rhymes "choose its mate" with "Sharon Tate" or the line that suggests the cock survived so long because it was stuffed in one of Josef Mengele's socks. Satan's jukebox is stuffed with lengthy workouts in classical and rock style, so the short, sharp and shocking work of Angry Samoans makes for a change from the likes of The Grateful Dead. Back from Samoa boasts some brutally short blasts of punk; only "Ballad of Jerry Curlan" is still going after three minutes and a few other sonic assaults – like "Gas Chamber" - are up there with "…Hitler's Cock" for tastlessness.

The band's belligerence and don't give a shit attitude led to them being banned from L.A.'s top venues when "Get off the Air," their rant at Rodney Bingenheimer (who might have been a relic from the hippy era but was also a major mover and shaker in the music scene of the west coast) was unleashed on Inside my Brain (1980.) After which their self-serving, sicko humour and total disrespect became a trademark. Angry Samoans stand on Satan's jukebox for a whole raft of bands, before and after, who taught impressionable listeners that self-regard outranked respect to your elders, the worst gags are the best gags and all the reward you need is a bunch of normal folks waving fists in your face.

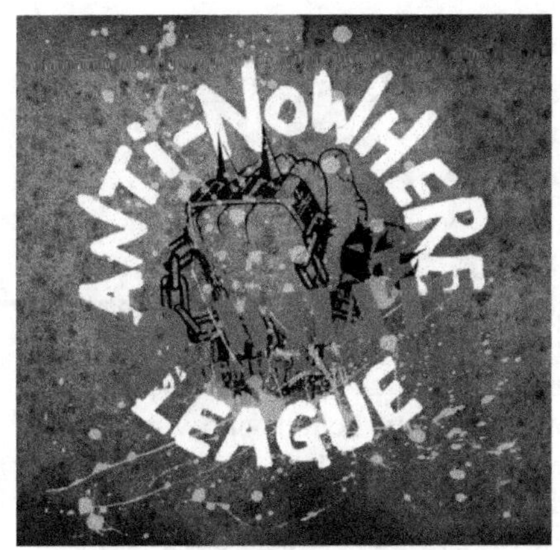

The Anti-Nowhere League: *So What?*

Satan sez: Early eighties hardcore punk anthem that's also a hit, sort of.

The "hit" status of this happy piece of hardcore punk is easily explained." So What" is so stacked with profanities and shot through with gross out claims that it was never going to snag any airplay. It's also the definitive Anti-Nowhere League (ANL) anthem. So, the genius solution to getting everyone to know and love it involved slapping it on the B side of the band's first 7" vinyl release in 1982. When the A side, their storming cover of Ralph McTell's folk standard "Streets of London," spent five weeks on the UK charts, peaking inside the top 50, most of those buying the single flipped it at least once, to be confronted with a driving punk stormer. A stormer that opens with the line "So fucking what?" before setting up a call and response lyric in which one set of achievements: "I sucked rock And I even sucked an old man's cock… I've fucked a goat, I've had my cock right down its throat…"

Are battered down with blank responses: "So what, so what, you boring little cunt…Who cares what you do?"

That pretty much is it. It roars along in this vein for just over three minutes, doesn't outstay its welcome and proves itself so damn infectious, funny and downright catchy that the lively variations on the gross and grotesque make a strong case for the cleverness of swearing and causing offence. The song blitzes through minor problems "I've had fleas" and equates them with worse "I've jacked up until I bleed" and makes every indulgent evil sound like one more inconsequential chore. It's possible to over-indulge any consideration of the song, claiming the whole thing as serious nihilism on the basis that everything is reduced to the same level of pointlessness with the steady "so fucking what?" retorts, but that's only half the strength of this song.

ANL named a tour after this song and their live career to this day sees them playing it to frenzied audiences. Metallica have covered it and it's a staple of their gigs too. Both bands prompt and indulge audience response. That, basically, is why this one makes the Hell's 100. If ever a tasty, sugared and infectious pill, was perfectly honed to drag good timers over to the darkside then "So What" is that animal. A youngster giggling over a first hearing of this catchy corker is someone who may well start imaging spewing up on "a pint of piss" or lingering on the speculation of how, exactly, and old man's cock might taste. This sugared pill is punk's unassuming Pandora's box, and, well into its fourth decade of action, it isn't going away just yet.

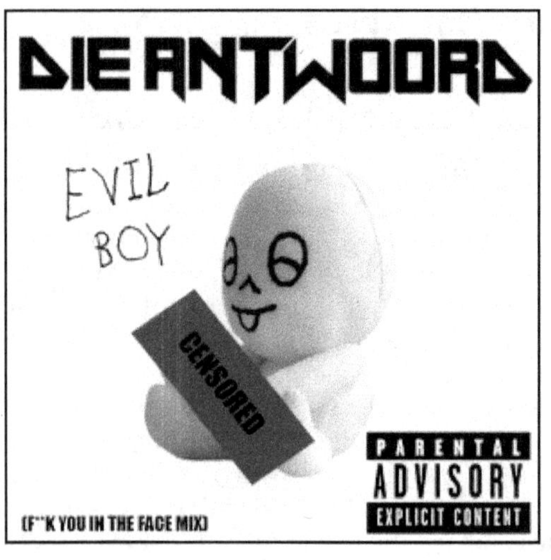

Die Antwoord: Evil Boy

Satan sez: Yeah, that's the general idea.

Die Antwoord ("the answer" in Afrikaans) are a South African rap-rave steamroller who manage to have it both ways most of the time. Often laugh out loud funny along with their barbed messages, their work celebrates trash culture and freely lifts sounds and visual styles abandoned by others. Their work has made massive impacts in some territories like South Africa and the US. Other places – notably the UK – haven't rewarded them with chart placings. The front line includes Ninja (aka Watkin Tudor Jones) and Yo-Landi Vi$$er (Andr du Toit), a couple in real life, and their dynamics are key to Die Antwoord's shtick. There's no shirking shit lives, violence and the usual rap material but often with a male/female battle going on in the middle, and Vi$$er winning out by taming the Ninja beast. The best example – arguably – is the video for "Pit Bull" with Ninja trussed up as a fighting dog, ripping throats and bossing the block until Vi$$er turns up and charms him.

"Evil Boy" is shameless big dick bragging with a guest verse from rapper Wanga, delivering his words in Xhosa (the language of a Bantu ethnic group.) The video is posturing on the edge of parody with Ninja's packet in his pants waving wildly about before Wanga wades in with a rap refusing the traditional manhood ceremony of his people (and thereby rejecting a circumcision.) So, there's serious intent behind the whole thing but there's also the sense that every set of values is there to be torn apart. Die Antwoord manage the same trick as a few others on Satan's jukebox, sitting right on the borderline of what's serious and what's seriously funny and taking their tools where they find them. Their celebration of "Zef" culture is central to everything else in their act. Vi$$er has explained this as having style and being sexy despite being poor, something Die Antwoord have turned into a badge of honour. Many rap and associated acts may have this angle but the fan art created by followers of Die Antwoord and their expert steering through success and trash culture has kept the strong in this area. Vi$$er's image – a trash culture albino with a very unique sense of style – is also right at the heart of their Zef power, and a blatant challenge to more mainstream notions of fashion.

Die Antwoord do the work of the Lord of Darkness, like many rap acts, because they rip up rules and make a case for their own take on bossing their turf on their own terms. Their humour is infectious and their reference points wide enough to help them escape and all of this says we don't need any help other than our own. Nowhere near as overtly satanic as – say – Flatlinerz – but powerful, personal and seriously funny when it has to be.

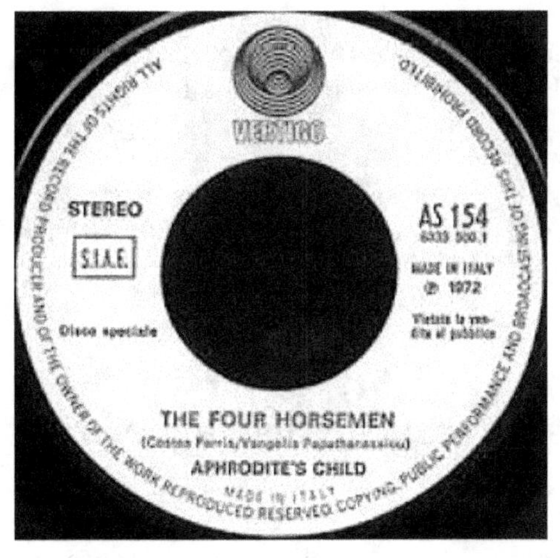

Aphrodite's Child: The Four Horsemen

Satan sez: Ah, the sound of a destructive apocalypse, it also has something to say about The Book of Revelation

The easy points to make concern the contents of the song and its parent album. "The Four Horsemen" is pretty much what you'd imagine, blistering and gloriously pompous prog rock played by Greek virtuosos at the height of their creative powers. This song re-imagines a key scene in The Book of Revelation as the most accessible chunk of a sprawling double album. Seriously, what's not to like? From a satanic viewpoint, this song, and much of the 666 album, records the moment in The Bible when the few are saved and the Lord of Darkness sweeps up the whimpering masses for whom it's simply too late. So, this 1972 cut looks forward to a happy time, well, a happy time for Satan, and brings it to life with Demis Roussos' vocal cutting cleanly through the crowded mix and some truly admirable fret wankery from Silver Koulouris. We could bang on, but, basically, this is the perfect fusion of needlessly complex prog rock, a mind-blowing concept and ripping your imagination from you and forcing it to take on board the end of the world. All this, and it reminds you that humanity is, largely, unable to save itself, most of us are doomed to eternal damnation and we'll discover this as a shit-storm erupts around us and our insignificance is rammed down our collective throats.

Satan also loves it for another reason. Forget that this sounds nothing like Abbey Road and consider that much of the explosive power on show here is the pent-up aggression of a band falling apart and forced to endure a painstaking recording process to gather the various parts of the sprawling masterwork, all of which made perfect sense to keyboardist Vangelis Papathanassiou. So, it took an apocalypse, to record an apocalypse. One reason it took the listening world years catch up on the true unapologetic majesty of this monster was that the band were history before the album was out. Granted, it also took much of the listening world to catch on to the fact that a Greek band were as gleefully up themselves as any bunch of English public schoolboys. Seriously, what was going on with all that bollocks about lambs kipping on New York streets? Didn't Genesis have the balls to tackle something really challenging? You know, like The Book of Revelation. So this is an Abbey Road job. In the car park they couldn't stand the sight of each other, in the studio they turned in audio gold, knowing all the time that the work was great and they'd never be able to tour it.

Gavin Baddely's awesome tome Lucifer Rising discusses this work, memorably describes Demis Roussos as a "kaftan-clad blimp-falsetto" and rightfully claims 666 for Satan on the grounds of both its contents and the vibe channelled with massive force throughout. The blimp falsetto was already being groomed for solo stardom, but his fleeting vocal performances on the album really leap out of the speakers, and it's arguable whether anything in the best-selling balladry that followed saw him better this performance. Apart from anything else, his intonation is clear and concise and the story he's telling is superbly painted in clear images. This song opens with: "And when the lamb opened the first seal, I saw the first Horse. The Horseman held a bow…" From which point, with the headphones cranked up, the scenery imagined when you close your eyes beats anything the best CGI has yet placed on a cinema screen.

It's fucking awesome, end of! And if you can feel the end of the world coming simply through the power of great rock music, you can sense Satan approaching because your butt just became his. Satan may change the contents of his jukebox, but he's unlikely to mess with this one.

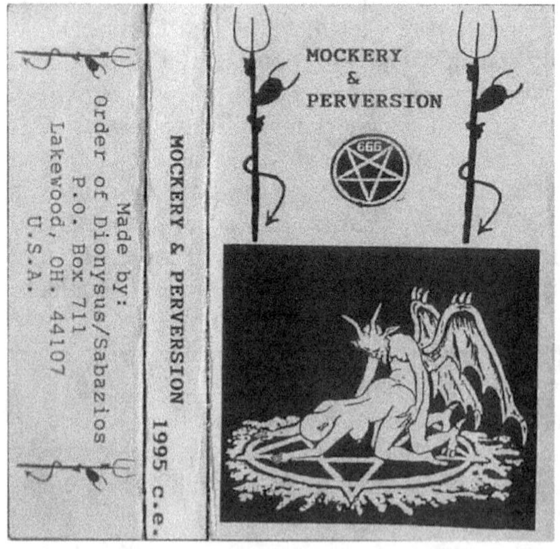

Joe Aufricht: Perversion Side

Satan sez: Me and Joe, we go way back.

There's an evangelical army, and its countless associates, out there doing righteous work to stem the tide of stuff discussed in this book. On the other side there's the likes of Joe Aufricht. Creative types, forces of nature, and unstoppable in their channelling of the dark side. Aufricht's on/off unleashing of his innermost demons has produced a stream of consciousness and a fusillade of filth fit to make him a genuine cult hero. A cassette artist in the nineties he has been rediscovered in the age of the download, and shared on blog sites like Glorify the Turd where the dregs of the music business are celebrated. "Perversion" is one side of a cassette release: Mockery & Perversion (1995.) Glorify the Turd note: "you may wish you were dead after about ten minutes of this shit!" That comment is in reference to the "Perversion" side of the tape. It's also the kind of backhanded compliment that means most to Joe. Glorify the Turd's commentary on the "Mockery" side of the tape sums up Joe's art superbly: "The uninitiated may listen to this and think they are listening to some guy trying to be weird / offensive / sophomoric and while, indeed, it does sound like that, I can assure you that you are dead wrong to think so. Understand that and clear your mind of all illusions to the contrary. Joe is not joking around on this thing—he is totally serious. Once you have fully grasped that fact, it starts to take on entirely new dimensions and the real fun begins."

Basically, Joe's tapes are intimate rants, filth filled, endlessly riffing on the thoughts most of us wouldn't want to share and ceaselessly inventive around descriptions of gross out acts. At the start of the "Perversion" side of this tape Joe is looking to get "horny" with anyone, including "pregnant chicks on roller skates" from which point on his sexual obsession is acted out in raps, snatches of song apparently invented in the moment and random sounds he makes with his mouth.

For the most effective results it's advisable to play this madness on headphones and see exactly how long you can survive it. When this guy gets into your head the danger is he'll take you over in a truly scary way. Joe is highly intelligent, intuitively creative in the manner of a good stand-up and – apparently – emotionally stuck at the moment of his sexual awakening. Seriously, character development in the context of this autobiographical rant about perversion amounts only to the fact that in adulthood he's better with the one-liners and talking to the opposite sex than he used to be. When, as a kid, he'd crawl under school tables to stare at girls legs. He might be more educated but that's only given him more insight into why he's decided to stay stuck, emotionally, at the moment his hormones first kicked in.

The fact he keeps this going for one side of a C-90 (if you're young you might want to Google what a C-90 was) without letting the energy level flag is part of the car crash fascination here. This is a sound recording fit to mess with the most balanced of minds, and probably, the most objectionable of Joe's legendary cassette period releases simply because it's a sex-obsessed diatribe on a level likely to deprive the most ardent feminist of hope. There are moments even Joe's most devoted admirers would struggle to defend, even as jokes. So, be warned, this isn't to everyone's taste. But it's a fitting addition to Satan's jukebox because the sheer tonnage of gross out invention here makes it clear that the dark side of the human mind is endlessly inventive. And, because Joe is living proof that no amount of well- meaning and morally righteous messages aimed at the world will begin to make a dent in minds like Joe's. As an aside Joe is also in an extreme metal band, but we'll leave you to Google all of that.

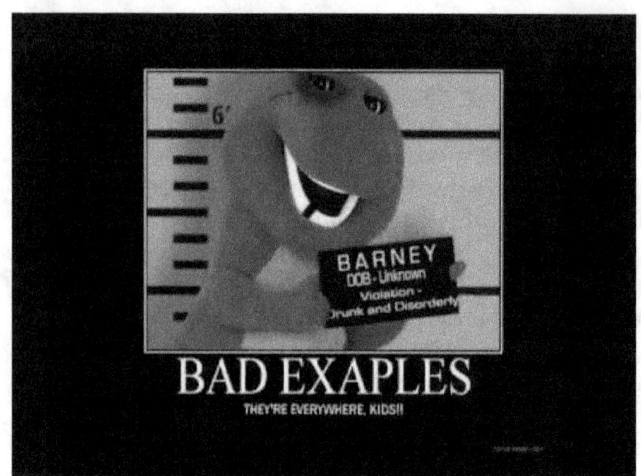

Barney the Purple Dinosaur: *I Love You*

Satan sez: It ain't the size, it's what you do with it!

This fleeting fragment of kiddie-friendly schmaltz is best known as the standard closing song of episodes of Barney and Friends, starring Barney the Dinosaur. With its blatant steal of a tune from the timeless and child-friendly "This Old Man" and lyrics that see no dividing line between family and friends – "I love you You love me, We're a happy family, With a great big hug and a kiss from me to you. Won't you say you love me too" – this is cutesy corporate American kiddie music at its very best. Barney closes every episode declaring his love for the watching kids, and – in the final line of the song – reprising "Won't you say you love me too?" It's cuddly, affectionate genius, completely comfortable and fit for a worldwide franchise, which Barney most certainly is.

Satan's slammin' to the song comes from an entirely different and somewhat surreal life the song has led. We can only skim the surface here but if any of what follows intrigues you we would strongly recommend burying yourself in the seventh chapter of Jon Ronson's book The Men who Stare at Goats, a stupefying stroll through the labyrinthine logic of PSYOPS (psychological warfare) as delivered by the US military, post-Vietnam. Chapter seven centres on the use of loud music and flashed strobe lighting directed at Iraqi detainees (mainly held in a shipping container) in their home country. "I Love You" featured in heavy rotation on the playlist for this activity and the chapter goes on to discuss the ethics and logistics of paying royalties when music is so used.

What is beyond dispute is that the intention of such work is often to bring on the Bucha Effect (aka Flicker Vertigo) a disorientating condition involving nausea bordering on epilepsy. The extent to which this combination of tinnitus inducing audio torture and relentless flashing lights succeeds in this aim is debateable, as is the amount of useful intelligence gained in such a way. For those unwilling to navigate Ronson's book there is – as of this writing – a 2008 Guardian article by Clive Stafford Smith freely available online which discusses the same issue, making the following points: "According to US military authorities, it was God himself who first wrote the strategy of 'torture by music'…Joshua's army used horns to strike fear into the hearts of the people of Jericho,'… the most overused torture song [by the US] is I Love You by Barney the Purple Dinosaur." The whole point of the overkill of this kinder classic is to render it as "futility music." Futile, that is, for the prisoner to hold a position of non-co-operation because such actions will only result in yet more exposure to: "I love you, you love me…"

A fringe benefit of such activity is the chance for the torturers to present their actions as little more than an "all round to ours" session where the contents of an iPod are shared with a few guests before a friendly chat leads to shared understanding and the passing from one side to another of useful information. Clive Stafford Smith, Jon Ronson and a few people they interview present some insight into the mental horrors that really unfold. It is to those horrors that – we would humbly suggest – the Evil Lord turns his mind as he punches the buttons to blast Barney from the speakers.

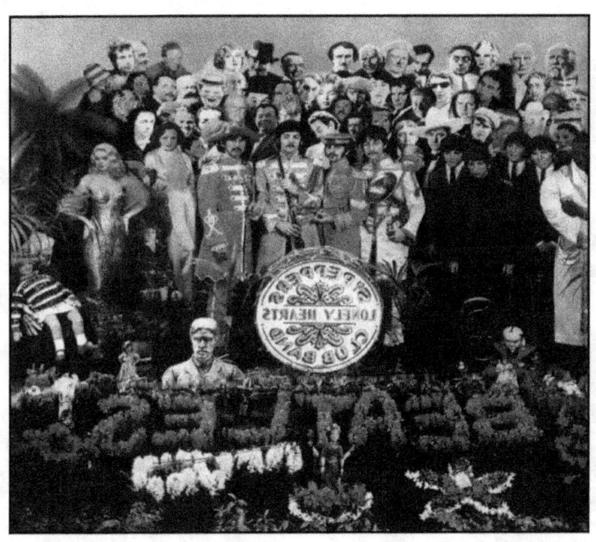

The Beatles: Locked groove at the end of Sgt Pepper

Satan sez: Deep and meaningless. But it's done good for me.

Let's keep this simple. The whole back masking/ demonic subliminal messages shebang owes mightily to The Beatles. It also owes a mighty debt to demented people in general, paranoid demented people in particular, and the raging hunger of the young and impressionable to believe in something greater than mundane human reality. Rant over! A great deal of The Beatles' importance to the whole mess is down to their massive record sales, the ceaseless screaming that drove them off stage and into the studio, and the fact they could command amounts of time and money to record that others could only envy. They were free to experiment well ahead of most of their peers. Another rant over!

The locked groove that ends Sgt Pepper's Lonely Hearts Club Band contains – according to the most reputable sources – "random gibberish" and Lennon and McCartney saying "Been so high" (Lennon) plus "Never could be any other way" (McCartney), though you'll find claims it is "Never could <u>see</u> any other way." Because the jumble of voices overwhelms the listener there are claims and counter-claims about what else is there. Paul McCartney once said in an interview he got so fed up with the hysteria about the whole thing he sat down and gave the locked groove a listen, only to hear "We'll fuck you like supermen."

More time and effort has been poured into analysing these fleeting sounds than has been devoted to much longer and more significant moments in other musical careers. For as long as there are people hungry for the darkness and willing to hear secret sounds where others just hear noise this phenomenon will continue. The Beatles' recording career is the best documented of any act, ever. But that doesn't stop people hearing things the band, and most of those researching and writing about them, say was never there in the first place.

Sgt Pepper was a much smoked to and dissected album back in the glory days of vinyl, a situation that frequently involved the record being on a turntable and spinning long after the music had stopped. Therefore, people reeling with the effects of weed and rambling mentally were subjected to the locked and repeating groove on replay for minutes at a time. Metaphorically at least, their heads were fucked with on a fairly large scale.

All the evidence suggests the whole thing is deep and meaningless, but – over the years – it's done the business for the Dark Lord. Doubtless this plays like a comfortable and familiar old hit when he puts it on the jukebox.

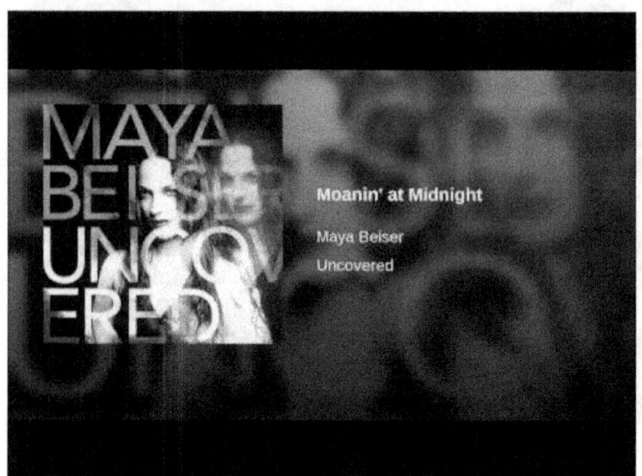

Maya Beiser: Moanin' at Midnight

Satan sez: I've uncovered a cracker here (arf!)

The world isn't exactly short of classical musician ice maidens, flirting with their highbrow craft and an image of designer darkness wherein their steely cool erupts in moments of musical passion. Cellist Maya Beiser is most certainly that animal from the tips of her fuck-me stiletto heels to the torn riffs on her covers of rock classics. She's on the jukebox not because the Lord of Darkness is so credulous as to fall for the marketing shtick when some record label rebrands another classical artist. She's there because – despite the clichés – she makes this world her own. When she gets it right she mashes the craft that made her a top string player with the ability to get into the darkness that inspired the originals and make the feeling live again on her terms. The Uncovered album that offers up "Moanin' at Midnight" as its second cut is more notable for the major rock standards – "Black Dog," "Back in Black," "Lithium," "Wish you Were Here" – covered. In tackling Howlin' Wolf Beiser is truly at her best. John Peel once memorably described Wolf's "Goin' Down Slow" as the sound of a man falling apart, and that's where Beiser takes this track. There's a fluidity and beauty to her cello in the opening moments but the sense of her channelling Wolf's immense, near bestial, voice gradually overwhelms the track whilst the minimal percussion keeps things uneasy; giving the work the same scraping vibe of Tom Waits' more skeletal cuts. The fact that Beiser both holds the tune and permanently builds the threat of the whole thing falling apart is the real key to channelling the painful end of the blues, and reinventing it for the second decade of the twenty first century in a classical setting. Taken in whole albums at a time this is often too dark and claustrophobic, rubbing shoulders with company it keeps on Satan's jukebox this little dark gem is mix-tape gold.

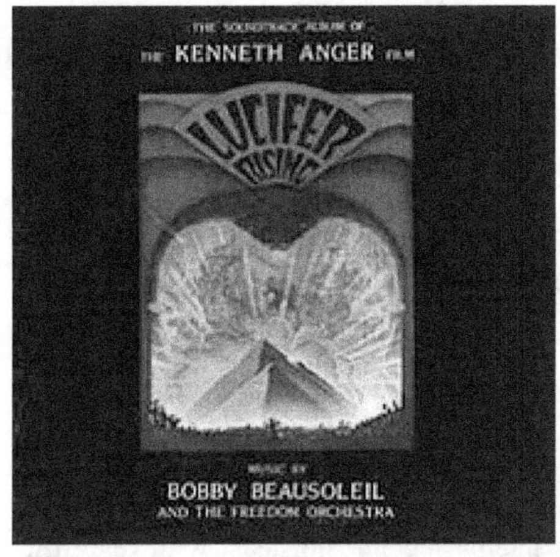

Bobby Beausoleil: Lucifer Rising pt.3

Satan sez: From the famous OST album.

It would take you considerably less time to listen to both soundtracks for Kenneth Anger's Lucifer Rising movie (Beausoleil's and the unused work by Jimmy Page, also discussed in this book) than it would to chase down and try and unravel the various claims and counter claims about how each composer became entangled in the movie and what – if anything – the impressionistic and bizarre final cut of the film actually means. The gist of the story is that Beausoleil, a noted guitarist and generally great musician on the L.A. scene in the sixties, got himself involved with Anger when the director originally began work on the movie. Various stops and starts were made on the project which moved between London and California and at times involved both The Rolling Stones and Jimmy Page. Page was duly recruited for soundtrack duties. The entry on Page's NOST (not the official soundtrack) elsewhere in this book discusses the Zep man's parting of the ways with Anger. By the time that happened Beausoleil was serving a life sentence for his part in aiding the Manson family with their campaign of mass murder. However, he lobbied and Anger listened, and the legendary soundtrack for the movie was recorded in jail. At which point in the story you can veer off and investigate the various legends about how Beausoleil acquired and used his instruments, and what – exactly – you are listening to as the album unfurls.

Satan's jukebox currently boasts the third part of the soundtrack. "Lucifer Rising pt.3" opens with a misty droning melody and slow crescendo on cymbal, there's more than a hint of Jimmy Page in the sounds before a keyboard and the drone begin a slow and slightly malevolent dance. More rock than much of the music on the soundtrack, this one also tells a story, carved out in a riff slowed to walking pace which falters before rising and taking on a rough edge. Gradually the track unfurls into a broad landscape with a hint of lingering evil. Musical figures emerge and play around, a slow pulsing beat drives the story forward and splashes of keyboard bring a sense of peace and closure, but always that slow drone lurks in the background.

Elsewhere on the soundtrack similar ideas to this get expanded to hypnotic levels (pt.5 and pt.6) and a slow disturbing saunter on electric guitar battles a blasting trumpet in the kingdom of the prog keyboard (pt.1). Sean Trane, reviewing the whole album online on the Prog Archives notes: "the whole albums (sic) circles around early Barrett-less Floyd and early Ash Ra Tempel music. Ranging from the mysteriously cosmic to the solemnly grandiose to the flabbergastingly beautiful, this music can only astound you, even more so knowing that it was created in prison."

Kicking aside the legend and rumour surrounding the whole caper and concentrating purely on the music, Beausoleil delivered a work of lingering menace and compelling darkness, the best moments of which stand their ground against the other works on Satan's jukebox.

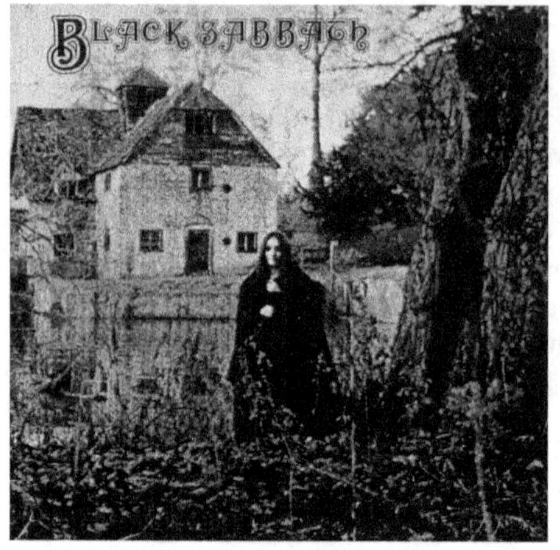

Black Sabbath: N.I.B.

Satan sez: (Adopts air-guitar pose) Der-der-der-dun-der-der/der-der-der-dun-der-dun/ Der-der-der-dun-der-der/der-der-der-dun-dun-dun

The fourth track of the awesome self-titled debut by the band that set the metal agenda. "N.I.B." is truly the stuff of satanic legend (not least with regard to its title which is often understand to mean "nativity in black" or "name in blood.") The alleged meanings of the title and much else you might find online linking "N.I.B" to unspeakable depths of depravity are, according to Sabs' bassist Geezer Butler, basically bollocks. The official line regarding the title is that it refers to a thin goatee beard sported at the time by drummer Bill Ward, which resembled the nib of a pen. However, this one is certainly amongst the very strongest in the slew of songs that have gone on to influence the channelling of darkness into music making since. More than the Stones' "Sympathy for the Devil" "N.I.B." is a touchstone of satanic rock because it personalises Satan and makes him a figure of some empathy. The story of the song involves Satan falling in love and changing his outlook, and the words are directed by Satan to the unnamed object of his desires. And, it is all the more of a classic love song because when he promises her the Moon in the opening verse, we know he's in a position to deliver it: "I will give you those things you thought unreal, The sun, the moon, the stars all bear my seal." In case anyone is in doubt about who is doing the promising the lyrics reveal it clearly soon after: "Look into my eyes, you'll see who I am, My name is Lucifer, please take my hand."

Beyond which it must be said, early Sabs are about as good as it got, anytime, anywhere with any band. Their album Black Sabbath (1970) only hit #23 in the US and #8 in the UK but one glance at its platinum selling status in the US says everything about why this album, and its similarly massive selling siblings matter. Like AC/DC the Sabs combine a potent power behind their riffs and the perfect deployment of their basic musical forces. That fact has made their early catalogue a touchstone for generations of music fans and kept the old sounds selling year on year. The Sabs are so simple and so powerful they positively incite the listener. In 1970 you could look at the likes of Led Zeppelin or Eric Clapton and marvel. But the power of Black Sabbath is the power to believe you can enter a guitar shop and – sooner or later – be like them. The riffs are instant earworms, the words are deep feelings honed into lines that don't require the listener hold an A' level in English to decode them and the collective strength of the band is their capacity to deliver all of this with cohesion. A proper band, not a collection of egos and excursions.

The Sabs were, and are, an everyman band with an effortless power behind their strongest punches. Black Sabbath (album) hits the ground running and never lets up on the quality. So "N.I.B." carries more authority because it's driven by a classic riff, placed literally in the middle of the seven tracks that make up one of the most influential metal albums of all time, and it's as good as anything on that album.

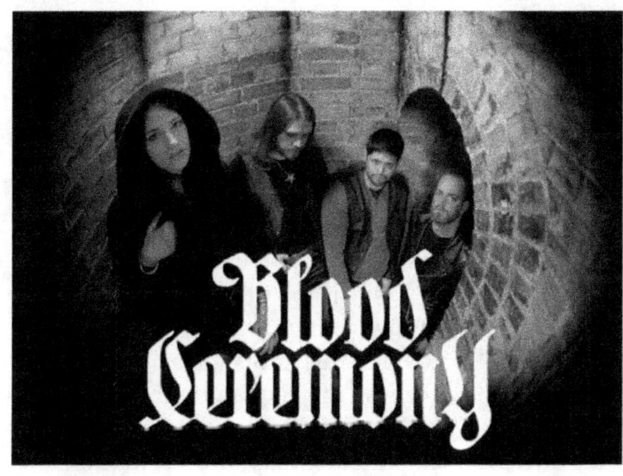

Blood Ceremony: Into the Coven

Satan sez: Did she say "Satan's bong?"

Twenty first century doom metalists with a retro touch so hard and heavy they frequently sound like a head on collision between early seventies Sabs and Jethro Tull. The Tull tweaks and assorted excursions into prog territory are generally led by singer Alia O'Brien as she channels a dark hippie sensibility into the sound. Her efforts have given the band both a visual focus and a distinctive and seductively soothing quality that lulls the listener in to their heart of darkness. It's debateable whether "The Coven" is a sincere statement of the band's true nature as dabblers in the Crowleyesque version of the dark arts or simply a very accomplished realisation of the music they all grew up on. Sitting three tracks into their self-titled debut album "The Coven" opens with the awesome: "They smoke black drugs with Saturn's bong" before wandering through a trippy account of airborne witches flying toward a "Quaalude eye" and ending "In a perfumed black mass with reptile gongs." Seriously, this is the perfect distillation of dark imagery, some whiffs of acid folk, and an affirmation that every satanic message apparently secreted in the earliest generation of heavy metal actually meant something. It's also a challenge to the grandchildren of the original metal crowd to gorge themselves on the Sabs, Curved Air and any other patchouli-scented vinyl and claim the realities within for themselves.

In the unlikely event that any of the original ranters about the evils of seventies Sabs and their followers still take an active interest in the output of current record labels Blood Ceremony are a nightmare incarnate. They are proof positive that the original power of that music lingers so strongly that some young people in the present century want, more than anything else, to go back a few decades and relive the sounds with the original spirit still intact. Rise Above Records, who released Blood Ceremony's first album, describe this as "flute-tinged witch rock." Hell, yeah!

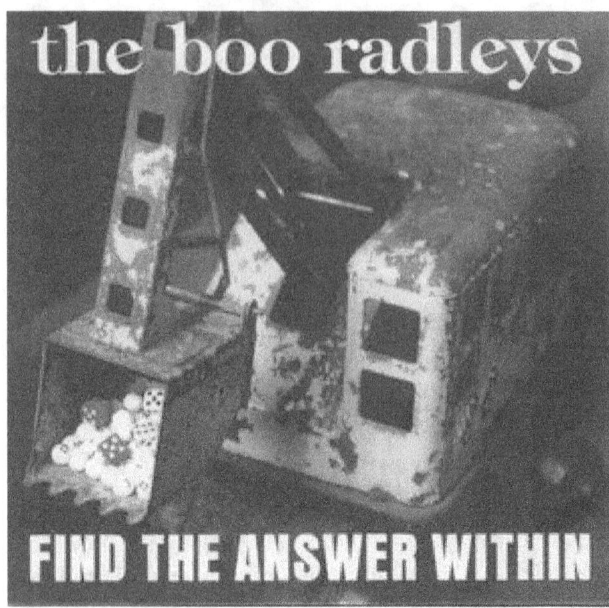

The Boo Radleys: *Find the Answer Within*

Satan sez: No crumbs of comfort for lathered up Lucifer hunters!

There are podcasts, online rants and a slew of slathering anti-Satanic rants out there suggesting backward masks (i.e. moments in recorded songs wherein words are inserted being sung/spoken backwards) are the spawn of the Devil, and a one way ticket to ranting insanity and worse. In a spirit of fair mindedness the present authors are prepared to consider this proposition but several decades of acquainting themselves with these - apparently – devilish ditties has, thus far, convinced them the various backward mask/Satan/gateway to insanity shticks are all utter bollocks. Incidentally, we're not alone in this experience*

Exhibit A in the authors' argument, and – therefore – probably a favourite where the fires of Hell are stoked, is this four and a half minutes of prime alternative rock. Culled from Wake Up!, The Boo Radleys' sole chart topping album in the UK, "Find the Answer Within" surges forward with the effortless tunesmithery and joyous jangling guitars that were a hallmark of the highest profile era of the band. Their finest moments are characterised by the fleeting nanoseconds between the tune entering your ears, and burning itself on your brain. "Find the Answer…" is up there with the best of the Boos, but it delivers one, literal, twist as a line goes by backwards. Not hidden, not even skilfully blended amongst other sounds. Up front in the mix, big, blatant, backward masking. Begging the question: WTF?

In 1995, when the song first saw action five cuts into its parent album, it took time and effort to secure the means to play it backwards and uncork the demonic despatch that surely lay within. Those able to make such efforts were rewarded with a tuneful and harmonious passage of the band warbling: "If you like a lot of chocolate on your biscuit join our club." On second thoughts, that last word should read "Club." For those still scratching their heads (especially those living outside Great Britain) it should be noted that this slogan, and the melody sung by the band, are lifted from a well-known advertising campaign promoting the Jacob's Club brand of chocolate covered biscuits (still showing strong sales after a century of popularity in the UK and Ireland.)

As a metaphorical middle-finger lifted in the face of slathering anti-Satanic ranters everywhere, highlighting their propensity to ado much about nothing in general, this backward mask this is hard to beat. Put crudely, it's devilishly funny.

*With regard to the proven effects of backward masking we recommend reading the academic paper "Forward and Backward Maskingwith Brief Chromatic Stimuli" by H. E. Smithson and J. D. Mollon. Let's just say, their peer reviewed and erudite discussion of the subject doesn't see the problem in the same terms as the most rabid religious ranters who have expressed their opinions in this area.

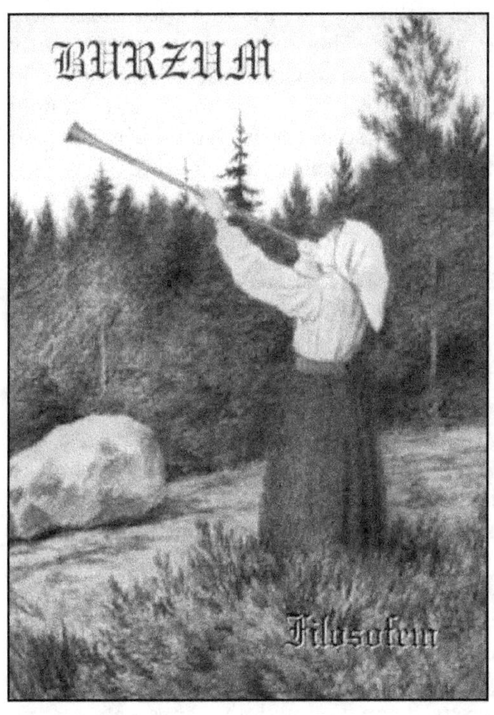

Burzum: "Rundtgåing av den transcendentale egenhetens støtte" ("Circumambulation of the Transcendental Columns of Singularity")

Satan sez: Classic dark ambience (Hell yeah!) Catchy title (NOT!!)

The nineties Black Metal scene in Norway is well chronicled in the eminently readable *Lords of Chaos* by Didrik Soderlind and Michael Moynihan. A major player in the most extreme goings on was Varg Vikernes, Burzum mainstay and a man with a vivid and dark vision he channelled into intense and chilling black metal albums. With churches burning and the competition to be the blackest of the Black Metallers also hotting up, something had to give. Burzum and their rivals Mayhem were the clear leaders in deeds of extremity, until Mayhem found themselves a member short, their lead guitarist - Euronymous - having been fatally stabbed, by Vikernes. Vikernes was convicted and imprisoned, he argued self-defence but his broad smile at the moment of receiving a 21 year sentence did little for his chances on appeal, even if it confirmed him as a Black Metal cult hero. He was also convicted in connection with arson at several churches. So the man rocked with Satan, end of.

Denied access to the usual tools of his trade – guitars and drums – Vikernes spent time in jail composing and recording two albums of an altogether different type; dubbed "Dark Ambient." The first of these releases; *Daudi Baldrs*, is – arguably – a masterpiece of disturbing musical ideas and bears repeated, if uneasy, listening and doubtless sees regular action on Satan's iPod. However, the dark ambient, minimalistic, introspective general mind fuckery that exploded on Burzum's two jail albums was already in existence whilst Vikernes was at liberty to kill and torch the odd place of worship. "Rundtgåing av den transcendentale egenhetens støtte" (Circumambulation of the Transcendental Columns of Singularity) is 25 minutes of circulating minimalist mesmerism so calm as to be catatonic. The dark beauty pouring from the speakers is, if anything, enhanced by a gleefully alternative approach to recording. Most of the Filosofem (released 1996 but recorded 1993) album was cut under deliberately demanding conditions. A stereo (as in equipment for playing music, not recording it) amp provided the route from guitar to tape and on the vocal tracks – which this isn't – the worst available microphone was used.

"Circumambulation…" trickles delicate sounds with a slow insistent rhythm (akin to slowly dripping water) and brings in an idiotically simple guitar riff. This delicate bundle trips lightly over 25 minutes. Taken in isolation this could be Norway's response to Brian Eno, taken in the context of an album of low-fi black metal this is nihilism writ large in an infuriatingly directionless deluge of pointless beauty. The fact it achieves so much, whilst wilfully using so little in musical and production terms, is something of a darkly magical act in itself.

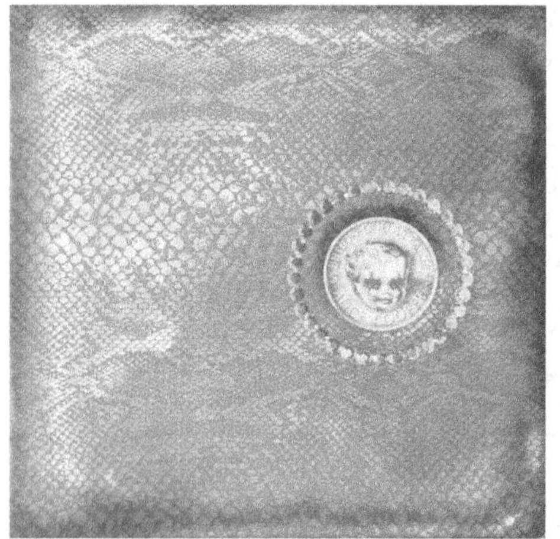

Alice Cooper: I Love the Dead

Satan sez: He's kidding, kiddies.

In 1973 the original Alice Cooper band were at the height of their powers and success. It was only later in that decade that their lead singer struck a deal to go solo that continues to reward the surviving members of his band by paying them for the rights for him, alone, to continue using the bankable name. The Billion Dollar Babies album is a watershed work between the hard rocking and sleazy dirt of the band's earliest outings and the theatrical/pantomime villain shtick that continues to make Alice (the man) such a bankable live act. Satan's jukebox needs at least one of the musical demons who drove a generation of religious writers to distraction with the, apparent, satantic onslaught of their work. Who better, frankly, than the guy who led the pack, Alice Cooper?

These days Cooper is a recovering addict (though one of the most successful in the history of the music business) who openly admits to never having cheated on his wife, and to being a born again Christian. But he still has it, sort of, both ways. He plays the Alice character and the old hits in big arenas for months on end around the world. And, his newer music is uncompromising, railing as angrily as the material in his past catalogue. If anything, he's angrier and more focussed with age. Back in the glory days, as a few his fans spotted, he could be laugh out loud funny.

Self-elected types with a sense of moral justice seldom saw him in that role, taking the horror imagery and claims that his stage persona came from contacting a dead witch via a Ouija board as gospel. In fact, the name story, and most of the other urban legends including the one about him killing a cow onstage with a rectal insertion of dynamite were utter garbage. Alice Cooper (the name) came – almost randomly – from the name of a character, fairly low down the cast list, in the television drama Mayberry R.F.C. When "School's Out" became an international hit in 1972 the Alice Cooper band were able to command impressive levels of time, money and guest talent to make their definitive album.

Billion Dollar Babies is that animal, the perfect purveyor of grim jokes, consistent digs at middle-American values and barbed asides suggestive of real perversion in the ranks. Rolling Stone stood, largely, alone in failing to recognise it as a great record. In time it would become a touchstone for the morally righteous to regard as designer depravity of the worst kind. Which, to a certain extent, it is. By default Billion Dollar Babies (album) remains a high spot for such moral panics because it was a well-established work when the early eighties evangelical onslaught really took against the music industry, since when other moral panics, like shoot-'em-up computer games and the evils of the dark web have presented threats to the well-ordered home that make the dangers of listening to rock music look tame.

"I Love the Dead" has a few tough acts to follow. Played end to end Billion Dollar Babies finishes with this track. By the time the listener arrives at the end of side two the horrors and grim gags have rattled past. "Hello Hooray" with its sense of showmanship leads into a selection of comic horror including the cynical political sideswipe of the other big hit – "Elected" – the sleazy nod back to past glories -"Raped and Freezin'" – a gorgeous piano ballad kissing off to an old love – "Mary Anne" - in which the twist in the tale reveals Alice (the man) to be singing to another man, and the showstopper on side one "Unfinished Sweet." "Unfinished Sweet" is the key to understanding the power of "I Love the Dead." Each song runs, just about, long enough to qualify in having some epic qualities and each employs some brilliant cod dramatics and sound effects. Indeed, "Unfinished Sweet" is a genuine shocker that woke up Alice's fans. If you've read a smattering of the other entries here you'll grasp that rock music comes a poor second to avant-garde art or simply recording real horror if you want to provide shocking sound recordings. But "Unfinished Sweet" has a few chilling moments. Alice sings about going to the dentist, being told his teeth are fine but his gums have to come out (arf! At the oldest joke on the album) and then instead of the expected guitar solo to follow the doom-laden riff the band work in the sound of a dentist's drill, truly horrible if you are wearing headphones and don't know what's coming.

But "I Love the Dead" shades it for Satan's jukebox because this one tackles a real taboo head on and was strong enough to wind up thousands of credulous sorts to make arguments that were only ever likely to convince Alice's fans, and others like Alice fans, that the self-elected moral sorts hadn't a fucking clue. It is what you'd expect. Mini-epic, leaden, theatrical rock with a lyric unrepentantly in praise of necrophilia. Alice loves the dead "before they rise" and is oblivious to a "rotting face" because "I have other uses for you darling." Bring on the doom-laden riffs (again!) cue the comedy orgasms and mix the whole thing with enough echo on the main voice to suggest Alice is singing some of song from inside a large box. Seriously, there are people with no sense of irony who believed every word and saw Cooper corrupting the innocent youngsters of America. Some searching questions were raised in response, like hadn't young American minds been more corrupted in the recent past when they were conscripted and taught how to kill the Vietcong? All of which kept the arguments raging for a few years. But all of which also ignored a fact obvious to Alice fans. This is a sick joke, well executed, end of. If "I Love the Dead" says anything profound it may well reveal that the Alice Cooper band's love of sick and novelty records extends to a knowledge of Jimmy Cross's "I Want my Baby Back" wherein a bereaved man digs up his dead girlfriend and also sings the final chorus with his head – apparently – in a box.

Cooper's career benefitted for many years from the fact that people who didn't know much about rock music appeared to believe him capable of the things claimed in urban legends. When others did commit real acts of atrocity, like biting the head off a bat (though Ozzy has always maintained he believed it to be rubber when it was thrown onstage) Alice's influence appeared to be all over the worrying developments.

Alice (the man, today) is genuinely at war with the satanic, but from a position of some tolerance and understanding of the dark side of human nature. He's learned lessons the hard way, through his addictions and the fact alcohol almost cost him the long and strong marriage he has enjoyed. He's always seen theatrically and humour as strengths in his work and he isn't about to apologise for that, for Billion Dollar Babies or for "I Love the Dead."

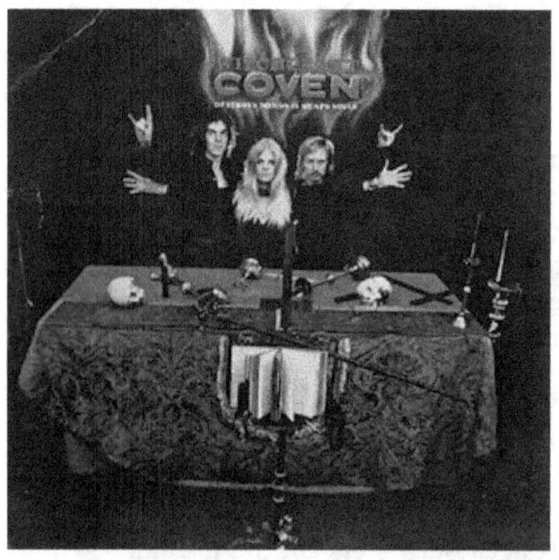

Coven: Black Sabbath

Satan sez: What's wrong with you humans, this lot should be massive!!

Coven should've been, like, massive. They were there at the start of satanic rock, flirting with the borders of metal and folk and being amongst the first genuine rock bands to have an in your face rock chick out front who packed more balls than most male frontmen at the time. We could rant on or we could just give the stage to Grim Kim who posted on the Metal Sucks website a few years ago: "Coven are credited as being one of the very first rock bands to embrace occult imagery and outright Satanic references, and chanteuse Jinx Dawson also claims to be the true progenitor of the 'devil horns'...Suffice it to say, Coven and Ms. Dawson are owed a fuckton of royalties from pretty much every extreme metal band ever!"

The inside gatefold of their debut album is the first rock artwork to display the devil horn gesture. The words "Hail Satan" are also clearly visible along with an inverted cross. Did we mention that the band signed their contract with Mercury Records in their own blood? So, they rocked, for Satan, then. And "Black Sabbath" opens the 1969 debut album with a strong statement of what this band did to damn near perfection. It rocks, but it's melodic and displays folk and prog touches at will. It also tells a story with a consummate command of language, the kind of command that thrash metal and its offshoots would make a trademark twenty years later. And, "Black Sabbath" poises itself perfectly on the edge of comic book/comedy/ earnestly satanic narration:

Bubbling pots of ungents and potions,
Flames revealing the obscene motions.
Old hags murmur in evil ranting!
Voices grow louder and join in the chanting.

All of the above is pushed out there with power and hypnotic performance by Jinx Dawson who was simply born to front a band with evil intent. Over the course of the whole album she roars without ever losing the perfect pitching of the notes and leads her clan with a command of vocal pyrotechnics that puts everything from a stage whisper to full throated Robert Plantisms into the mix. When she's called on to – like – just sing, she has the emotive authority of a traditional power balladeer.

This band were influential above and beyond the reach of most of their peers. Their first album even ends with over 13 minutes of a black mass but Satan's jukebox already has that need covered, so it's "Black Sabbath" the satanic snack simply packed with godless goodness that makes Hell's hot hundred.

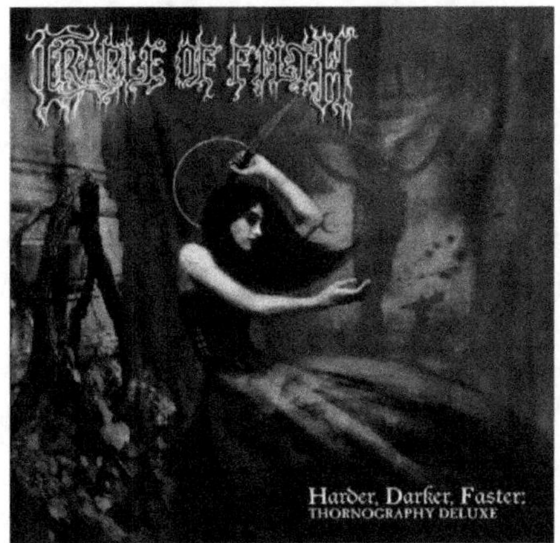

Cradle of Filth: Libertina Grimm

Satan sez: You say "sell out" I say "get in!"

Cradle of Filth are part of the revolving stage of reliable performers on Satan's jukebox and the whole point of him having a decent track from a decent album rather than one of their more obviously satanic early offerings is that this band, and their fans, are trusty mainstays of extreme metal. There are loads of bands out there capable of finding a fan base, defining a style and mining their particular winning formula for the best part of a lifetime's work. There are a select few who take this art to the level of continued international success and knocking out albums that continue to interest and innovate. In that department Cradle of Filth (est. 1991) are up there with the likes of Hawkind, The Grateful Dead and The Cure; all bands with a visual style, some sense of lasting values that inform their career and a lengthy track record of ensnaring a die-hard fan base who won't let go but will take the ideas they hear in the music and spin them off to inform their own lives.

Frankly, all of the above amounts to the kind of reverence towards graven images we're warned against in the Ten Commandments. Cradle of Filth don't cut it as arch Satanists. Nowhere near as influential in that area as forerunners like Venom. They aren't a patch on the church burning and rival murdering that saw their Norwegian counterparts vilified and one of them receive a life sentence. The criticisms that have been poured onto the more accessible albums in their collection have some merit too. The band did link themselves to Sony records and Thornography (2006 – released on Roadrunner) which hosts "Libertina Grimm" is a prime example of fierce extreme metal rocking with one ear on the radio friendly, all of it mainstream enough to allow major rock magazines and big selling live events to include the band. As with all true cult bands there's enough intelligence behind the whole caper to allow them to ramble on about it having meaning. In the case of the album title the band's own rap on this included: "The thorn combines images of that which troubled Christ, the crown of thorns, thus intimating man's seeming desire to hurt God and also, of the protecting thorn and the need to enclose a secret place or the soul from attack. An addiction to self-punishment or something equally poisonous. A mania. Twisted desires. Barbed dreams. A fetish. An obsession with cruelty. Savage nature. Paganism over Christianity. The title can also represent a sexual attraction to religious iconography as in the case of the 'possessed' Lourdon nuns." So, it's specific enough to carry a real focus, and general enough to allow in loads of free thinking amongst the fans.

"Libertina Grimm" has that possibility writ large all over it, presenting a character. Dani Filth, mainman of the band since the start, said: "Libertine Grimm is another gothic character who is actually an amalgam of many different women. She is sexy, erudite and possessed of an extraordinary wit, but this is counterbalanced by an unhealthy appetite for self-destruction and flights of morbid fancy, brought on by dark secrets, terribly chic drugs and wild, sexual abandonment. She is a gluttonous Miss Muffet; the fairy-tale girl who ate the Big Bad Wolf; and the beauty who slept with one eye on the coming talent. Libertina Grimm is every goth girl's coven mistress."

At which point you can stand back in cynicism at the fact they've just given every female fan the perfect role model template to play with and provided some mental wank fodder for most of their male fans. Or you can see Cradle of Filth for what they really are; master explorers of a broad sweep of the darklands, unafraid of showmanship and entertainment and expert extreme rockers. "Libertina Grimm" packs all of these ideas into erudite verses, all of which perfectly skirt serious intent and cracking turns of phrase: "She was Alice through the glory hole/ An ejaculate misconception/ Disney-esque, the high priestess/ Of greed and deepest dark deception".

And: "Fantasy and candy stores/ Snow White and the seven straws/ Smoke and mirrors on all fours".

Thornography charted all round the metal world and made the lower reaches of the main album lists in both the UK and US. Not something extreme metal acts have traditionally achieved. "Libertina Grimm" roars in with a simple, strong, riff, revs with a growl and descending lead guitar melody padding out the sound, riffs up enough to build the anticipation and then delivers lines like those above for the best part of six minutes. A crowd pleaser, in a collection of crowd pleasers from a reliable band. Cradle of Filth are an entry point for impressionable minds finding themselves attracted to something dark. To put it crudely a twelve year old girl, devoted to Harry Potter, might find herself ensnared by this, at which point she's probably lost to another life that might have included riding ponies and generally being nice to her elders. Once she's on board she might be persuaded to listen to some of the other stuff in this book. On that score she might also feel an instant affinity with Cradle of Filth who have a habit of being even handed, sexually speaking, with the characters praised and explored in their songs. Early corkers like "The Black Goddess Rises" from Total Fucking Darkness (1992) established from the start a belief in female strength and potential. Not something a lot of their metal peers were doing at the time. The messages in the band's lyrics have gone alongside female imagery on their album covers. If general music fans know one thing about this band, it concerns the infamous "Vestal Masturbation" t-shirt from 1996 which included an image of a masturbating nun, breasts bared, and the striking legend: "Jesus is a cunt". The predictable backlash did no harm to the band's profile and even their most extreme visuals, like that t-shirt, could be argued to be images of female empowerment. The band even employed a female vocalist – Sarah Jezebel Deva – for 14 years.

So, this lot are firm favourites on The Devil's Jukebox, and if he ever tires of the tunes he has, Cradle of Filth are likely to be around long enough to bang out a few more just as good.

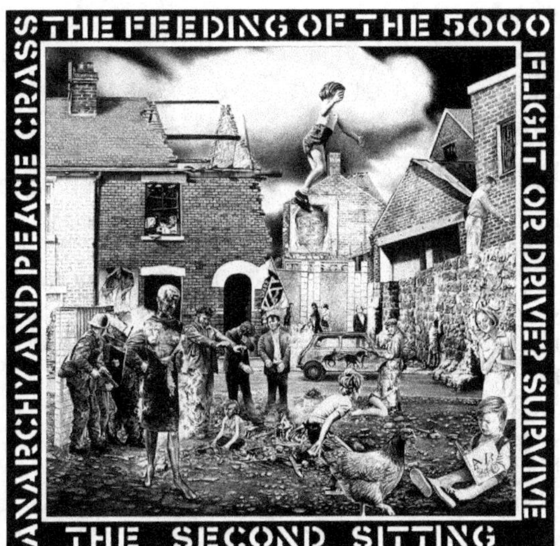

Crass: Asylum

Satan sez: "impotent fucklove prophet of death". Oi! Bob Dylan, match that!

The reason many vinyl copies of Crass' The Feeding of the 5000 album have a silent two minutes entitled "The Sound of Free Speech" is that pressing plant workers refused to knock out albums including "Asylum". Granted, this is a pressing plant in late seventies Ireland, still a country guided by the Catholic Church, and Crass were arch anti-establishment anarchists unwilling to compromise any of their artistic punk vision. The fallout of the stand-off saw Crass take control of their own production, and re-instate the track, which also saw action in a different form as the single "Reality Asylum." With feedback and electronic effects Eve Libertine starts a spoken word assault on Christ and all he stands for; recasting the Son of Man as a selfish and inconsiderate attention seeker who has damaged the human race, and the place of women in particular. The power of the message to persuade and, oddly, to entertain is enhanced by a poetic wordplay that works in strong profanities with consummate skill, making for enough memorable lines to make the whole thing feel considerably longer than the real two minutes and a few seconds.

At this point, we'd suggest the curious simply Google the lyrics and check the complete wordage out. But, a few choice lines follow: "Down now from your papal heights, from that churlish suicide, petulant child…He hangs in crucified delight nailed to the extent of his vision…You [Jesus] dug the pits of Auschwitz, the soil of Treblinka is your guilt, your sin, master, master of gore, enigma…Jesus died for his own sins, not mine".

Like we said, it's a spoken word "assault" on Christ and all he stands for. Strong stuff with powerful rather than tuneful sounds to support the rant and the reputation of an uncompromising anarchist-punk band behind it. Crass badges which recast the A in the band's name as the classic anarchist symbol were popular at the time and the band's policy of keeping their record prices lower than the competition also ensured their work got heard; though the content of their albums generally precluded radio play. So, many were drawn to Crass because their marketing, though always set up in opposition to slick commercial ventures, had some skill. All of it ramming home the message of authenticity central to Crass. Duly drawn in, the audience could be relied on to actually listen and think about what they were hearing. Crass were never likely to be best sellers but the original Feeding of the 5000 album hit the top of the UK indie charts and the re-issue, with "Asylum" duly restored to its opening slot on side one managed to reach #11 in the same chart. All of which means the band got inside young minds and Satan doubtless still feels thankful to them.

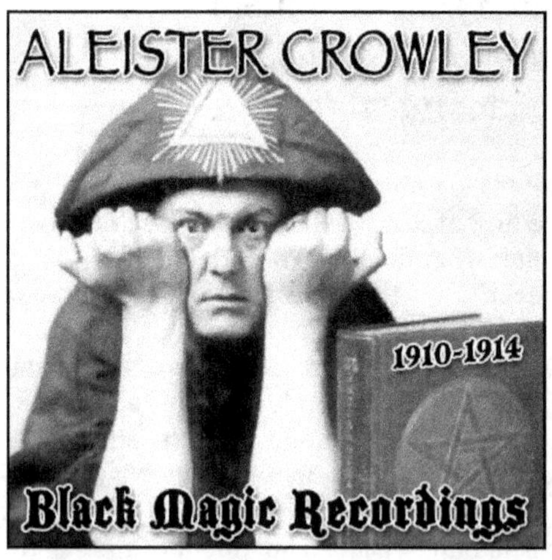

Aleister Crowley: The Pentagram

Satan sez: Mah boy, doin' mah business.

What Lucifer makes of some of his subjects in Hell is anyone's guess. It isn't always the most like-minded people who make the most stimulating company. And, if your work or social choices bring you into contact with too many people like you, the results can be stifling. Essayist, poet, necromancer, mountaineer, opiate addict, sexaholic…yeah, well, Crowley (1875-1947) wasn't one for a single vice when 24/7 dark side options were in the offing. So it's entirely possible Lucifer finds Crowley's presence an exception to cloying acolytes, lacking in imagination.

Crowley was cool, then and now, and, as befits a proto-rock star he also tried his hand in the early twentieth century cutting a few of the early wax cylinders, collecting an output that remains widely available in scratchy low-fi downloads, secreted all over cyberspace. Most of these spoken word pieces of agreeable occultism present Crowley reciting rites, enunciating in

Enochian (an occult language) and generally straddling the razor's edge between full-on incanting of evil and consummate showmanship with some ease. A charismatic figure who has enjoyed lasting fame as an icon in various corners of counter cultures (Led Zeppelin's Jimmy Page once owned Crowley's former gaffe; Boleskine House on the shores of Loch Ness) Crowley has dragged many to the dark side, several of whom have stayed the course.

It's likely Crowley's lifestyle, his copious output of written work and the enduring myth surrounding all his achievements is the driving force in his unending celebrity. But, the little sound nuggets have their part to play. So, just over a minute of the man celebrating demonic symbolism in sound, with that rising and falling cadence that pitches his delivery somewhere between high church Anglicanism and prime period Laurence Olivier, may well find occasional favour on The Devil's Jukebox.

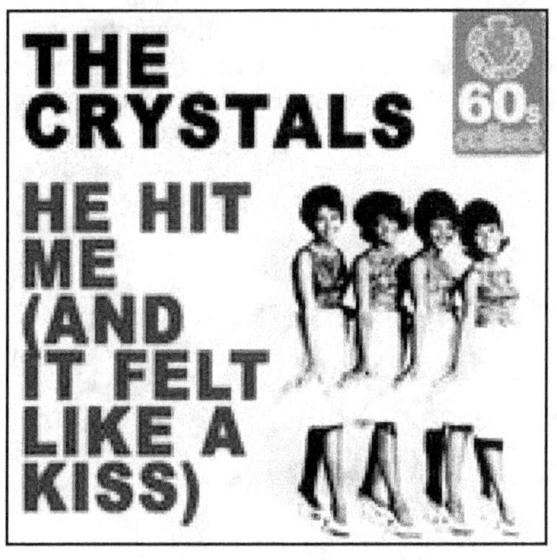

The Crystals: He Hit me (and it Felt Like a Kiss)

Satan sez: Carole King wrote this?! Get in!!

When Hole played a cover of this song on MTV's Unplugged show Courtney Love introduced it with: "This is a really sick song," and gave the song the proverbial kiss off with an ironic "nice feminist anthem" at the end. Amy Winehouse frequently cited this Phil Spector produced Goffin and King tune as a favoured and influential song in her life. Which is why it spins on Satan's jukebox. It's a soulful teen anthem with a plot. The singer's boy hit her but "it didn't hurt me" and – in any case – she was maybe asking for it after admitting being with "someone new." The simple story goes on to reveal the singer is "glad" because after her straying is duly punished the making up between the pair brings tenderness and she feels wanted. Great tune, The Crystals had talent to burn and Phil Spector was – metaphorically speaking – on fire in 1962.

Elsewhere in this book The Donays' version of "Devil in his Heart" is discussed as an example of simple girl group music with the capacity to lure the easily led into the ways of depravity and darkness. That pill is sugared compared to this strong concoction. Lyrics aside, this is pure pop genius. The melody is catchy enough to establish itself from the start and varied to the point it doesn't outstay its welcome; all of the above being aided by Spector at his inventive best, bursting with ideas and not overwhelmed with budget. A simple bass figure and scraping percussion is gradually joined by other sounds and as the tenderness overwhelms the singer the backing girly harmonies and string arrangement stand in contrast to the stark opening, suggesting the cuffing brought her back to her senses and strengthened the romance.

Since its release the song has led a strange life, shunned by radio it remains the least played Crystals' A-side. It didn't chart on either side of the Atlantic and marked the end of Barbara Alston's lead vocals for the group. Darlene Love took over for the follow up ("He's a Rebel") and the band scored their only US #1. "He's a Rebel" and "He Hit me..." have some similarities in their idolising of bad boys, but in terms of political correctness they are miles apart. For all its lack of success "He Hit me..." remains cultish and revered, as evidenced by Hole's love/hate relationship with the tune and the way female singers with a strong sense of their own identity have been drawn to it, even if – like Amy Winehouse – they've avoided producing a cover version. The Motels, who's Martha Davis was a strong front woman, turned in a storming cover on their All Four One album (1982.) So "He Hit me..." haunts the music industry the way a demanding and highly unsympathetic role in a drama haunts the theatre. Tackling and interpreting this dark material is likely to appeal to a few more female singers in years to come. Writing for All Music Guide Dave Thompson said: "It was a brutal song, as any attempt to justify such violence must be, and Spector's arrangement only amplified its savagery, framing Barbara Alston's lone vocal amid a sea of caustic strings and funereal drums, while the backing vocals almost trilled their own belief that the boy had done nothing wrong."

Satan doubtless loves it, more – probably - than he loves the deliberately dark "She Kissed me (it Felt Like a Hit)" by Spiritualized.

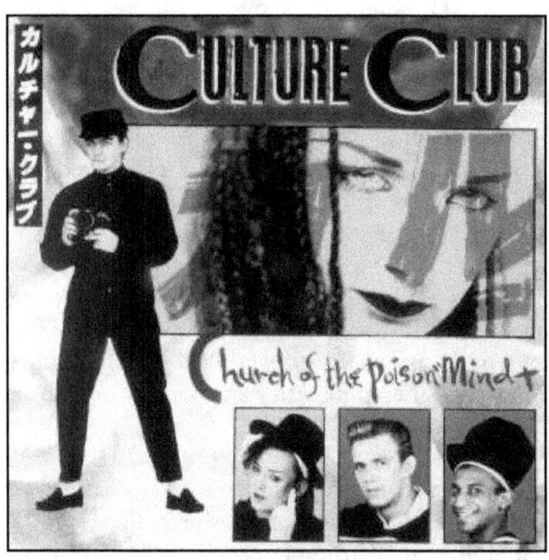

Culture Club: Church of the Poisoned Mind

Satan sez: Mah guilty pleasure, and one for the kids.

This catchy little corker saw top ten chart action on both sides of the Atlantic and led the promotion of the band's second (and by common consent best) album; Colour by Numbers. In the UK only David Bowie's "Let's Dance" could keep it off the top spot. For all their bright colourful pop charm and the insane earworm qualities of their very best songs, Culture Club riled the righteous in two ways. Firstly, there are transparently dark moments in their lyrics. The band, well, particularly Boy George, had strong opinions and the pretty polemics of some of their hits, like "Do you Really Want to Hurt me?" and "Victims," had a habit of slowly ambushing listeners with thoughts of what, exactly, might be going on when George sang lines like: "Pull the strings of emotion, Take a ride into unknown pleasure..." ("Victims.")

Half the problem in terms of the mild panics unleashed by Culture Club was the gender bending notion of the wildly effeminate Boy George out front wooing the first MTV generation with a combination of his cuddly charm and casual disregard for the kind of strong gender values held by the Christian right. The fact he pissed people off on an industrial scale, if anything, encouraged George and gave his band some credibility amongst more serious music fans who regarded much of the bouncy MTV friendly pop as garbage. Certainly, the likes of Jacob Aranza - evangelist, preacher and author on the satanic end of the music business – found George a daunting challenge and the music of his band a veritable mine of depravity. For the sake of balance at this point we should note that the highly recommended – by us that is – online Encylopedia of American Loons notes of Aranza: "At least Aranza helped make youth rebellion in the Eighties more exciting. Apart from that, he is a disastrously insane fundie, combining Taliban ideology with extreme paranoia and conspiracy theories, always a delightful combo." Aranza – who once accused The Captain and Tennille of producing a song designed to get kids hooked on ecology - got particularly worked up in his second book on backward masking when he discussed "Church of the Poisoned Mind."

The song is an elliptical tease, addressed by the singer to one other person with "desolate loving" in their eyes, charting a love/hate relationship which appears to use dancing and music as a metaphor "the beat, I had to fight to make it mine, That religion you could sink it neat. Just move your feet an' you'll feel fine." Frankly, the lyrics don't give that much away. You could, just about, read it as a kiss off to Christianity in general from a sexually flexible singer sick of church driven bigotry directed at his kind. That is why some of those taking their values directly from scripture had a particular problem with this song making the US top ten. Then again, maybe the "church" in the song is a metaphor for a vindictive attitude that doesn't allow the subject of the song to appreciate the singer's love. Or – shock bloody horror – maybe the four members of the band who combined to write it just threw random lines together that, sort of, worked wrote one of their catchiest choruses which repeated the phrase "Church of the poisoned mind" over and over and then high-fived each other when they heard the results because they knew they'd nailed a winner. Apart from anything else Culture Club never sounded quite so shamelessly Tamla Motown as they do here with the call and response chorus and Helen Terry's assertive voice turning the gender politics on its head as she sounds like the strong one in the vocal to and fro.

Decades after the event it seems pretty tired and laboured to look any harder into all of this but, it is worth noting that whilst much of middle-America melted before the effortless class of Culture Club's finest songs there were others, notably in the south, fuming with increasing ferocity at the thought of their country showing such love to such a fey looking bunch. But the band, well George, stoked these fires convincingly, never more so than when he thanked the Grammy Awards for bestowing the band with the Best New Group of the year award by noting that New York knew a good drag queen when it saw one.

Where previous androgynous acts had made something of a big image deal of the whole affair, Culture Club never pretended to be anything other than a really good pop group hell bent on writing hits and enjoying the party for as long as they could make it last. They were, and are, fun and because of that they got to young and impressionable minds at an early stage in their development. For some, that remains the work of the Devil.

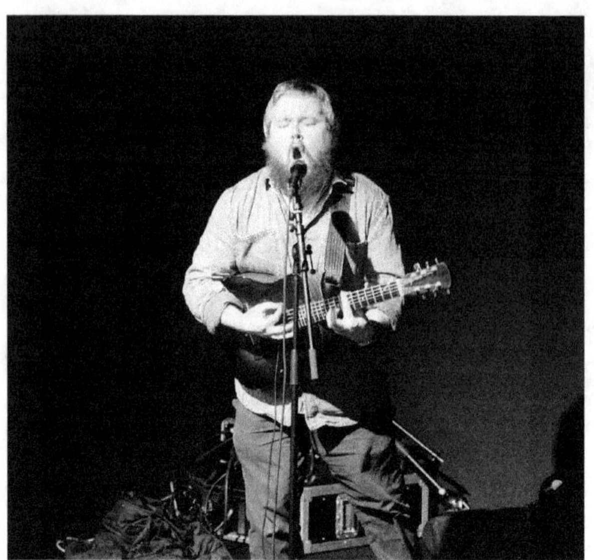

Richard Dawson: *Poor Old Horse*

Satan sez: Harrowing howling of the highest order.

Not to be confused with a sentimental song of the same title, this 2013 a Capella cut by rough-hewn Geordie folkie Dawson chronicles the slow agonised death of a horse in a tanners' yard. From the outset it's obvious the unloved old animal can't survive, and the tanners go about their duty with a resignation and carelessness that only prolongs the agony. Struck with a spade, stabbed and overwhelmed the stoic old animal fights and presents a tough challenge to the men who glance it a blow, feel its wrath as it fights back, set about bludgeoning the animal, break one leg with a spade, stab its collar bone when they seek the heart and – finally – gather together to hold it down in its final agonies. All of the above is told with no music and a strained bellow on the chorus that mimics the hopeless protests of the horse, rising and falling like desperate cries and never offering comfort. After the bleak slaying the men go their separate ways each with a different comfort on offer, one to see his sleeping baby, another for "a cup full of ale" but all – apparently – only able to snatch a brief respite from their grisly trade.

This truly is music fit to turn a wedding into a wake, all the more so because it's told with a sense of truth about the death of a working animal, registering our valuing of horses only for their ability to work and the need of men for money. The tanning trade in this song involves manually killing a magnificent animal because only its skin and meat are of value in the end. At best the situation called to mind is a bleak necessity, at worst it's a knowingly cruel trade, arguably hellish, that brings out more bestiality in the men than the noble animal they kill. It's also a great performance from Dawson, but that's just makes the horror all the more vivid.

The existence of music so dark, without recourse to conjuring up fake demonology or wilful wanders into shock tactics is a reminder of how hard, brutal and generally pointless real life can feel. Running a shade over five and a half minutes this tale is long enough to burn itself into your psyche, prolonging the listening agony even as it grips you by the ears and refuses to let go. All of which, breeds despondency, and that's always good for business on the dark side.

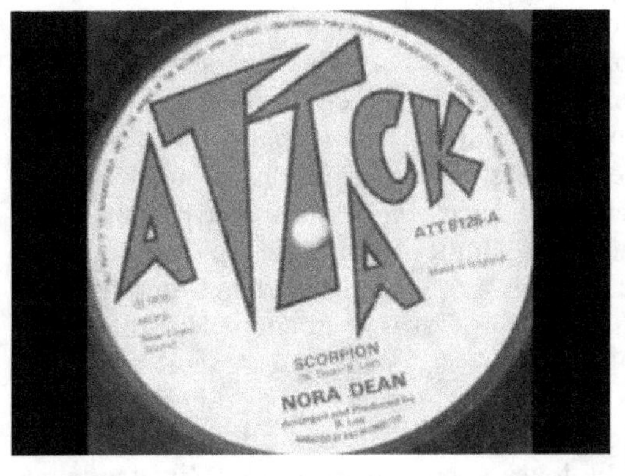

Nora Dean: Scorpion

Satan sez: Oh Mama!!

One of those fleeting, fun, guilty pleasures for which jukeboxes were created in the first place. On those odd occasion when Satan slaps his iPod on shuffle it's likely that these little gems crop up as his triple CD of the Trojan X-Rated Box Set punts them into the mix. As we trawl his personal jukebox we find "Scorpion" a gleeful piece of prime 1975 smut in which the singer meets a man with a "scorpion in his underpants" and howls in mock horror to her "Mama" as she tries to come to terms with the discovery. Had we trawled the jukebox a week or two either side, it's likely some other interchangeable cult classic would be doing the honours in this slot, maybe even another one by the same artist. Dean covered exactly the same tune and discovered "Barbed Wire" in his underpants, so we'll assume this is a singer mining a winning formula rather than a genuine tale of a brush with serious injury. In any case, Nora sings both songs as if she's barely repressing a laugh now and again and recounting a life changing sexual event.

The cultish end of reggae – recorded on shoestring budgets and bursting with low-budget invention and characterful lead vocalists – often relied on sexual innuendo and the most blatant double entendre twists to carry the appeal. This far down the line the sheer tonnage of this stuff, both rediscovered and awaiting rediscovery, is mind numbing. It's also life affirming for the lord of Darkness as he regularly updates the tunes with a lighter touch on his jukebox. This one is pretty much what you'd imagine, chugging along agreeably, smirking its way through a catchy romp and not outstaying its welcome. It betrays no hint of genuine evil, but it's utterly unapologetic about its earthy humour.

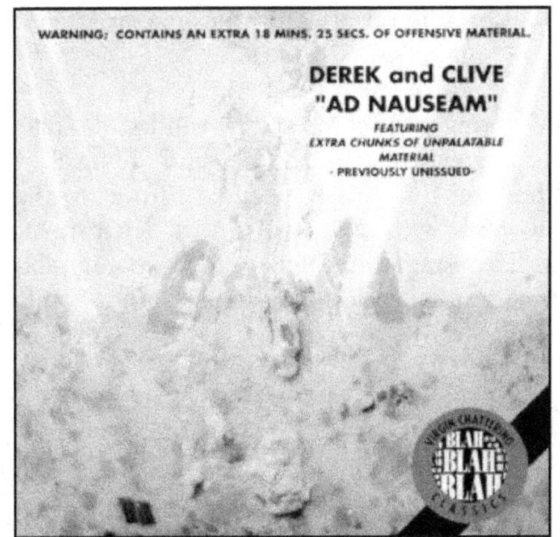

Derek and Clive: The Horn

Satan sez: Dick jokes, the way we do 'em in Hell.

Rolling Stone described *Let It Be* as "a cardboard tombstone". They weren't deaf to the merit of songs like "The Long and Winding Road" or "Across the Universe." They were, however, mindful of the way the variable quality control betrayed a band in break up and the variable contributions of each talent to the particular tracks meant even the best moments were hollow triumphs. Peter Cook and Dudley Moore's first two Derek and Clive albums were ramshackle and drunken affairs, sporadically brilliant and worthy of their cult status. *Ad Nauseam* (1979) marked a change in approach, more focussed, boasting the longest and most surreal of their recorded duets. It also presented a personal vitriol and animosity directed from Cook to Moore that saw Moore depart during the recordings, never to return. *Ad Nauseam* shows the Derek and Clive masks slipping visibly. The original characters had a nominal back story as toilet cleaners and stuck mainly to their London accents. *Ad Nauseam* has a higher proportion of sketch based spoken word, Cook refers to Moore as "Dudley" during a vicious, and very funny, attack on British television legend Bruce Forsyth. Some of the sketches are character based, and better timed and focussed than anything on the first two albums. "Horse Racing" presents a field of runners with names like The Prick, Big Tits, Vagina and Arseole and milks the ensuing possibilities of their positions: "The Prick might just have got up in the last few strides, but I wouldn't like to put my money on it." "The Horn" is the longest and most ambitious audio sketch the pair ever attempted. Its jokes about British Prime Minister James Callaghan "that oily heap of shit" and even Margaret Thatcher and the recently deceased Pope might have dated, but the darkly comic musings on being sexually excited by everything other than your own wife are still disturbingly funny. It's also the last time the pair used their Oxbridge minds and vast reserves of comic inventiveness to savage established religion. Recorded around the time Monty Python were making a movie suggesting that any lucky Palestinian chancer wandering around aimlessly a couple of thousand years ago might just get mistaken for the promised messiah, "The Horn" catches satirical comedy with a religious slant at the point where knocking solid establishment targets was still a staple of the act but the bizarre twists of clever logic had to be mixed with some down home dirt if the work was going to play well with the emerging alternative comedy crowd.

Derek and Clive hit that borderline and walk it with expertise, occasionally dipping when the chemistry between Cook and Moore stalls the surreal flights of fancy. Clive (Cook) leads us out with a riff on the sight of the recently deceased Pope John Paul 1st being so well turned out in his coffin that it gave him "the horn" after which a 23 minute furore of fertile comic invention ensues, the running riff being that just about anything gives Derek (Dudley) the horn. There's one notable exception to this rule because Derek's wife simply doesn't do it for him and Clive gets him to realise that his bearded wife is, in all probably, Jesus Christ and: "you're in shtook, mate!"

On the page it isn't funny, delivered with the comic timing and on the spot invention the pair had, even in these dismal final days, "The Horn" is in shamelessly bad taste and unafraid of the most offensive twists to make a gag. Indeed, the tracks originally deemed surplus to the parent Ad Nauseam album are graphic shockers to rank with anything in this department, "Valerie's Hymen" – for example – features Derek discussing cutting his wife intimately and destructively with a carving knife. The stuff is out there now; Valerie is discussed in a bonus cut on the Derek and Clive Come Again album.

"The Horn" is a standout and highly ambitious achievement on the cardboard tombstone that buries the brilliant partnership, and it still plays in those places where the listeners can't get their gags deep or dark enough.

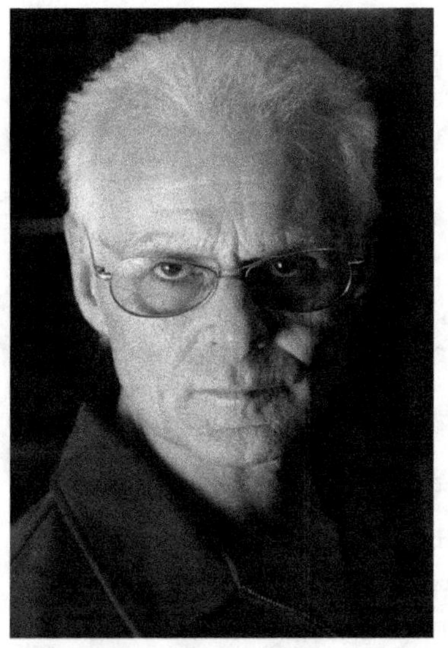

Michael Des Barres: *Teenybopper Death (He Loves you Bernadette)*

Satan sez: Seventies pop of the most deranged and dark persuasion.

Good luck tracking down a vinyl copy of this seldom seen tranche of tasteless seventies (1974) tack. The Devil's Jukebox doesn't contain this track for its musical merits. It's a solid slab of seventies songwriting with a nod towards early sixties death discs and some pretentions to being a "serious" stab at investigating a tragedy. Slated as the first solo single from British aristocrat (nah, seriously, Google him) Michael Des Barres, who had recently ceased fronting the band Silverhead, the 7" was rapidly withdrawn when the realisation of what it explored caused instant controversy. Lyrically the A' side dealt with the tragedy that had unfolded in May 1974 after David Cassidy announced concerts at Glasgow, White City and Manchester would be his last. Burned out and, frankly, on the wane (his final single for Bell Records stalled at #9 in the UK charts) 24 year old Cassidy was nevertheless besieged by teenage girls wherever he went but at the second last show, at London's White City stadium, one section of the crowd surged forward once they'd caught sight of Cassidy. Girls fainted, others trampled on their prone peers and an event-hardened medic from St John's Ambulance compared the resulting carnage to stuff he'd seen over thirty years before in the blitz. By the time the medic and his mates got involved 14 year old Bernadette Whelen, unconscious and utterly helpless in the heap of bodies, was already fighting for her life. On May 31st, three days after Cassidy had gone onstage again in Manchester (to a depleted crowd of 8000 – since many parents had banned their daughters from the gig), Bernadette Whelen lost her fight for life without ever regaining consciousness. The subsequent inquest recorded death by asphyxiation with the coroner citing Bernadette as a "victim of contrived hysteria" and suggesting that "trendy, high platform shoes" were a contributing factor in the number of girls who fell over in the throng.

Michael Des Barres, apparently appalled at the events, duly wrote "Teenybopper Death." Some internet sources also link Nick Lowe with the writing of the song. The song drew mixed reaction, instant outrage and rapid deletion. It was mentioned in the British music press but you won't find it listed as having a catalogue number in the well-researched history of the Purple label. So far as the present authors can establish, the official release was aborted and the track doesn't do duties as a bonus cut anywhere on a CD or even appear on YouTube. Purple Records – mainly the EMI owned recording home of Deep Purple – kept faith with Des Barres for a short while. Since when this song remains one of those ultra-elusive seventies curios, revered as much for its rarity as any hitherto unappreciated musical qualities. It's even beyond Larry Lurex (Freddie Mercury)'s one and only single in its ability to remain virtually unobtainable as a 7" single. Tracking down an evidence trail of the single's existence on line isn't easy, though sound hounds and those with a ghoulish angle to their memories haven't easily forgotten. A typical example of such being "Mike" who responded to the freakydigger blog site in 2007: "The Bernadette Whelan tragedy also spawned a cash-in tribute single ("Crushed in the front, it was no publicity stunt") from Michael Des Barres, then of Silverhead, later of the Power Station, which went out on Deep Purple's vanity label. You can imagine the outrage."

It's likely that the copy on The Devil's jukebox is pristine, and is savoured occasionally as his Lord of Darknessship considers both the gormlessness of massively hysterical human crowds and the unending ability of humanity to drag dark art works from the depths of human despair.

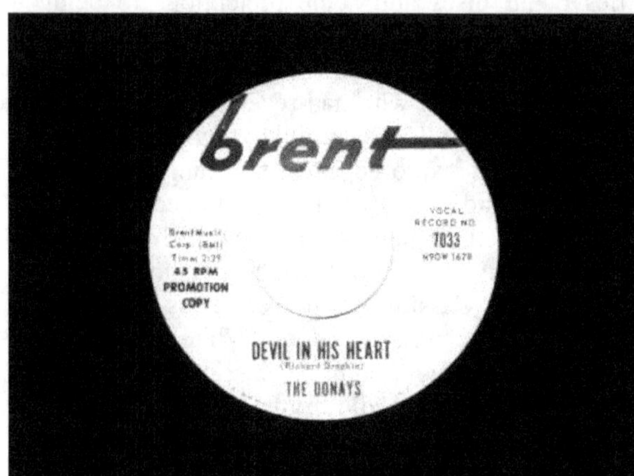

The Donays: Devil in his Heart

Satan sez: And she'll be seeing the real one one day.

So let's do the geeky bit and then talk Satan's jukebox. Everyone knows "Devil in her Heart" is on With the Beatles, but not that many people could say that Robert Gordy wrote it or that it was first released as "Devil in His Heart" by the all-girl band The Donays, appearing on Correc-tone Records. The sentiments are, arguably, more poignant when the gender politics are reversed and the song is performed by an obscure group who come across this far after the event as talented but essentially normal people. Lyrically, it's a pretty simple set up. A woman, hopelessly in love, believes the worrying qualities she sees in her man can be tamed by her love, and by bringing out the good she sees in him. But there isn't that much hard evidence. His eyes "tantalize" her, his lips "really thrill" her and when he holds her he says he really loves her. Elsewhere, for all the reminders of the Devil in his heart, she's the one saying she can't believe he's really that bad.

This is gorgeous sixties teen fodder, aimed at young (mainly female) record buyers, and offering them support for their own romantic dreams. The kind of superbly sugared pill that says "so what if he put his brother in hospital when they argued about who got the top bunk, he's nice really." You've got to wonder where, exactly, the innocent trusting love in the lyrics might lead the singer. What, for example, does she do when the loveably devilish guy whips out the handcuffs and suggests he link her wrist to the bedpost? He's loveable, right, it'll be fun, what could possibly go wrong from there?

If Satan slams to this perfect pop pleasure it's because he knows that misplaced trust can be the first step on the highway to Hell. He knows that recruitment to his clan thrives where evil is seen as attractive and that there are fools born every minute. Okay, this is just a pop song aimed at impressionable youngsters who wanted desperately to believe in the message. But it's also so insanely innocent and simplistic it could just about incite a riot in the wrong place. It's unlikely, for example, to be on heavy playlist rotation in your local women's refuge. Rant over!

It's also a nostalgic little gem from the days when all pop music wanted to do was to swap its nurturing charms for teenage dollars. Ironically, The Beatles and their ilk were the beginning of the end of that world. This stuff inspired them, but they took the messages and ideas to more complicated places, after which the world would never be the same. Indeed, if you knocked a twenty first century version of this charmer up today, it might make more sense to call it: "He's got the Devil in his Heart (But I'm Risking Nothing Without a Pre-Nup.)"

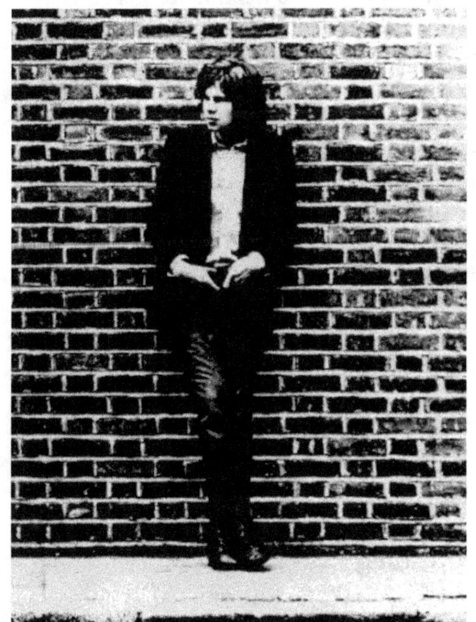

Nick Drake: Black Eyed Dog

Satan sez: Ah, the hellhounds, forever on your trail.

Recorded in July 1974 the balance of opinion identifies this skeletal and haunted song as the final recording by Nick Drake. It's likely many of those reading these words are up to speed on the basics of Nick Drake's story, so we'll keep the overview brief. For those of you not acquainted with the man, the internet is dripping information and speculation. Drake (1948-1974) recorded three albums in his lifetime and left enough material unreleased for a substantial compilation; Time of no Reply. Drake performed some gigs, for which eye witness reports and reviews remain mixed. Some suggest he was mesmeric, others that he lacked the ability to project himself and didn't come across beyond the front rows. There is no footage of Drake performing. Drake's fortunes had sunk so low by the time of his death that the story of his final release says everything about the problems he faced. Drake turned up at Island Records with the tape for his final official album – Pink Moon (1972) – in a bag, leaving it at the desk where he wasn't even recognised. When the album came out Island took advertising in the music press saying they were proud of their artist and proud to release it. But the short and very basic album didn't chart. Drake's death in November 1974, aged 26, was officially ruled a suicide via overdose of prescription medication. The verdict was disputed by some in his family and remains contentious. By this point in his life even the loyal Island Records had parted company with him and he no longer enjoyed the financial retainer with which they'd supported him. The critical and commercial indifference that dogged his career gradually turned. None of Drake's official albums – Five Leaves Left (1969), Bryter Later (1970) or Pink Moon (1972) – charted, though they have all achieved gold record status on the back of ongoing sales. Ironically it was the rag bag Made to Love Magic (2004) that finally broke him into the UK top 30 albums, almost 30 years after his death. Made to Love Magic and Time of no Reply both include "Black Eyed Dog."

"Black Eyed Dog" is slow, haunted and basic, even by the intimate standards of Drake's simplest work. Lyrically it's as chilling as any blues and simpler even than songs like Robert Johnson's "Hellhound on my Trail." The singer sees a black eyed dog calling at his door, the dog knows his name. This is death incarnate and – though barely 26 when he recorded the song – Drake is clear: "I'm growing old and I wanna go home." As a channelling of stark depression, honed into a song but passed on to the listener with very little interference this is a cold dose of reality.

One listen is usually enough to get, that for Drake, death might have been a welcome visitor because life was a challenge he struggled to master. There's much writing out there about Drake, thankfully his life and legacy has bred a fan base of thoughtful, intelligent followers, many of whom take inspiration from his work rather than endlessly rehashing the tragic poet/ doomed youth clichés. On the positive side "Black Eyed Dog" contains Drake's artistry as much as the more ambitious and orchestrated tracks that make his first two albums such a positive experience. But this is dark, uncompromising work that touches the point of breakdown, and offers no hope other than the relief of something ending.

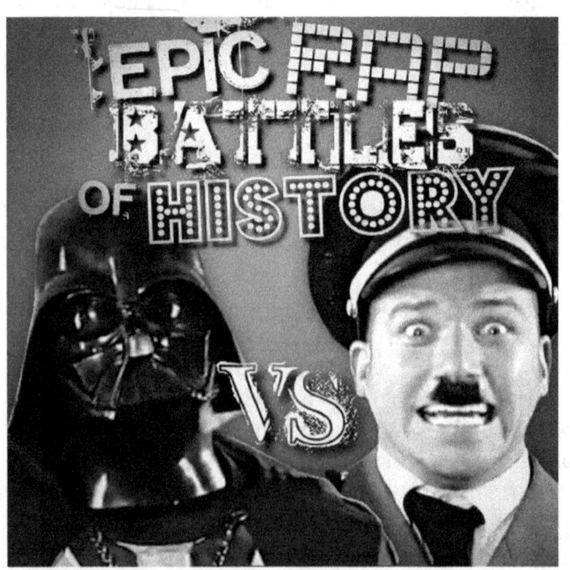

Epic Rap Battles of History: Darth Vader vs Adolf Hitler

Satan sez: Lucifer's laughs are let loose with this lil' beauty.

The music has rapid choral blasts and the kind of noodly electronics that suggest a familiarity and fondness with first generation computer games but from the opening seconds when Hitler screams; "Screw you you big black cunt…" this is a forceful fusillade of fermenting anger, played for laughs, there and gone inside two minutes and all the better for its fleeting assault on your ears. Such blink-and-you-miss-'em battles are the stock in trade of a recording outfit who have their tiny niche carved to perfection, taking in some politico stuff (Barak Obama vs Mitt Romney) and some genuine gangsta (Blackbeard vs Al Capone.) Vader's heavy duty asthmatics up against Hitler's high-pitched rantings, however, are a mite above the more mundane jokes and this cut is the jukebox favourite.

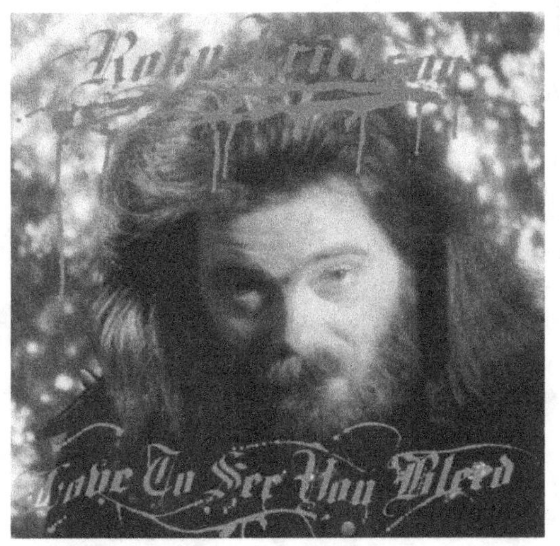

Roky Erickson: Love to see you Bleed

Satan sez: A ripping yarn.

The bulk of Erickson's musical career has been spent in various states of mental distress, creatively trawling some hitherto unimagined artistic ground between Syd Barrett's music and Charles Manson's philosophy. Thumbnail biographies present the man as a prime acid casualty and unwitting victim of harsh public services (both medical and law enforcement), though the truth is more complicated. Erickson had already shown signs of paranoid schizophrenia before arrest for possession of one marijuana joint saw him face up to ten years in prison. State laws on drug use in Texas were brutal in the late sixties. Opting for an insanity plea (possible because he already had an established record in this area) Erickson was hospitalised. It was – near enough - the end of the Thirteenth Floor Elevators, a band worthy of being considered psychedelic legends.

Erickson was finally released in a confused state in 1974, since when his sanity and fortunes have staggered through periods of creativity, chaos and catastrophe. The low points have included telling the world his body was hosting a Martian and being arrested for mail theft (though he was never convicted because the offence largely comprised gathering mail from neighbours who had moved away and taping it, unopened, to his own walls.) The high points have included some sparky work with the help of good musicians and producers, a brief return to big label action with CBS and a slew of the strangest and most bizarre psychedelic rock recorded in the last 40 years.

But none of this has been easy, and sometimes the work released is up there with the most disturbing audio artefacts ever offered for sale in the name of entertainment. "Love to see you Bleed" is one such animal. The title track of a patchy 1992 collection, this is the stand out on the set for two reasons. Firstly, it's as harrowing and downright scary/strange as anything the man ever recorded. Secondly, this is spoken word Hell on earth time. With nothing more than Roky's intoned voice and words, you are up close and really personal with psychotic madness.

It might be there and gone inside two and a half minutes but this audio assault is addressed to "you" and presents a searing set of images; "see you bleed down whole side of face and cheek…my, how your blood is really dripping, love drip…all those deep gashes, thick slices must sting blues…" Seriously, the graphic description of the psychopathic poet gloating over the final moments of a victim already fatally suffering is out there in the very worst way. Sick to the point of psychosis, vivid to an unforgettable degree and hate filled beyond normal horror product; this is a genuine nightmare turned into an album track. In its best moments the

Love to See You Bleed album is listenable and catchy, and much of Erickson's work onwards from the mid-nineties has managed to improve on this level of achievement as, gradually, the man has found some trustable friends and a loyal audience. Some of the worst moments in his stop-start solo career, including the track currently under discussion, were made worse by deals and management that left the artist, already established as prone to paranoia, feeling used. At best, "Love to see you Bleed" is a catch all revenge fantasy channelling years of pent up anger. At worst it's a description of what the man (or indeed any of us) might actually be capable of if we channelled our inner beast and cared nothing for the consequences.

PS: "Thick slices, meat hunks…BLE-E-E-ED!!!"

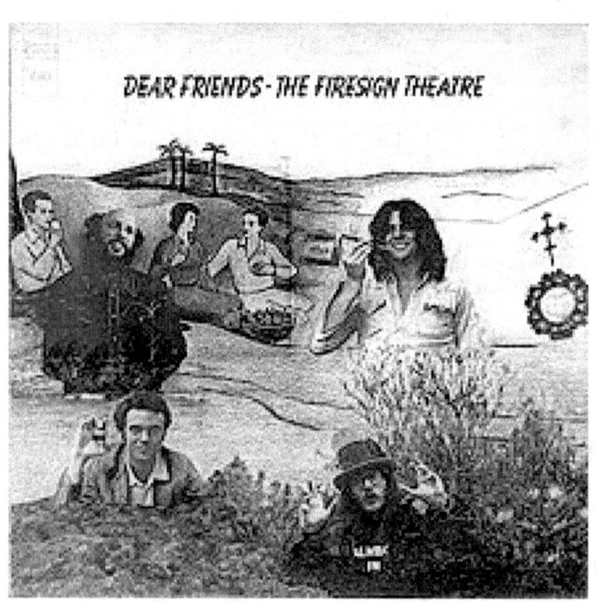

The Firesign Theatre: Dear Friends: Opening Sermon

Satan sez: A missionary missive from "the land of reversible cups and sanitary pedestals."

Time hasn't been too kind to The Firesign Theatre. The LA based comedy troupe hit their heights early on, since when their particular brand of genius has been bypassed by time and technology. The four Firsesigners (so called because all have Zodiac fire signs – an act the more reactionary religious types considered satanic in itself) - have proven resilient and able to adapt but their early recordings (improbably on the major Columbia label) still elicit the most critical respect. Basically, The Firesign Theatre produced recorded comedy involving dense narratives, surreal plot twists, multi-layered jokes and enough audio trickery to make their best works worthy of repeated plays. In the 21st century there are two obvious downsides to any rediscovery of their early genius. Firstly, their early albums demand devoted listening; any attempt to play them in the background and/or dip in for a few minutes, is largely pointless. The rules involve: long attention spans, headphones, volume well up, closed eyes and treating the whole production like you would a well-loved book. Secondly, their magpie-like marauding of all elements of popular culture in search of jokes has dated. Newbie fans simply have to trust that some of the jokes and diversions, like the occasional straying into radio adverts and the like, are superb parodies of contemporary American culture of the time.

Basically, these guys grew up in post-war USA, and their style suggests that from their earliest conscious moments they were critical of mass commercialism, tuned into to radio and its infinite possibilities of mental scenery and possessed of imaginations so explosive that real life would always seem dull. For British, and all lands once-owned by the British, listeners, The Goons (as in the radio shows produced by The Goons) are an obvious touchstone. Another way into the Firesign universe might be to imagine what might have happened if Monty Python had relocated to hippie-central west coast USA. But, where the Pythons considered albums a diversion from the televisual work the Firesigns treated the form as the perfect repository for a brand of surreal humour that found a turned-on, semi-stoned audience willing to go with the journeys on offer.

If you're still reading then the main point to make is that the deep and mischievous comic logic of the The Firesign Theatre probably sits in a treasured folder somewhere where Satan stores a vast tonnage of music. Doubtless he has most of their albums there. The fleeting introduction to their Dear Friends (1972) album, which opens a side of vinyl entitled "A Properly Religious Opening" is a chucklesome reminder to the Dark Lord of why he'll always love these guys, and sits on his jukebox to be shared with visitors. It is, what you'd imagine; a cod sermon delivered on the edge of high church style spouting cleverly about nothing in particular with a gospel choir humming quietly away. Our achingly sincere preacher asks us to share in "That great old hymn; 'By Order of P.D.'" at which point the choir erupts into a chorus of "Towed away, towed away, where do you go when you're towed away." For added comic effect the track title – as written – puns on "Toad Away." There's enough religious irreverence to piss off the truly righteous and enough surreal humour to set the scene for another bizarre adventure, which duly follows. But, like a treasured Monty Python sketch, this is basically your starter for ten more (or the whole album.)

S'cuse the rant but; there's a surreal aspect to the onslaught of evangelisation by the likes of Jacob Aranza and the PMRC on the music industry. This occurred back in the days – mainly the eighties - when a small percentage of the world and its collective dogs seriously believed rock music was pumping the Devil into both ears of the young and impressionable. You can still read their rants about the evils of the Electric Light Orchestra, Hall and Oates and other AOR giants playing with satanic symbols and lyrical asides. But…where the fuck were the evangelicals and overly concerned parents when a small slew of AOC (album oriented comedians) were plying their trade? The Firesigns make Satan's jukebox because their work is truly out there, encouraging the kind of deep thought and creative twists of imagination that suggest everything you know is wrong and the only knowledge you can trust is self-knowledge. In that respect they are up there with the high IQ funsters like Monty Python and Peter Cook and Dudley Moore (Derek and Clive.) Elsewhere Cheech and Chong mined a fertile furrow of the most gormless stoner gags. These acts, and a few others, turned out product on album, sold it to the same people who were listening to the likes of the ELO and near enough demanded these listeners follow their logic to get the gags. Cheech and Chong in particular were a living advert for a weed-heavy lifestyle that flew in the face of hard working values of all the "straights" in western culture. The Firesigns and their ilk were a living advert for questioning everything, especially the established pillars of society, you know, like the church. Did the crusading hordes simply miss these comics time and time again, or were they (the hordes) simply too damn dumb to get the gags (even the most gormless Cheech and

Chong gags – like the one in "Dave?") We could, maybe, attempt to start a conspiracy theory suggesting Satan protected his own comedians so they could go about their evil work. But, it'd be pointless to punt that idea out here because anyone reading this book is too smart to fall for that shit, right?

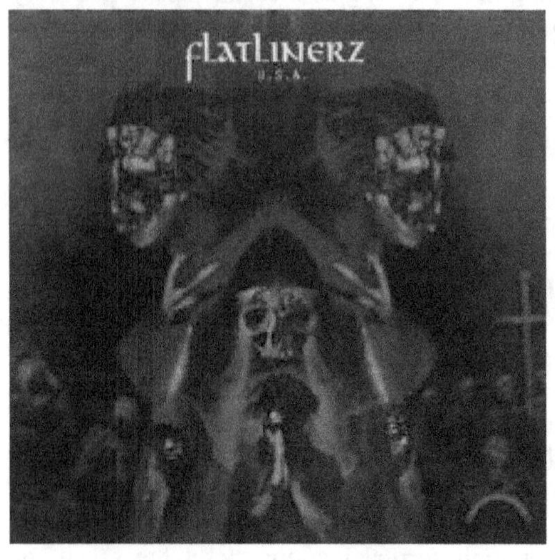

Flatlinerz: Satanic Verses

Satan sez: "Your souls, just a morsel that I crave."

Credited with instigating the term "horrorcore," Flatlinerz erupted from New York in the mid-nineties, made an impact for a couple of years and then split, only to reform in 2014. The album U.S.A. (Under Satan's Authority) brings horrorcore into being, offering up a collision of hip-hop, hardcore and "horror" (as in stuff clearly inspired by slasher movies and an impressive knowledge of satanic lore.) "Satanic Verses" was culled from the collection as a single. The sight of the band up to their elbows in guts in the video sets it apart from the other mid-nineties offshoots of gangsta rap, so too the lyrics: "Bodies pouring and to the grave/Studying scriptures but you can't be saved so behave/ Your souls just a morsel that I crave…" The satancore stylings are up there with the hard end of dark metal, though every word is clear on the single and the whole thing trundles by slowly enough to put the images in the mind of the listener. This is a vision – quite literally – of Hell on Earth. Worse than gangstas getting even with everyone by way of gunfire because U.S.A. (Under Satan's Authority) adds another dimension to the degree of trouble in that land. To be fair, lyrically this crew have it both ways. Their vision of Hell still leaves them fighting their corner: "My mic is the passageway to the land of the livin.'" Their vision of Hell is also played for some grim laughs and the kind of shock tactics that scare the audience before leaving them reeling from the adrenaline and feeling alive because they survived the shock. References to David Koresh, David Copperfield (because Flatlinerz make bodies disappear like he does) and Satanic Verses are also up front, suggesting the crew have an agenda built on savvy arguments. As an aside here, there was some savvy in the band's deal with DEF JAM. Flatlinerz man Jamel Simmons is nephew to Hip Hop mogul Russel Simmons, DEF JAM owner and co-founder. So, the band might not be in league with Satan, but their connections helped land them a deal with the one label capable of making them cool by default. All of which was good for Satan too.

Flatlinerz are flirting with Satan in ways that make him cool to black inner city kids (and all those white grammar school boys in England who just love gangsta rap.) And, Satan is alive, well and at the heart of this shit. Flatlinerz are feeling his presence, telling America to wake the fuck up, and not entirely hopeful that their mic, and their means of escape from the unfolding hell will help others.

Like they'd say if this were a movie; be afraid, be very fucking afraid!

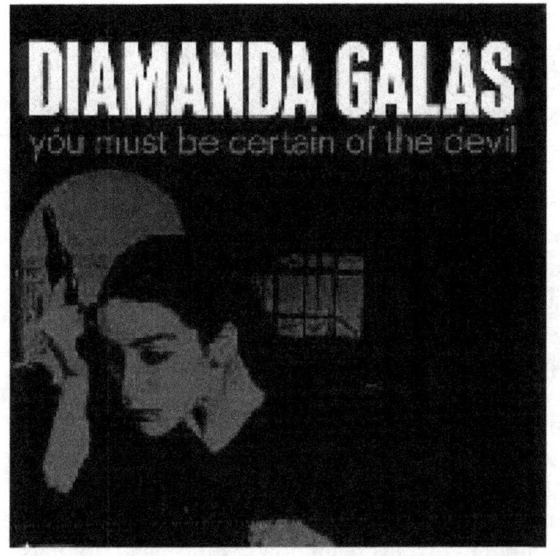

Diamanda Galás: This Is The Law Of The Plague

Satan sez: Indignant, angry and aimed at the church, what's not for me to like here?

This lengthy and extreme chunk from a live recording, made in 1990 at Cathedral of St. John the Divine in New York City, comes from The Plague Mass. A lengthy performance piece by vocal artist and avant-garde performer Diamanda Galás. The whole work mourns the loss of her brother to AIDS but it is way more complicated than that. Despite the setting Galás is also raging at the complacency of major American institutions, including the government and America's religious establishment, especially the Catholic Church. Plague Mass uses banging and echoing percussion and the myriad possibilities of the performer's exceptional vocal range and acting abilities to push the sonic envelope into areas of extreme discomfort. "This is the Law of the Plague" is the second individual track on the resulting album and the longest piece in the whole performance. It employs a litany of religious pronouncements to mock Christian dogma in the face of the growing AIDS crisis, banishing AIDS victims and all associated with them as "unclean" and repeating the mantras to the point of overkill. The cult selling work has become a touchstone amongst the most ambitious and influential outsider music available. It has also generated countless words of description, all of which leaves the present authors bowing to the erudite assessments offered by genuine experts on composition, like Airek Beauchamp. Discussing "This is the Law of the Plague" on the Sounding Out website he notes: "[Galás] incorporates elements of glossolalia, colloquially known in religious communities as 'speaking in tongues,' a speech act that embodies voice by implying a physical loss of control of the body as well as the casting off of concrete linguistic structure. Galás's use of glossolalia deliberately blurs the border between spiritual possession and the madness inherent to AIDS as the virus passed through the blood/brain barrier of its human host.

"Aided by electronics, Galás's vocals begin as the chant of orator. Punctuated by a throbbing, sparse single drum-beat, her sickened, keening crawl of words enumerates in detail what it is that defines a person as unclean. The language is precisely enunciated, each word sharply edged and cornered…Slowly, Galás's voice rises to the shriek of a pious, avenging angel, a shrill, wail shimmering with vibrato communicating the sound of a raptured body, rent in chaotic ecstasy. Eventually her ululations are submerged in a bath of primordial babble, a place where language moves in every direction through a body somehow more permeable, a sonic space that Deleuze would describe as topographic, that is, possessing heights and depths. Enacting and inviting the babble of the mad and the afflicted maintains a red line on the tolerance of the listener's psyche before returning, without ceremony, to the sparse and cold incantations of the church. Here queer(ed) timbres push the audience to limits well past the reaches of patriarchal or accepted sound; Galas plays along the edge of tolerance before dropping the audience abruptly back into the decidedly colder and less humane sonic tropes of an unforgiving religion".

So it's no wonder Satan slams to this one, then. To put things crudely, "This is the Law of the Plague" and the whole Plague Mass straddles the line of satirising a religious mass whilst also acting in exactly that capacity, albeit in a secular way. Indeed, it's the fact that it is both a mass and requiem and also a harsh questioning the way the morals of a country or an organised church actually operate that make the work so powerful. Like most majorly influential outsider works – Captain Beefheart's Trout Mask Replica and the like – Plague Mass occupies that strange twilight world in which a handful of people can't stop writing and banging on about it, loads of people – kind of – know what it is, but it's played sparingly on radio and seldom even sees action on a car stereo if there is more than one person in that car. Seriously, this thing clears rooms and reminds passengers in a vehicle that they could walk. In an ideal, or at least slightly more tolerant, planet Earth some online campaign would catch fire and a mixture of sincere support and freethinking experimentation would lead to mass downloads and take "This is the Law of the Plague" to Christmas #1 status all over the world. And Simon Cowell would start the following year advising talent show contestants they should aim for the same levels of artistry at all costs that Diamanda Galás exhibits here.

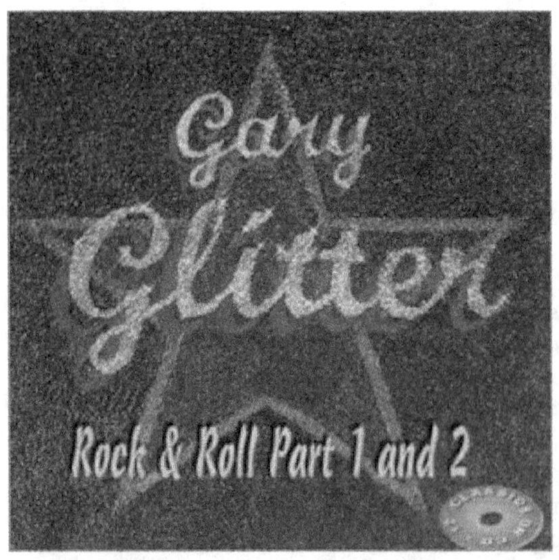

Gary Glitter: Rock n Roll (Part 2)

Satan sez: Long-term theme song of the New Jersey DEVILS, a nice little earner for GG and me.

It's unlikely that anyone sussed enough to actually want to read this book will be ignorant of Gary Glitter's convictions for sex crimes, or his general status as a British national disgrace. Then again, if you're – say – American…

The whole reason Lucifer might light up on hearing this song is the sweet convoluted contortions of its after-life and staying power in the face of the artist's monumental fall from grace. The story of this song is also a massive insight into a few of the musical world's more unpredictable twists and turns.

Musically speaking Rock n Roll (Part 2) is three minutes and ten seconds of primal pumping glam rock power. Glitter rides the wave of big drums, grinding and basic guitar and incessant hand claps to lead the chant: "Hey…" in this vision of bestial rock n roll simplicity, stripped back to something a caveman wouldn't struggle to understand. It hit #2 in the UK, launching a career in Glitter's home land that would land him three #1 singles, national treasure status in two separate eras and a level of celebrity fit to see his processions down various red carpets greeted by paparazzi photographers shouting "Leader!" in the hope he'd turn to be photographed. That's "Leader" as in "Leader of the Gang", title of another massive Glitter hit and the source of a chilling lyric; "There's no one like the man I am." Hades must have howled with laughter when that one gave Glitter his first UK #1 (and howled again at the thought the B-side was called "Just Fancy That".)

So, Glitter is doubtless a favourite for the full-on evil he unleashed, but that's only half the ironic mirth attending Glitter's simplest and most enduring floor filler. Glitter's hit career was lengthy and impressive in the UK, a few other UK-alike territories (Australia and Ireland) also supported him well into his declining fortunes, but in the USA Rock n Roll (Parts 1 and 2) was his only top ten single, and Glitter only ever troubled the lower end of the US lists once more. In that mighty home of music sales the man remains, as near as makes no odds, a one hit wonder. Which – sort of – has been the making of him in the USA and other territories.

Like many of the glam rock royalty Glitter rose from an unknown grafter to chart regular in rapid order. Such a trajectory was a mixed blessing in 1970s Britain with its high top rates of tax for the biggest earners. A few pop stars went from rags to riches so quickly their chances of salting stacks away in clever tax avoidance schemes were always going to be limited. Not so Marc Bolan, incidentally, who brilliantly set up a discretionary trust, avoided a skinning by the tax men and was doing way better than the rest of the competition until he died suddenly and left an offshore trust in charge of his future earnings, with no real responsibilities other than to keep on stashing the cash. But, we digress too much.

Glitter, by contrast, crashed and burned financially by the end of his hit period only to rise again – oh the irony – playing student unions packed to the rafters with those who had once been his teeny fans, and then rebuilt his brand – oh oh the irony – by branching out in the nineties to tour an annual thundering, hit packed, "Gang show" where many of his original fans brought the family, including the kids, to see the most bankable rock n roll pantomime on the road. Seriously, the man, and his "family entertainment" were beloved to the point he could rebook venues a year ahead, and venue and artist could sleep easy knowing the tickets would fly out of the box office.

Then he took his jammed computer to be fixed, saying there were files of "a personal nature" he couldn't access. Seriously, PC World thought they were trying to help him unblock the accounting for the fortune accrued from his revived career. Since that day in 1997 when the staff of Glitter's local computer supermarket found themselves gawping at child sex images Glitter's brand has been as toxic as that of any musician, anytime, anywhere. But he's still loaded. It may escape a casual watcher of television news or reader of a paper, but Glitter's various court appearances and those moments when the press doorstep him show consistently that everything from the clothes on his back to the location of his London home remain impressive. Granted, such riches are of limited use when you're in jail, but in the period between losing his live audience and losing his liberty the man still lived well.

That good living is down mainly to a fortune stashed from the years of live gigs after the first major comeback and to Rock n Roll (Part 2.) The B-side of the first hit is the one Glitter song known and loved in those parts of the world where the man, as in his name and image, meant little. Kevin O'Brien, a PR genius who worked for various hockey teams was the first major mover to take the song with him to whip up crowd hysteria, since when it has become a staple of sports events everywhere. Often known as "The Hey Song" (on the basis that this is about the only intelligible word Glitter sings.)

Another genius aspect to this near-gormless mish-mash of music and banging is the silences, which have proven useful to various sports crowds as they insert their own favourite sounds. New Jersey Devils' fans took to inserting refrains of "Hey you suck" into the playing of "Rock n Roll (Part 2.)" News of Glitter's infamy spread far enough in the USA and Canada to gradually halt the wanton use of the song, though for many years he could rely on hundreds of thousands of dollars pouring in purely from this song winding up sports crowds, and that fortune hasn't dried up, merely slowed down.

His UK infamy is such that tabloid press stories frequently use his Christian name in the opening paragraph and then drop "Gary" in favour of "vile pervert" thereafter. But much of the world remains in ignorant bliss with regard to Glitter, let alone his sexual proclivities. And "Rock n Roll (Part 2)" is so brilliantly brainless you get the whole point in seconds. Listeners; perhaps that should be experiencers, of the song don't even require any grasp of the English language.

As an insight into the life of a song this is a salutary lesson to anyone intent on penning hits. FFS, this corker makes "Louie Louie" sound refined and ambitious, so if you want 'em to last, keep 'em simple. As of the writing of this book Glitter's ass may busted, big time, but his biggest hit continues to kick ass in return. The moral majority, to date, have been able to slow, but not stop, this juggernaut.

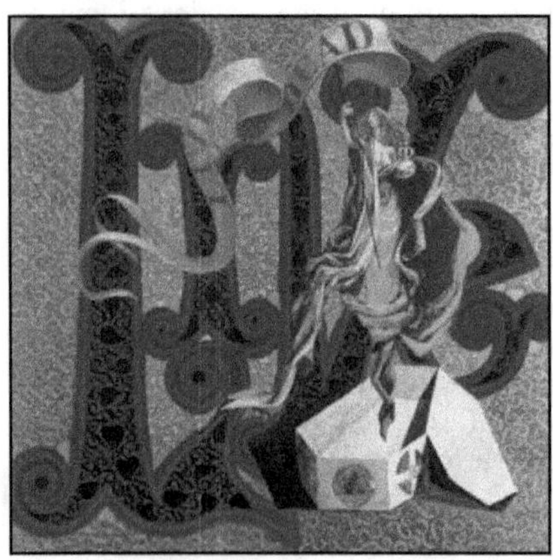

The Grateful Dead: Dark Star

Satan sez: The sweetest of secular sacrements.

In the convoluted, contradictory and claim-ridden history of popular music's most mesmerising moments there has never been another composition like The Grateful Dead's "Dark Star." Generally absent from any high-profile list of the greatest rock anthems, largely ignored by the popular end of radio and covered only by those suicidal enough to compare themselves to true legends, "Dark Star" remains both a law, and a lore, unto itself. The story of how a two minute 44 second single that failed to trouble any chart became an expansive addition to classic live shows and, in turn, became the touchstone by which Dead directions and the innermost thoughts of band-members could be gauged, is available online if you want it.

"Dark Star" remains – to all intents and purposes – peerless. Any attempt to compare and contrast it with another composition of similar vintage might, just, help a novice grasp the complexity of the situation; it doesn't tell you what immersion in this most elusive of musical experiences might feel like. "Dark Star," like Tubular Bells, works best when experienced in its slowly unfolding entirety. And, like Tubular Bells, "Dark Star" exists in revisions and re-workings, all suggestive of the fact that its creators never saw any one performance as the final statement. Like Hawkwind's Space Ritual "Dark Star" is an event, and deeply cosmic, even if the space explored is inside the mind. And, like "Stairway to Heaven," "Smoke on the Water" and several other classics it has become a signature work of a band able to boast many career highs, and a defining work they never thought of as such when it was first created. Bear in mind, the first released version is a single! When the BBC produced an ambitious and far-reaching history of classical music in the 20th century one rock track seeped into the series. During a discussion of minimalism and other classical music that overlapped with rock in the late sixties The Sound and the Fury allowed a portion of "Dark Star" from the version on Live Dead to run underneath a voice over.

For the purposes of this discussion we need only establish three more things: firstly, "Dark Star" became such a legendary item in Dead sets that those in attendance would gain respect from their peers for having been lucky enough to have the experience. Secondly, "Dark Star" remained an unpredictable, randomly expanding monster and a focus for experimentation and the Dead's most daring and inventive moments throughout its tenure as part of their performances. Thirdly, despite a reticence about performing "Dark Star" that – sometimes – lasted years, the Dead had clocked up over 100 performances of their most distinctive work by 1993; and at this point the Dead's Phil Lesh commissioned collage artist John Oswald to mix and explore these recordings with a view to creating one almighty composition based around varied performances of "Dark Star." That masterpiece of creative compiling is now available as the Grayfolded album.

So, the work has grown and expanded over the years, the Dead's totally permissive policy of freely allowing bootleggers to record gigs and, subsequently, freely allowing online posting of such recordings means there are countless versions of "Dark Star" a few clicks away when you log on. "Dark Star" is a rite of passage for dead heads and functions like a sacrament to the faithful. Like those claiming UFO abduction or direct communication with a deity, the dead heads who experienced key performances at first hand are revered in their community. All of the history and behaviour described so far in this entry equates to the sinful behaviour of following other gods and making graven images; as specified in the Ten Commandments. As a functioning creative force The Dead are – more or less – dead and gone, now. But, their magnificent mass lumbers on and still snags converts. We'll assume, because it's the easiest point of access if you are unfamiliar with this track and want to check it out, that the version on Satan's jukebox is the best known and semi-official nailing of a definitive performance, the one that appears on the Live/Dead album.

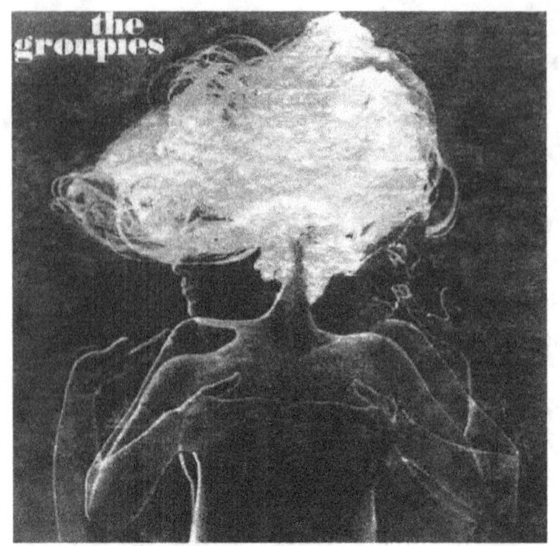

The Groupies: The Groupies

Satan sez: Ah, the sex, that goes with the drugs and rock 'n' roll.

There's a massive irony in finding this entry nestling so close to Gary Glitter in the alphabetical running order. The sexual power of famous rock performers, and their appeal to young females, is the fuel for this spoken word album. Incidentally, whilst we're banging on about that we should also point out that Cliff Richard's close proximity to Rectal Smegma in this book is also an alphabetical accident. Basically The Groupies (album) is what you imagine it might be. A late sixties recording, since reissued on CD featuring a group session (arf!!) with some of America's top groupies of the time. Foremost in the conversation is Cleo Odzer (1950-2001.) This is middle-America's worst nightmare about its sexually promiscuous daughters, writ large over two sides of an album. There's rambling conversation, poor recording quality and – not that it matters on a jukebox – some fairly cheap artwork on the original album. But this is an insightful discussion of groupie culture that presents girls old enough to know what they are doing, talking intelligently about choices made and lessons learned. It's also an insight into a culture where some groupies specialise in musicians of a particular type (guitarists being popular) and the American contingent rate their English counterparts as "weird." The discussions of the behaviour of British musicians, the dangers of sexually transmitted diseases and some of the darkness that goes with the territory (like the odd bruises and the kinks that some musicians force on the girls) are all laid bare and treated with intelligence and a matter of fact confidence. The fact that some girls will accept a cucumber as a sex toy, and delude themselves into thinking this is about romance and a future is treated with some derision by the outspoken little brains trust recorded for this album. Though, the self-worth and obvious intelligence of the sexually voracious crew here is unlikely to impress anyone who sees promiscuity as sinful.

Technically speaking it's all one work, so Satan doubtless has the whole thing as a single sound file on his jukebox. He probably has a soft spot for Cleo Odzer too, she may even drop by to listen to her young self and reminisce. Her twin obsessions about sexual behaviour and making sense of the whole culture around it went on to inform her life, which included earning a PhD in Anthropology after studying the sex industry in Thailand. Her academic and authoring work went alongside being treated for drug issues. Odzer knew the whole scene from the inside and found some empathy with the Thai prostitutes whom she saw as inventive entrepreneurs, somewhat like herself. Odzer's death, in India, remains unexplained, possibly AIDS related and also possibly down to blood pressure and circulatory issues. Either way, the lifestyle that made her such a precocious expert and so self-aware on this album, brought her to hang out with Satan for eternity just before her 51st birthday.

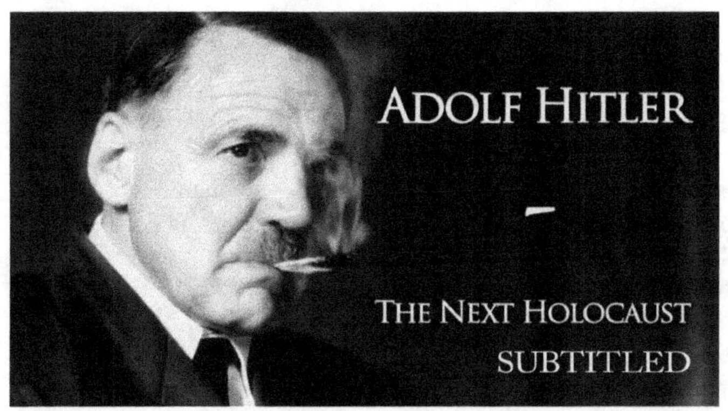

Adolf Hitler: The Next Holocaust

Satan sez: PaarrtyYY!!

A shade over two minutes of gleefully tasteless krauthop carnage with a jaunty rhythm and bass-voiced rapper overlaid with a ranting Adolf Hitler setting out the future agenda, the gist of which the present authors - who don't speak German – are reliably informed involves a little of the no more Mr Nice Guy routine and a lot of the old (almost) winning formula. Clearly, for all the effort put into a decent looping groove and enough melodic invention to place this at the pop end of the rap/hip hop market, the whole point here is blatant offence. All the more so because the resulting earworm draws some of its mirthful mischief from the deft placing of the kind of musical backdrop that would suit a trendy actor aiming to have a hit single downloaded by 11 year olds with the trademark incendiary oratory style of Der Fuhrer. The production does stink a little of economy but the short track doesn't outstay its welcome. Well, there is the issue of whether this "joke" was ever welcome in the first place, but where Satan's jukebox is concerned, that's not really a problem. Bad taste with poptastic bounce and a happy sounding take on the horrors of a new holocaust.

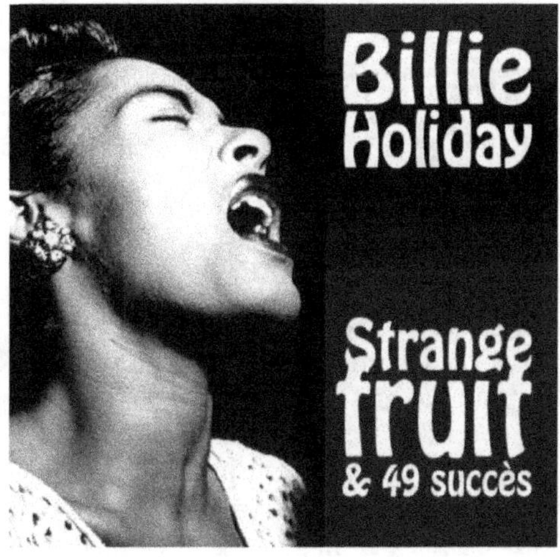

Billie Holiday: Strange Fruit

Satan sez: Lady sings the blues.

Men of "wealth and taste" have an appreciation of the finest artistic statements, and they come no finer musically than this 1939 recording. Holiday wasn't the first to perform the song and she didn't write it. But, as with Elvis covering "Hound Dog" or Sinatra tackling "My Way" this is a defining reading of a song and a defining moment for the singer. The song started life as a poem, written in 1937 by school teacher Abel Meeropol. The lyrics describe the sight and smells in the aftermath of the lynching of black people, their bodies are the "strange fruit hanging from the poplar trees." Like most classic songs the various parts of the legendary recording came together more by accident than design. The original poem was called "Bitter Fruit," leaving less room to find degrees of interpretation in the words. From Holiday's point of view the song was personal (reminding her of her father) and more than another addition to her set. Her wish to record it eventually won out over commercial considerations, though her label – Columbia at the time –

were not interested in recording or distributing it, fearing a backlash in the southern states. In the end it was Commodore Records who cut the first recording and arranged a distribution deal for the song that would eventually become Holiday's best-selling track of all. Though, originally, "Strange Fruit" was a B-Side.

After which, it's really pointless to go beyond stating the obvious. So many words have already been written on the subject. "Strange Fruit" is more than a recording of a song. Holiday sang it live at the end of her set, one bright light on her face, the band in near darkness and the arrangement restrained to the point every word was clear. Some critical comments liken her reading of the song to treating it as a prayer. Her 1939 recording has that reverent quality. But, it is a dark and bitterly surreal little beast, chronicling inhumanity and using the barest details to bring the utter horror to the imagination. There's hope, of a sort, but only because the moral message of the whole thing mocks southern, God fearing, America's self-image: "Pastoral scene of the gallant south/ The bulging eyes and the twisted mouth…" So, the hope depends on people seeing the strange fruit for what it is, and changing their ways. You could look at all that civil rights have achieved since Holiday first cut the song and see hope and progress. But, the bitter resonance of "Strange Fruit" would doubtless make perfect sense to everyone bereaved in the Emmanuel AME Charleston church shooting in Charleston in 2015, over 75 years since "Strange Fruit" was first released.

There is beauty in Holiday's performance and in the sparing arrangement and restrained playing, especially in the delicate improvisation of the piano part that starts the recording. "Strange Fruit" drips artistry because it has strength and authority in the story it tells. But it's also a recognition of the worst in human nature, and it makes sense so long after its release, because strange fruit of similar kinds still appears all over the world.

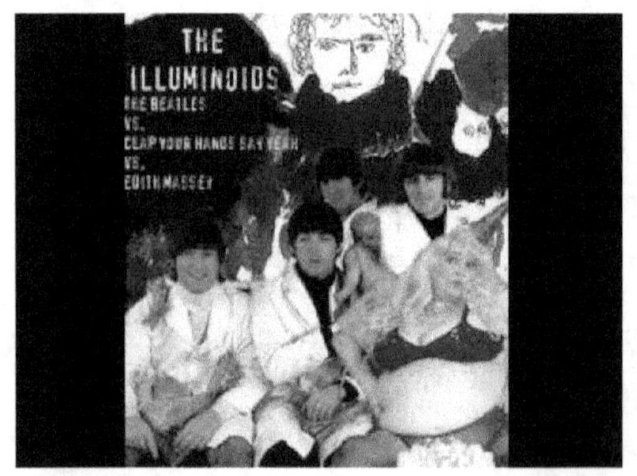

The Illuminoids: Satan Said Walrus Eggs

Satan sez: Messin' with the mystic and mashing up a treat.

We acknowledge the sterling work done on behalf of all mankind by the Music for Maniacs (M4M) blog site and – in particular – Mr Fab; head honcho of this admirable operation. M4M pretty much does what you'd imagine and does it superbly. When they blogged a compilation of music in tribute to John Waters' classic trashfest movie Pink Flamingos this track made the collection and M4M noted: "a mashup from 2007 that mixes Massey's 'Pink Flamingo' dialogue with the Beatles, over a stomping beat from Clap Your Hands Say Yeah. The Egg Lady meets the Egg Man, with special guest: Satan. One of the members of the Illuminoids was Howie Pyro, who took the name for his super-swell internet show 'Intoxica' from one of the songs on this here [Pink Flamingos] soundtrack."

Hell yeah! We imagine that Satan salutes the attitude, the achievement and the fun. In particular he salutes the sly hilarity that keeps a straight face as a song long associated with Beatle conspiracy theories is deftly intercut with references to the Lord of Darkness before a fragment of "eggman" related dialogue from Waters' movie turns up to make mock of everything. The whole compilation is a transcendental trash fest of titanic proportions and this track is a fitting finale to the whole shebang.

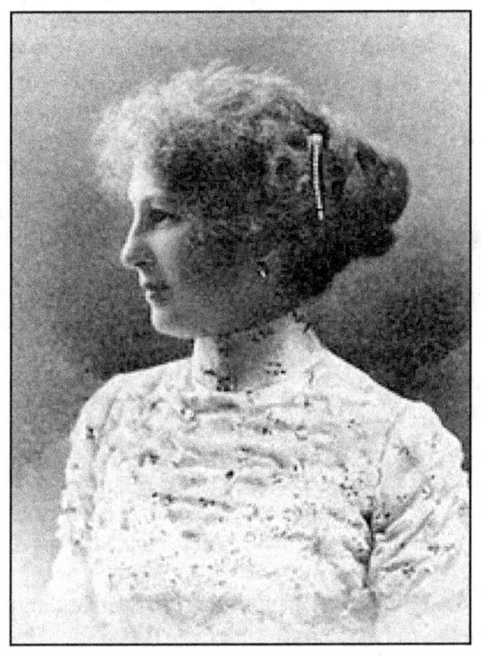

Leos Janacek: Elegy on the Death of My Daughter Olga

Satan sez: In the midst of life we are in death, in the midst of death, we might shake a few others up!

Olga Janacek (1882 – 1903) was the eldest child of composer Leos Jacacek (Leoš Janáček if you're being totally accurate) her youthful ill health and early death left him, literally, tearing out his hair. By the time of Olga's death her younger brother, Vladimir, was also dead and the composer and his wife faced a childless old age. He dedicated his subsequently published first opera to her and also – within two months of her death – had produced his Elegy, in her honour. Lengthy discussions of the work consider the reliance on traditional Russian verse forms and its musical references to traditional music, all produced in honour of a daughter who had shared her father's love of Russian culture.

However, Satan, and a handful of die-hard audio thrill seekers balancing precariously on the non-existent fence separating voyeurs from ghouls have a slightly different take on the piece. Years before high quality mechanical recording devices (in their early infancy by 1903) Elegy on the Death... goes as far as a classical composer could in actually recording the final moments of life. The early ebb and flow of Janacek's work reveals the way he set out to recreate the final shallow and rasping breaths of his dying daughter. Put crudely, the took the distinctive sound – better known to all and sundry in the days when large numbers of the well-appointed persons in the upper reaches of European society struggled and died with typhus – and notated it as the opening, and recurrent, motif of a classical work.

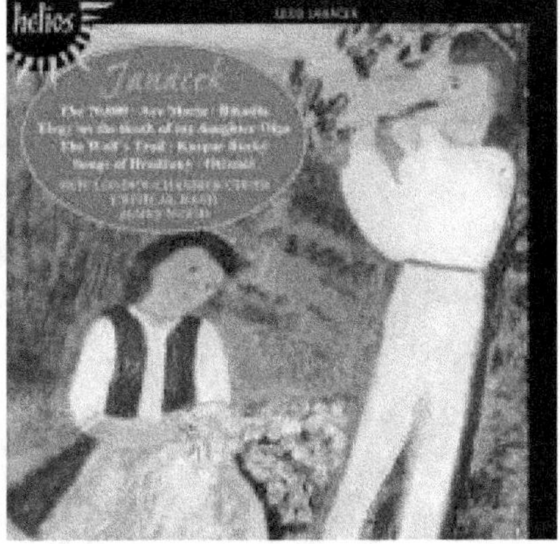

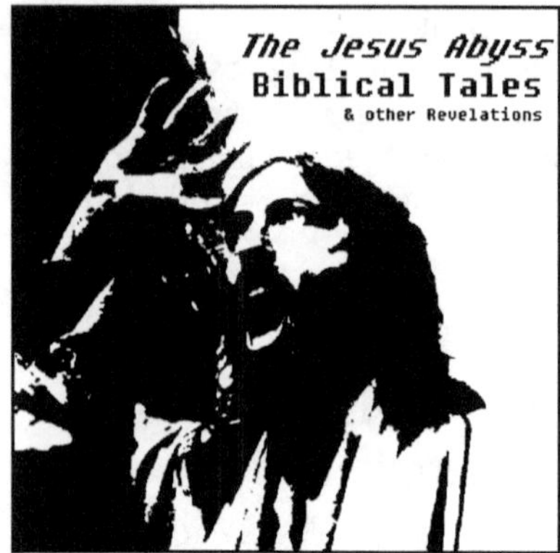

The Jesus Abyss: Forgive me Father

Satan sez: Chill out fella!

Hey up, we're going to get all wanky bollocks about an album that, basically, slams. But work with us on this one, there is a point to all this. The mainly dance oriented works of The Jesus Abyss sit on Bandcamp, agreeably available for free download and capable of offering up expansive mental voyages. The present authors would highly recommend Voyages of the Interstellar Mind Trip, complete with its generous samples of – amongst others - Charles Manson, Ronald Reagan and porn star Lacie Heart. For Satan's jukebox, however, we need something from their collection Biblical Tales and Other Revelations. The album visits their familiar dance territory but also branches off into cliché ridden church sounds and spoken word numbers as it repeatedly sticks classic Christian morality up against the everyday expressions of the human condition. For a concise summary of why selfishness and self-interest might, just be excusable in the face of the ongoing daily grind, this album's "A Child of the Thatcher Era" is an erudite expression of a frustrated generation. Similarly, "Who Needs God?" which precedes "Forgive me Father" is an agreeable litany of mainstream and cult heroes, including footballers and film stars, fit to conjure up memories of when we were mesmerized by our fellow humans, and drawn away from the righteous path. However, the short, simplicity and understated brutality of the final track is the real point of the album. Coming after the inventive journey "Forgive me Father" is a short rant in a confessional, listing sins. The confession runs alongside a chirpy choir singing a hymn, so we could, quite literally, be in a church. Since the good and evil battle has raged over eight tracks by this point we are listening in on a story we believe to have happened. The teller is sorry, and we've already heard him ranting in his cups and demanding: "stand me a beer and mourn the poor whores of Chatham," so we've shared this journey. The confessional rant seeks some redemption but delivers a gleeful little sting in the tail. The problem being the obvious problem with many confessions. Our man has enjoyed enough sex, drugs and rock 'n' roll to have reason to fear about his entry into Heaven. But, having acknowledged all of this he tells us, and the listening-in God: "I've fucking loved it."

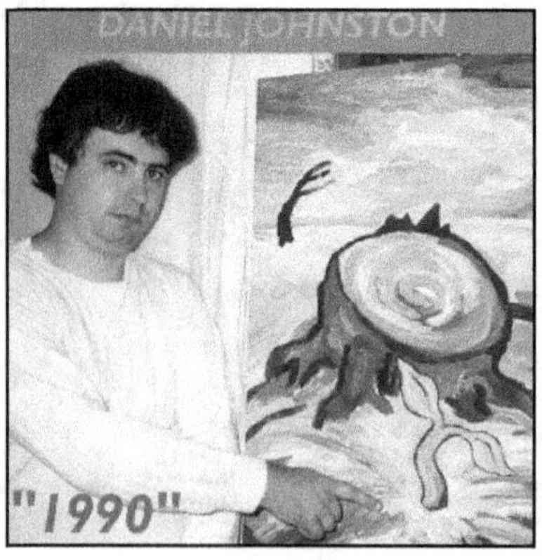

Daniel Johnson: Devil Town

Satan sez: Boy…I made you!

Daniel Johnson is a singer songwriter of the old school. A guy for whom the standard instruments generally suffice and the stories of his own life make up the subject matter. But those facts barely scratch the surface in getting to grips with a truly unique and compelling body of work. Far better, frankly, to watch one of the best music documentaries ever made: The Devil and Daniel Johnson, if you want a better insight. Johnson's life long battle with mental illness – which has been channelled and recorded in his output since the early 1980s – is the real deal here. Johnson's prolific albums account opened with the aptly titled Songs of Pain (1981), and has produced enough suitable tunes since to fill Satan's jukebox. "Devil Town" opens the album 1990 (1990, obviously) with just over a minute of personal pain and misery channelled almost directly from Johnson's soul to your ears. Johnson's songs frequently ignore standard singer-songwriter values (many run short, the instrumentation is basic, Johnson's voice rises and falls as much with his own demons as it does with a standard melody line.) So, in the unlikely event you knew nothing of Johnson until you opened this book, "Devil Town" is a useful introduction. This is as simple as it gets, Johnson sings solo with no accompaniment in a high, echoing slightly whining voice with a hint of early solo Neil Young. It's an introspective fragment that also sets up a typical dynamic in Johnson's work. He doesn't so much sing to us as allow us to intrude as he sings his thoughts back to himself.

With regard to its place on the Devil's jukebox this minimal outing leaps over many of Johnson's better known works because it is a simple statement of his relationship with the Devil. "I was livin' in a devil town, Didn't know it was a devil town, Oh lord it really brings me down, About the devil town…" Johnson states his friends were "Vampires" though it took him time to realise this. Longer still to realise he was also a vampire. And that's Johnson's ongoing presence in Hell explained in a few words. In the most general sense, the man has demons and has suffered with them for years. Johnson, unlike Wesley Willis, has never chosen to see this hell or these demons literally. His autobiography, poured into hundreds of songs and counting, is an ongoing battle with the darkness that overwhelms him regularly. The dilemma is that this same hell has defined his artistry and made him a figure to be revered by a die-hard fan base. Few of Johnson's listeners would choose to join him on his excursions to his private hell, but most of them wouldn't want to transfer their allegiance to more predictable and market friendly performers.

In another reality, maybe, a contented and anonymous Daniel Johnson would go about his life. But it appears Satan – however you might define such a being – always had plans for him, and still refuses to let go.

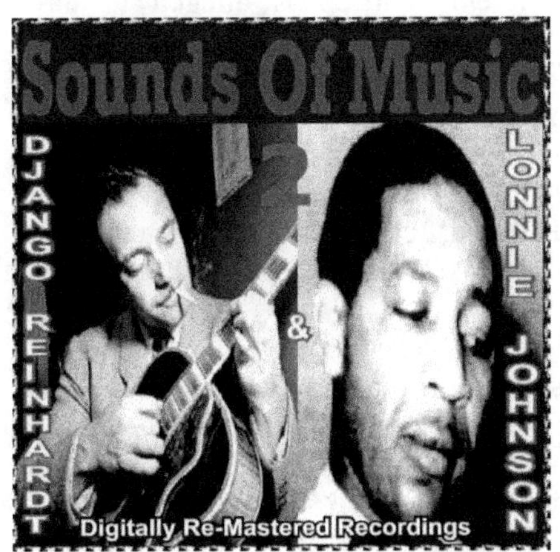

Lonnie Johnson: She's Making Whoopie in Hell Tonight

Satan sez: She isn't, but I get your point.

Alfonzo Lonnie Johnson (1899 – 1970) carved out a blues career that – in retrospect – puts him up there with the greats. During his lifetime he combined periods as a professional musician with periods spent working in mundane jobs. He was working as a janitor when rediscovered and encouraged back into the recording studio for a late period renaissance in his career. Johnson's main claim to immortality is his combination of consummate guitar skill with some deft songwriting and a very personal way of making the songs of others sound like his own. Johnson's version of the much covered "C.C. Rider" ranks with the very best. If he wasn't the first to popularise the classic guitar solo, played note by note with a pick, he was pretty damn close to the first. Johnson also straddled the jazz and blues borderline long before others made that territory their own and – perhaps more strikingly for his era – worked with racially mixed groups of musicians.

This barbed missive, recorded in 1930, is an uncompromising sideswipe at a teasing woman who has led the singer on and delivered a lot less in the bedroom than he was hoping for. The simple solution; kill her. Which is pretty much what's happening from the opening verse which ends with: "I'm gon' take my razor and cut your late hours, I will be servin' you right." The second verse makes it clear the singer has already passed the woman's "height and size" on to the local undertaker and by the final line of the song the deal is done and: "a coffin will be your present, and Hell will be your bran' new home." There's no suggestion the law will take exception to the summary justice or the singer will hear out any arguments about his own unreasonable behaviour. Uncompromising to a chilling degree and all the more unsettling because the guitar and vocal forge ahead with such a sense of certainty, this is grim humour of a simmering and satanic nature, or something worse.

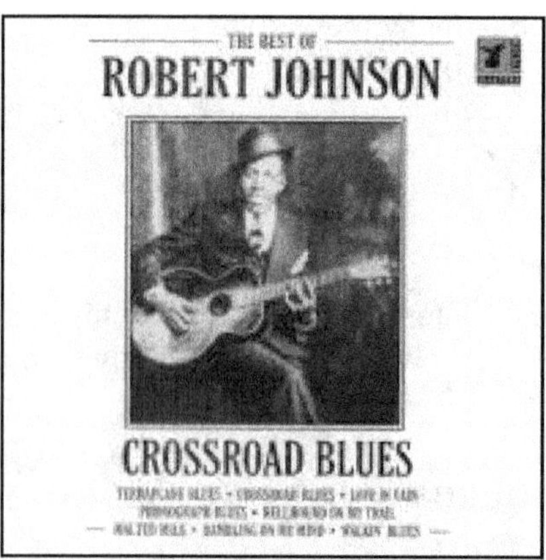

Robert Johnson: Cross Road Blues

Satan sez: Who cares what he's on about, bring on the credulous fools!

Robert Johnson (1911 – 1938) is a blues legend and – more than any other blues legend – the source of the myth that the best musicians sell their very souls in exchange for their talent. Elsewhere – like all over the internet – you can read copious discussions of the Faustian pact wherein Johnson is alleged to have sacrificed his eternal existence. In return Johnson – apparently – got the ability to create a small but definitive catalogue of acoustic blues on which most understandings of the how and why of all blues music has been based. Few catalogues of music anywhere on Earth have been so minutely studied. From blues historians to occultists of every hue, by way of music scholars and the utterly demented, Johnson's work is interpreted, re-interpreted and strangled to produce meanings the man himself may never have been able to anticipate.

Rant over! Whether "Cross Road Blues" (AKA "Crossroads") is remotely what some claim it to be is lost in this welter of wonderings. For many the song – of which there are two versions - is a literal account of a frightened and lonely Johnson, stranded and vulnerable to the point he recounts an actual deal with the Devil. This argument is supported by two other Johnson songs. "Me and the Devil Blues" offers up the line: "Early this mornin' when you knocked

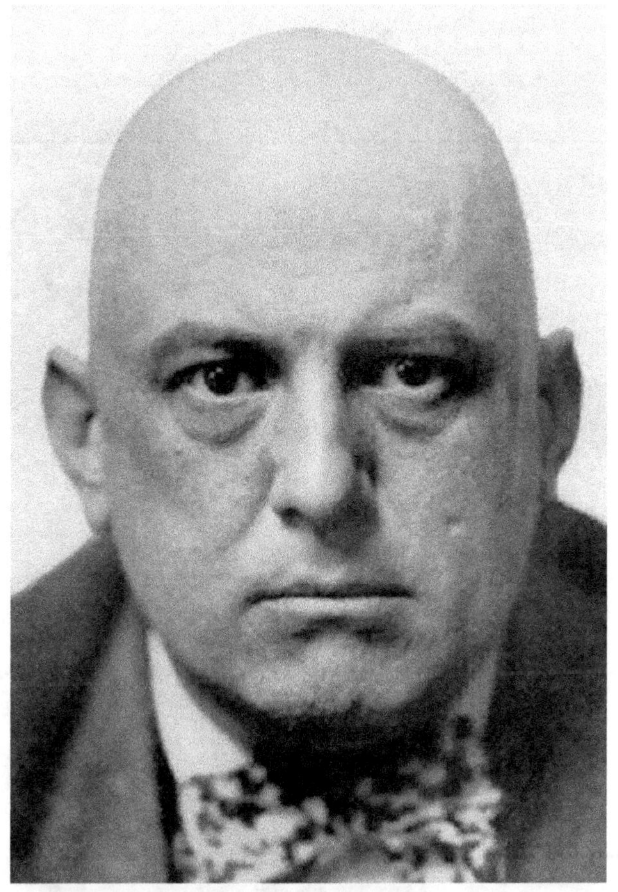

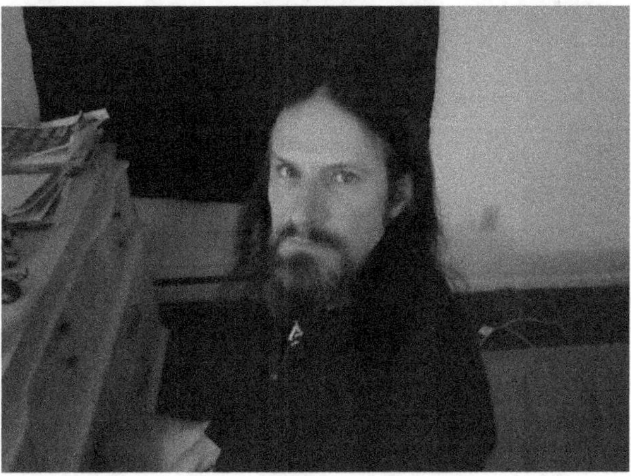

Aleister Crowley and Joe Aufricht – Life-long dwellers on the dark side and connoisseurs of depraved delights.

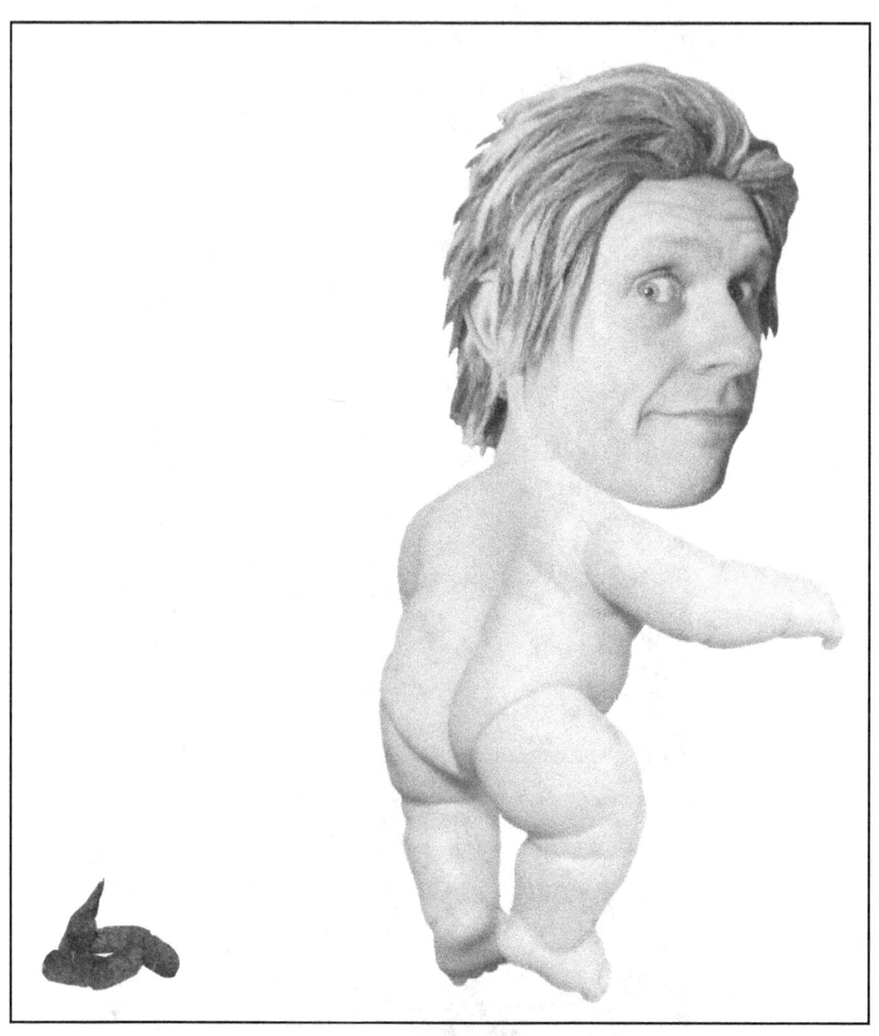

Typically puerile publicity shot from south east Essex kings of smirksome smut Kunt and the Gang.

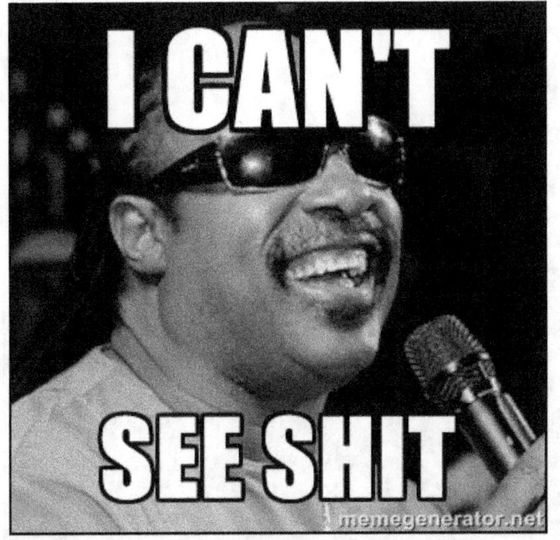

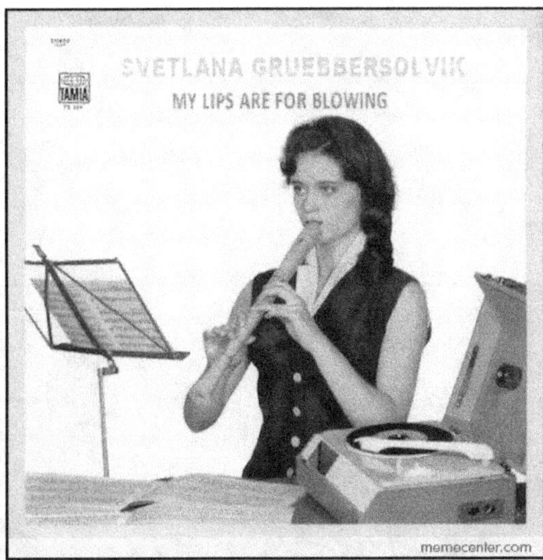

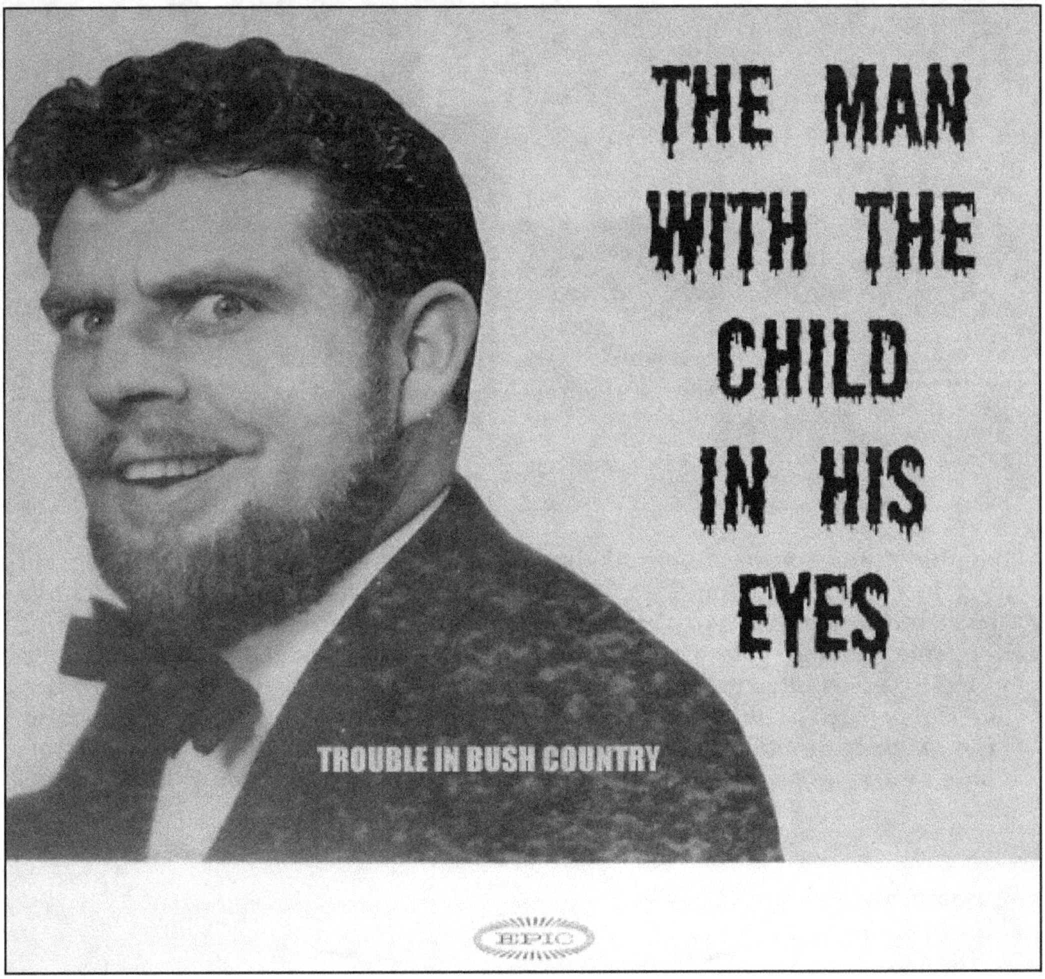

Internet memes, though if these records exist to be heard anywhere it is certainly in Hell

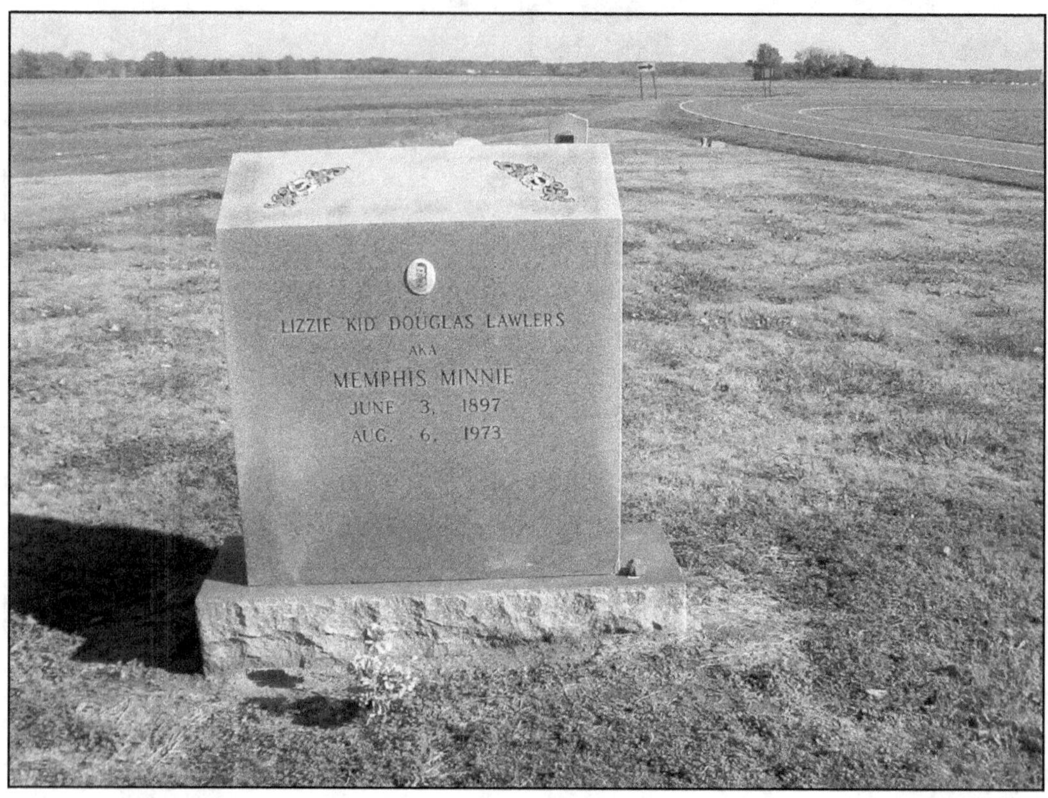

Memphis Minnie's gravestone and also a prime example of the way the world sanitises the darker side. Minnie's conversion to the church late in life may well have owed much to wanting to please her sister. The reverent tribute etched on the other side of her grave praises her artistry. The Stone was funded by Bonnie Raitt in 1996. The tribute reads: ***The hundreds of sides Minnie recorded are the perfect material to teach us about the blues. For the blues are at once general, and particular, speaking for millions, but in a highly singular, individual voice. Listening to Minnie's songs we hear her fantasies, her dreams, her desires, but we will hear them as if they were our own***

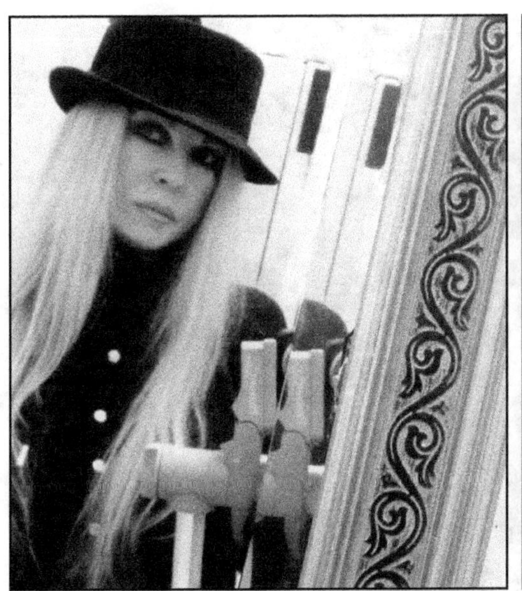

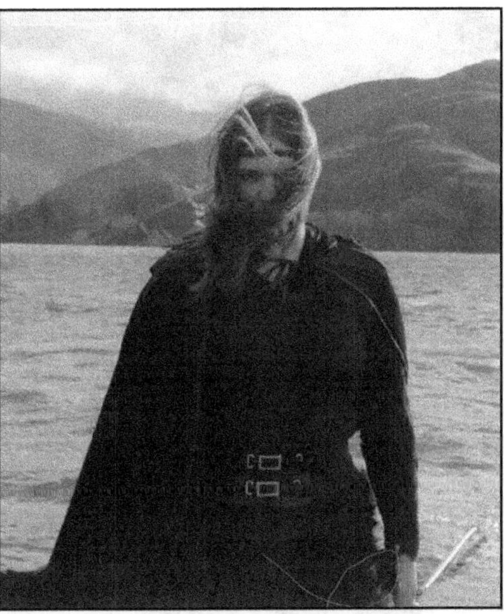

Jinx Dawson gets mystical with a mirror, Rose Kemp channels some windswept warrior- queen chic in the Lake District

Two fearless dwellers on music's dark side.

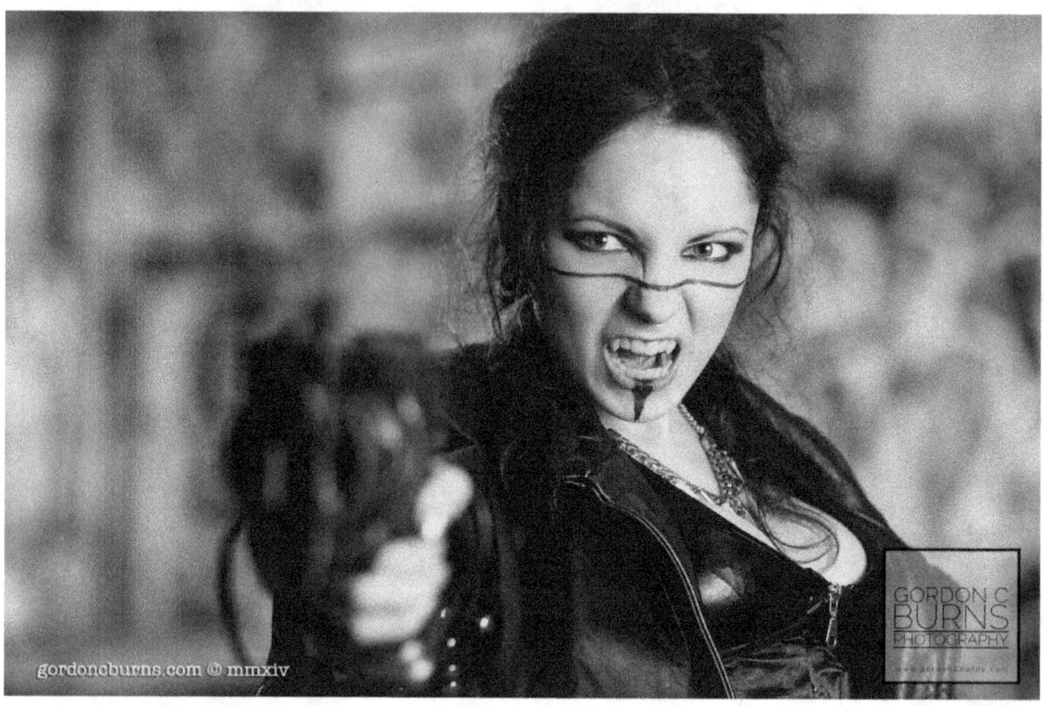

Photographer, model, author and generally unstoppable creative spirit Miss Kitty Grimm. Her name was inspired by the Cradle of Filth song Libertina Grimm (discussed hereabouts). Kitty's many talents extend to providing the fire photograph edited into the front cover of this book. It's such a shame her innocent young mind was corrupted by Cradle of Filth. Without this malevolent twist she might have, like, done something useful and interesting with her life!

upon my door, and I said 'Hello Satan I believe it's time to go". "Hellhound on my Trail" tells a story of Johnson struggling to stay just ahead of a demonic hound. Beyond which those hell bent on believing the demonic twist are reliant on seeing the lyrics symbolically. It's the same story – more or less – in both versions. The first take of the song has five verses, the second has only four. Verse one sees Johnson stranded at the crossroads, looking to hitch a ride and failing, in the second verse he bemoans his luck in failing to get the ride: "Didn't nobody seem to know me, babe, everybody pass me by". The identity of the "babe" he's addressing is never made clear but in the third and fourth verses she's addressed again as the singer gradually falls apart until: "Lord, babe, I'm sinkin' down" closes the second version of the song. The first version offers a fifth verse, compounding the misery by bemoaning the lack of a "sweet woman" in Johnson's distress.

From which point on it's in the ear of the beholder as to what is going on. The final verse strikes some as a frank admission that, lacking any human comfort, Johnson reveals he sold his soul. Well, either that or we've got a stark recounting of a, basically, shit day. Whatever, "Cross Road Blues" is amongst the finest in a matchless catalogue of skeletal acoustic blues, boasting a haunted vocal and a spookily effective and sparing guitar style that has spawned many imitations, most of whom haven't come close to Johnson's scary original.

What matters with regard to the Devil's jukebox is that generations of the highly ambitious and hugely credulous have stumbled on Johnson's work, and legend, taken the supernatural side of the story recounted above as the true version, and set off in pursuit of darkside options of their own.

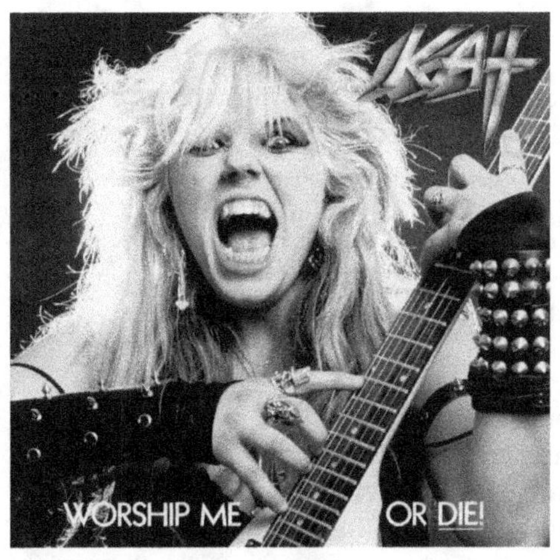

The Great Kat: Worship me or Die

Satan sez: Get down with the graven image.

Speed queen, guitar-shred girl and potty-mouthed princess par-excellence The Great Kat (Katherine Thomas) plays insanely fast and furious metal workouts, with a specialist slant on ripping into classical masterworks. Best known for head on collisions between the greats and her Great Kat style; releases like Beethoven on Speed and Rossini's Rape tell you all you need to know about the contents of those collections. But Kat (who incidentally was born in Swindon, England, and originally trained and performed as a serious classical violinist) has also played up every metal cliché to the point of owning them and reworking them to her own ends. Onstage she's a swirling blur with some variations of leather, lace and studs on show, blonde hair flailing and macho guitar stance solidly established. She's also happy to flirt with the satanic. We should probably mention "Satan

Says," a fairly obvious punt at reinventing the novelty notion of the bubblegum hit "Simon Says" in Kat's metal world. But for Satan's jukebox it has to be the title track from her 1987 album. The blisteringly direct chunk of thrash/speed metal takes no prisoners. Lyrically it's simple to the point of deranged megalomania: "If you don't do what I say/ You shall be struck down on the ground/ Dead! Dead! Dead!" That's us told, then. Later on it's: "Follow me, thrashers/ I have the power to decide who will live or die!" Which is pretty much the point of Satan slamming to this crazy kitten.

To be fair Kat is never knowingly undersold and her whole shtick suggests that deep down she knows she's funny too as she plays every angle of the she-beast to perfection. But Kat's claiming of the power to decide life and death has a point. Her guitar shred is frighteningly fast, her classical training powering the fret work (she also plays violin in her metal mayhem) and the power, musically, is a real and tangible force with just a hint of unholy terror when the notes come so fast, precise and sharp that they defy the ability to the human ear to register what's going on. At her best – including this aural wallop of a workout – Kat is a frightening force of nature.

"Kat rules! Kat rules!/ Kat rules! Kat rules!/ Kat rules! Kat rules!" Hell yeah!

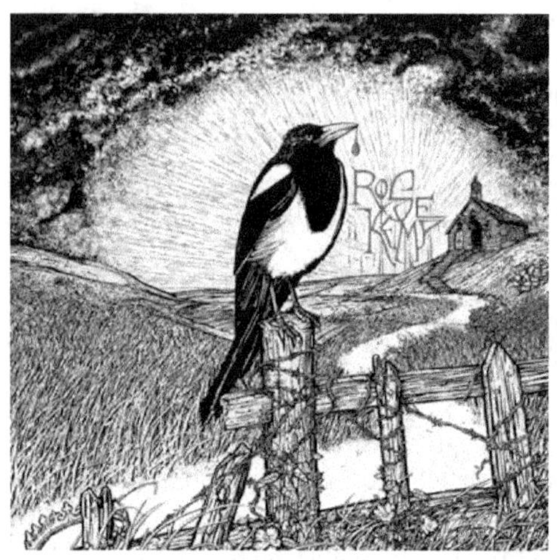

Rose Kemp: The Unholy

Satan sez: Attagirl! My English Rose

Singer/songwriter Kemp's take on darkness involves a tuneful, often lengthy exploration of themes and her own soul with a massive nod to acid and traditional folk and bursting eruptions of full metal storms. A crude assessment of the results might imagine her locked in her bedroom with her guitars and the entire Opeth catalogue, doomed to rekindle their dynamics with only her own resources. But that's unfair to the creativity and invention Rose brings to her expanding catalogue and – in particular – it's completely unfair to a collection of lyrics that embrace the dark and satanic as a ground in which to live and explore the meanings of life. Kemp's work produces a near-perfect fusion of lyrical insights with expertly deployed riffs and roars to punctuate the moments of highest drama. There's a sense in listening to Kemp at her best that she doesn't so much write this stuff as allow it to flow through her.

"The Unholy" for all its slightly unwieldy length is a truly accessible route to the heart of Kemp's current purpose. Lyrically, it riffs over a very short meditation of standing your ground, despite obvious problems: "I am the uncharmed/ Put down the red pen/ Or I'll cut your fingers off." The music soothes and surges at different points and develops a simple riff and melody, with random flourishes of instrumentation, to the point of setting up a truly hypnotic vibe. Kemp's earlier solo work is more folky and restrained (unsurprisingly so since she's the daughter of folk royalty; Maddie Prior and Rick Kemp of Steeleye Span.) But it's the darker music of her more recent solo output that has truly set a distinctive mood and tone for Kemp, and offered up some choice cuts suitable for Satan's own jukebox collection.

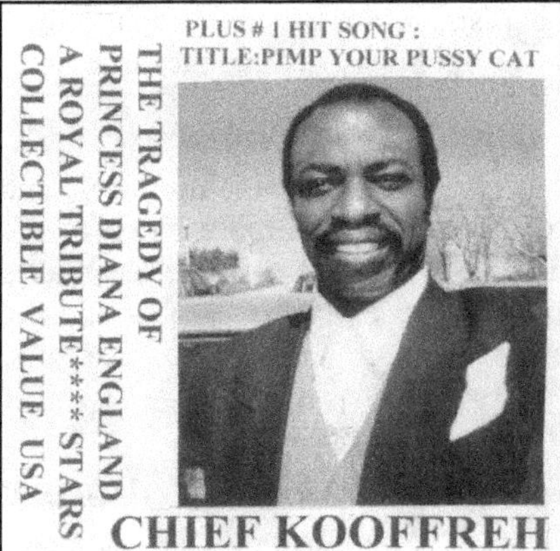

Chief Koofreh – Princess Diana of England/Accident or Pushed

Satan Sez: Dunno who's side he's really on but you have to love this guy

Koofreh's output is bizarre to the point it beggars belief. The easy point to make is that his work qualifies as rap. Beyond which, this is the kind of artist Spotify and its peers were made to promote. S'cuse the pun but, it'll likely be a cold day in Hell when a major record company come calling at Koofreh's door. Koofreh's prolific output is partly explained by the clear passion he takes to his work, though the fact that many of his original albums include the same songs as his other albums explains why there are so many releases. So too his endless harping on about the same themes, employing the same backing tracks and the same stable of simple sound effects. Koofreh dresses like a preacher, intones his tracks over basic backing and drops in the most clunkingly obvious sound effects on cue to keep the momentum going. In his tribute to Diana Kooefreh's observation that "the bell tolls" is followed by a cowbell. Job done. His cod theatrical delivery was probably never better than here, as he chokes back sobs at the thought of the death of the "English angel" and repeats "we miss you." That's more or less it with regard to the curious concoction.

Satan's particular love of Koofreh might take a little more explanation. Koofreh is up there with righteous epic fail jobs like Jimmy Swaggart in the collision of Christian spirituality and blatant carnality that informs our understanding of him. Granted, Swaggart's carnality – kind of – outed itself, since when he's done an admirable job of redeeming and reinventing himself. But memories linger. Koofreh's whole hustle is a much more blatant collision of heavenly sentiments and hard-on inducing concerns. If you sample just one YouTube video we'd heartily recommend "Jesus Christ Almighty Healer 'Heal my Life,'" wherein occasional shots of Koofreh walking are intercut with shaky footage of a busy street, but the whole nine and a half minute devotional rap is made more riveting because we're never very far away from another gratuitous shot of a scantily clad woman, many of them famous beauty queens and the like.

Koofreh's career long concerns have included falls from the moral high ground, in particular the falls of conspicuously beautiful women. His view – crudely – could be summed up as one in which a traditional devotion to scripture might save us all. But his grasp of reality is, at best, informed by his constant pondering over pictures and life details of these conspicuously famous and beautiful women. He is moved to produce tributes, like the one to "Shakira, Gwen Stephanie and Jennifer Lopez" that take their PR at face value. He also harps on about those occasions when his favoured females – like Miley Cyrus – behave in ways unapproved by the Lord. Koofreh blames Miley's dad for pretty much everything the daughter did wrong, or so his rambling rap: "Miley Cyrus, Vanity Fair, Daddy Soft Porn" suggests. Incidentally, if you avail yourself of this one on YouTube you'll hear a cowbell sound not too far away from the bell that tolls for Diana in the tribute song to her. You're doubtless getting the drift here. Koofreh truly is an artist almost beyond parody.

If Koofreh is out there doing work on behalf of the Good Lord it's debateable how welcome this work is in the wider Christian community. Truly, with cannons this loose much of the ensuing fall out is liable to result in friendly fire casualties. To put this in context, the chief's tribute to Diana is amongst his more focussed and technically accomplished works and the comments posted on YouTube in response range from seeing it as downright offensive to an ironic observation about it putting "'Candle in the Wind' in its place."

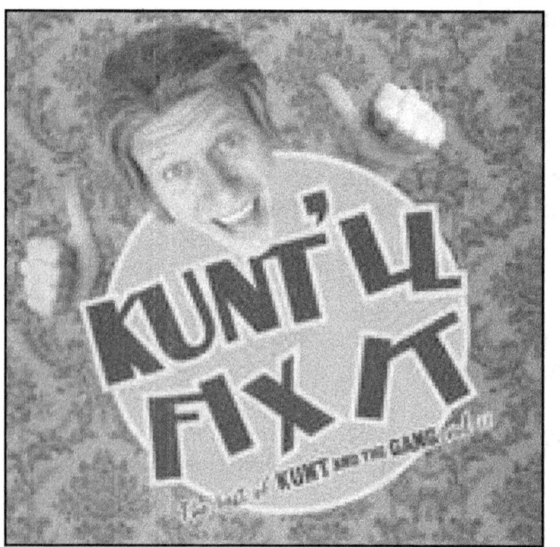

Kunt and the Gang: Jimmy Savile and the Sexy Kids

Satan Sez: LOL fun with Leeds' lowlife returning from the afterlife.

Kunt and the Gang (KATG) were south Essex comedy kings with a taste for the tasteless and a deft line in lyrical couplets. This is a perfect introduction to their peculiar genius. Malevolent mirth erupts as the singer is visited by Jimmy Savile, breezing in from the afterlife to put his side of the story that saw his posthumous reputation ravaged after the industrial scale of his child abusing began to emerge. Savile's defence – that the kids led him on – is at once the stomach churning self-justification of others caught in the same situation and delivered with such a light touch, simple melody and catchy couplets, as to lead us through the darkest arguments with a delicate comedy charm: "The kids were consenting, his shell suit bottoms were tenting," runs an early line, and it's doubtful if anyone else, ever, has rhymed: "He got them in his Rolls" with "penetrated their holes."

For the full KATG comedy caper experience we'd recommend their album-length *Shannon Matthews the Musical*, a sympathetic and, vaguely, hopeful trawl of an infamous faked kidnapping, but for jukebox purposes, "Jimmy Savile…" does the job every time. If, perchance, you're American or from some other part of the world spared the onslaught of

Jimmy Savile (one time "national treasure" of the UK) there is ample material online detailing a parallel career in child molestation that puts his depravity into the premier league of paedophilia. Now we've told you that, it's up to you whether you go online to check out the details.

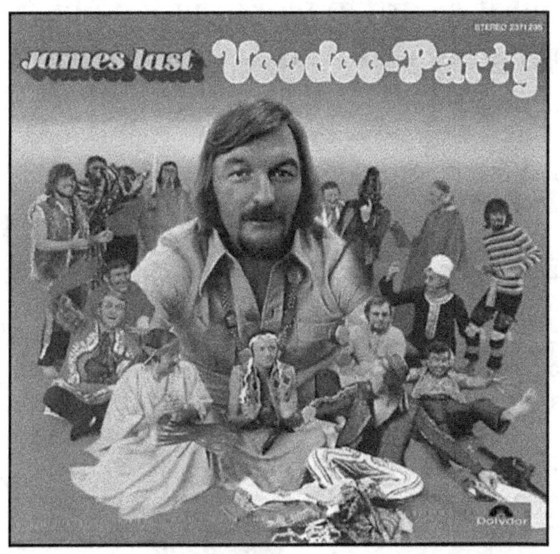

James Last: Mr Giant Man

Satan sez: Ho ho holy fuck!!

Culled from Last's Voodoo Party album, "Mr Giant Man" rubs shoulders with covers of Santana and Sly and the Family Stone as the trendy suited and bearded band leader does his level best to stay tuneful and embrace darkness. Some of the covers, just about, work. Last isn't Quincy Jones but he gets a modicum of the spooky vibe of Marvin Gaye's "Inner City Blues" even if Last can't resist some strident brass in the middle. He also makes a passable fist of "Mamy Blue," though this song had been covered and changed to the point it lacked a definitive version. Last's take on throwing a voodoo party clearly revolved around in re-animating songs to the point they stalked the speakers like the befuddled dregs of the walking dead; bland harmony singing substituting for a voice and simplified melody lines providing a facsimile of the original, and more soulful, licks. The Lord of Darkness may have taken a certain pleasure as Last's insatiable appetite to put his stamp on every possible theme for an album's worth of tunes led him to voodoo. Satan may even have nodded in approval when the odd sub voodoo chant like "U-Humbah" was dropped into the running order. But the cut that makes Satan's personal jukebox is an absolute jaw dropper. "Mr Giant Man" probably made Last's voodoo party because it's about a monster. But, otherwise, it's a Bavarian stomp, with rattling chains that sound like a warm up for a Screaming Lord Sutch session, call and response between the giant and the backing chorus and lyrics so unspeakably trite they'd be laughed out of a development meeting for a breakfast cereal commercial. The giant is planning a party, "everybody will be there" there will be dancing in a "giant way" and fun is assured. This is James Last's idea of slammin' at a Voodoo party, right? Granted, the lead trumpet does, briefly, attempt to push the envelope and scream a little. The fun for Satan and his followers here is surely the thought of the original album with its cack-handed mashing of rock and soul with some standard African rhythms and then this sore thumb of a novelty song. Well, that, and the notion that Mr Muzak had briefly gone over to the dark side. James Last did middle of the road music on an industrial scale, everything from his chart successes around the world (65 charting albums in the UK in his lifetime), his roomful of awards and a claimed 200 million record sales is massive. He was good at what he did, but to the ears of anyone remotely close to Hell the novelty strewn abomination that hosts "Mr Giant Man" and – in particular – the song itself are the kind of insane innovations that make Jive Bunny sound deep. The thought of Last briefly peddling this monster to his ultra-conservative audience is also life affirming, in Hell at least.

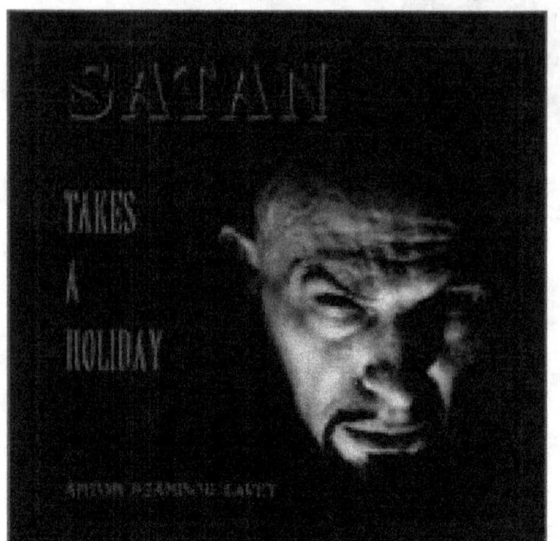

Anton LaVey: Satan Takes a Holiday

Satan Sez: Ah, a guilty pleasure, but it's hard to work out who has the guilt and who has the pleasure.

LaVey (1930-1997) did more than anyone of his generation to define and promote Satanism. A tireless promoter of both the brand, and himself, LaVey cut a dark, slightly stereotypical figure of an incarnate demon. He managed enough creative invention and media savvy to keep his cult celebrity alive for decades, earn himself the chance to hang out with the cutting edge celebs of successive generations and be a significant figure in the lives of others who would go on to develop popular aspects of the satanic, like Marilyn Manson. LaVey's Church of Satan and his popular writings, which gradually evolved enough thought for people to start discussing LaVeyan Satanism, were central to keeping his presence on the satanic scene both high profile and vital until the end of his life. On the down side his church, like many business empires run by an individual with a strong ego, soon descended into in-fought claim and counter claim. LaVey's wife and his estranged daughter were at loggerheads whilst the man's corpse was still cooling. So his brand, though influential and still popular, behaves like many popular brands when we get to the boardroom.

You'll notice, we've written an entire paragraph of discussion about Lucifer's poster boy and we haven't actually discussed the music. The dark and slightly jaunty organ tune that forms the title track to LaVey's album has a grim humour, and hovers on the border of comedy instrumental/ serious darkness/could've been film music. But it stands out on the album for a particular reason. Most of LaVey's long-player features the man, ahem, interpreting a range of songs, including some slushy balladry and standards done with a satanic twist. We could say it isn't his finest hour, but – thankfully – the whole cash-in caper runs well short of a full 60 minutes.

This far on from the recording and release it is probably fair to say that it must have seemed a good idea at the time, and with LaVey regularly photographed with Hollywood's high-profile and the cool rock elite it stood to reason he should make an album. These days autotune and some electronic trickery might well make the results more listenable and popular than they proved. If you haven't been initiated into this collection it might make sense to think in terms of the way Telly Savalas interpreted a series of pop standards in the mid-seventies, even taking his version of "If" to the top of the UK charts. LaVey talks and, sort of, intones his way through the vocal stuff.

He and Satan were pals, we'll assume Anton made it to Hell when he passed in 1997, maybe, the two of them knock a couple of buttons on the jukebox, and chuckle over this little novelty now.

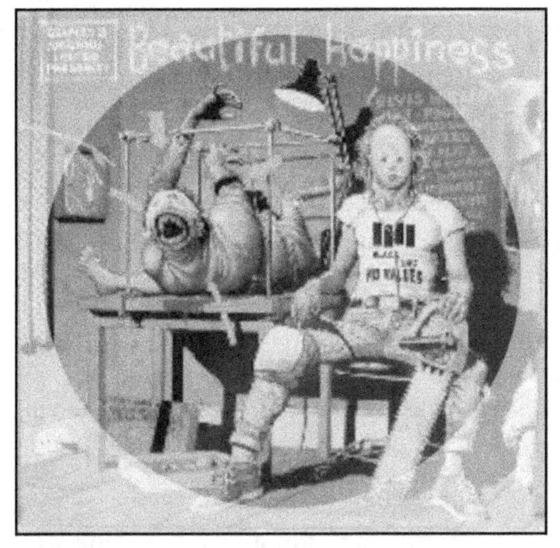

D J Lebowitz: Holiday in Cambodia

Satan Sez: Belligerent rant here reduced to bangin' tune!

The Dead Kennedys' second single is – arguably – their finest recording, a surf intro led piece of primal punk moralizing, ripping into the self-righteous and smug underbelly of rich America by contrasting the fortunes of their young with the grim realities of life in the Khmer Rouge/ killing field lands of Cambodia. All of the above achieved with a genuine corker of a tune and deep ironic twists in lyrics and music, especially when surf musical phrasing and punk politics collide under the chorus refrain of "Pol…Pot, Pol…Pot." Awesome, and if you want to retain some semblance of moral high ground whilst outraging half of the population, The Dead Kennedys' is a devilishly good name. Better, possibly, than Sex Pistols. What we're saying, in a round-about kinda way is that this song is superb and Satan doubtless slams to it. But the true strength of "Holiday in Cambodia" is that like the very best alternative anthems it survives maulings that would destroy lesser compositions. In fact, it's up there with the likes of "Smells Like Teen Spirit" in sounding great in those covers that truly distort the original sound. Duckmandu's accordion rich take retains the anger but adds an ethnic quality lacking in the original, Richard Cheese's lounge singer slaying of the tune plays up the "Holiday" in the title by transposing the grim sentiments to a Christmas tune setting and – as we take the current trawl of Satan's jukebox – we discover he is currently slammin' to this instrumental take from DJ Lebowitz. Lebowitz included this banging assault on American punk on his Beware of the Piano (1988) album.

For those unfamiliar with Lebowitz a short introduction: Lebowitz is a lounge piano player with a hard hitting and combustible style which sees him frequently turn standard piano playing – almost literally – upside down. The left hand, typically the rhythm side, intrudes on the melody lines whilst the higher right hand notes provide spot colour and flourishes rather than a lead melody. Lebowitz' extensive repertoire combines punk and alternative covers with his own originals (the latter often combining memorable tunes with gleefully smutty titles name checking the likes of haemorrhoids.) "Holiday in Cambodia" ranks amongst his finest moments because the strong hook, rumbling tension and explosive moments of the original provide the perfect platform for the pumping style Lebowitz has made his own since the late eighties. He hits hard and fast on the keys, conveying the narrative of the original without a single word or additional instrument. It's all the sweeter if – like the Lord of Darkness – you have a love for the original song and marvel at the myriad of creative visions it has unleashed.

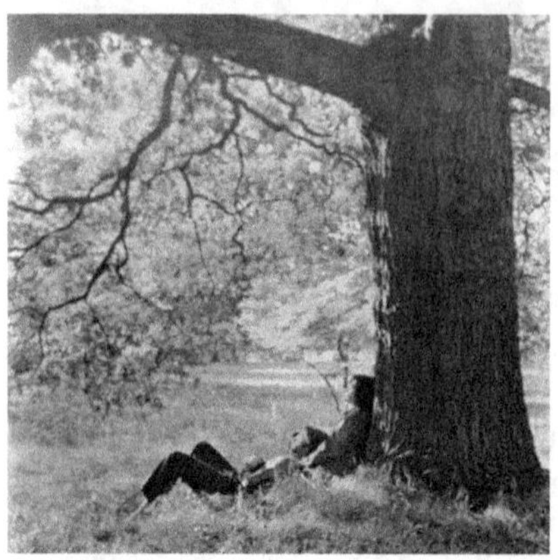

John Lennon: My Mummy's Dead

Satan Sez: 49 dark seconds hinting at human hopelessness and a harvest for the highway to Hell!

Lennon's undisputed masterpiece *The Plastic Ono Band* starts and ends with meditations on his mother. The opening "Mother" is missive of pain that precedes Lennon's "Primal Scream" collection in which he purges angst and disillusion with passionate and often screamed vocals over the starkest rock backing. As an aside from the present book the album also ends any argument about whether Ringo could drum; in the intimate musical settings the man is never less than brilliant, but we digress…

Having come to terms – sort of – with his demons and avowed himself of a faith in his life with Yoko, even if various religious and mystical touchstones (God, Buddha, I-Ching…), are lined up and lambasted, Lennon signs off with this lachrymose low-fi gem, borrowing the tune of Three Blind Mice to the point of near-plagiarism and plunging the listener (people gave a shit about albums then, devouring them from end to end) into a dark abyss of unresolved pain with his parting shot. If the great songwriter and channel of revolutionary fervour couldn't ultimately escape his demons, even on his greatest work, what hope is/was there for anyone? Apart from anything else, what hope does this fleeting fulmination on inescapable pain offer to any listener lacking their own Yoko?

Lennon's work wasn't Satanic in any overt way, but the positioning of this plunge back into the darkest recesses at the very end of the emotional roller coaster has doubtless done for the hopes of a few easily impressionable listeners over the years. Such twists of fate can be good news for the nether world.

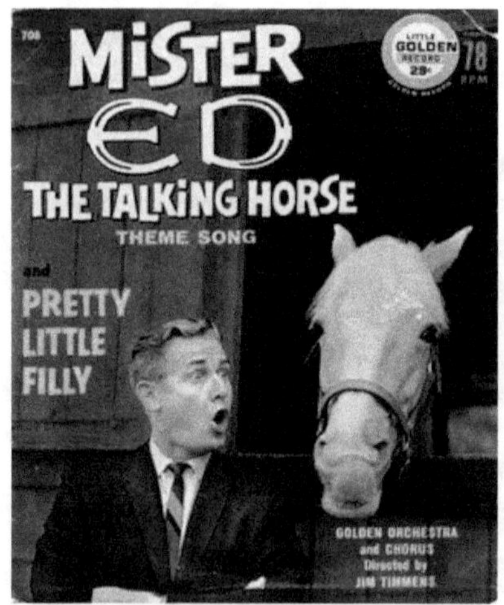

Jay Livingstone: Them from Mr Ed (A Horse is a Horse)

Satan Sez: "Someone sung this song for Satan?!" No way!

This clopalong cut of cod country and western opened the sixties sit-com Mr Ed, a piece of agreeable nonsense in which a talking horse (Mr Ed) only spoke to his owner, prompting all manner of comic misunderstandings (the owners wife got jealous of the time he spent with the horse, the highly intelligent horse was responsible for acts for which his owner was blamed etc.) The theme song was written by Jay Livingstone and

Ray Evans, and performed by Livingstone. The show was a rare example of a television comedy that started small and briefly exploded to become syndicated world-wide gold, although the essentially simple comedy idea at the heart of the whole caper was always likely to prove limited.

The belated explosion of interest in the song – over twenty years after the show was cancelled – must have stunned every surviving member of the cast and crew as it hauled Livingstone's work back into a truly surreal spotlight. The Mr Ed controversy happened at the same time Ozzy Osbourne was in court defending "Suicide Solution" and Michael Mills' evangelical take on the evils of masking in music was at its highest profile. So, perhaps, it is no surprise that an Ohio preacher named Jim Brown was minded to make a fuss about how the theme from Mr Ed (aka "A Horse is a Horse") sounded backwards. According to Brown, the fragmentary composition (which clocks in shy of one minute) includes the backward phrases "Someone sung this song for Satan" and "the source is Satan." Brown's PR skills and ability to incite others were strong enough to support an event in which 300 young people publically burned records and cassettes of secular music.

To be fair, the Mr Ed controversy is right at the comedy end of this cavalcade of Christian righteousness and even Brown believed the message, though audible, was never intended. He told the Chicago Tribune: "We had a copy of (`Television`s Greatest Hits`) and were just curious to see if there were any messages at all...sure enough, we heard the message. Satan can be an influence whether they know it or not...We don`t think they did it on purpose and we`re not getting down on `Mr. Ed`" Brown's army of clean living youngsters spared the copy of Televisions Greatest Hits including the Mr Ed theme when they incinerated other recordings.

As to how the satanic message is possible, it might be worth briefly considering the pun and scan heavy lines of the song played forwards. Sung to a cantering beat these include such tongue twisters as: "Go right to the source and ask the horse. He'll give you the answer that you'll endorse. He's always on a steady course. Talk to Mister Ed." S sounds proliferate, the odd N is in there and "Someone sung this song for Satan" can just about be teased out, if you listen hard enough.

Brown's more general point that "Satan can be an influence" whether musicians and songwriters "know it or not" is the real reason Satan might well have this one on his jukebox. Follow that logic to the closest conclusion and you're faced with the grim notion that your best musical efforts may be possessed, whether or not you want that to happen. Seriously, where – exactly – does this shit stop? Any lyric played backwards may just reveal some satanic snippet (especially when you allow for every sound in every language ever invented by man.) If you believe that your only options are to give yourself wholeheartedly to the Good Lord and dedicate every note played to his glory, or – like – shrug your shoulders, embrace the darkness, pick up a guitar and start improvising a few words, like: "A horse is a horse, of course of course, and no one can talk to a horse of course, that is of course, unless the horse, Is the famous Mister Ed!"

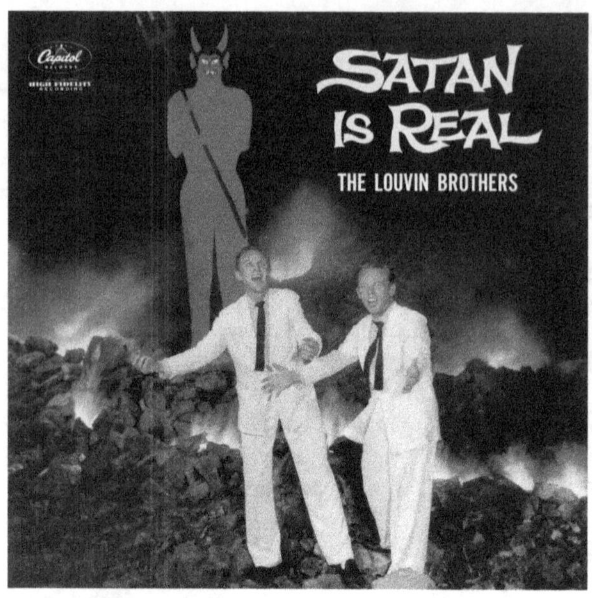

The Louvin Brothers: Satan is Real

Satan Sez: Hell, yeah!

Not one the Dark Lord listens to every day, but a reminder of his ongoing battle with the forces of good, and some victories along the way. "Satan is Real" is the title track of an album of simple, passionate country music by a brotherly duo who shared both a love of the Lord and an explosive antipathy towards each other. Despite their common Christianity the Louvins exploded in much the same way as the brothers Everley, Davies, or Gallagher. These explosions coming for largely similar reasons; i.e. one brother (Charlie) had the long game and protection of the brand uppermost in his mind, the other (Ira) was partial to a party along with the work. As an ironic aside that befits in this book, Ira battled drink problems for many years and encountered much alcohol-related trouble. Without the drink he might have escaped a string of failed marriages, being shot by one of his wives (she claimed self-defence on the grounds he'd just been beating her) and having a warrant issued for his arrest for driving whilst drunk. With the warrant pending, Ira was fatally injured (oh, the irony) when a drunk driver hit his car on the 20 June 1965.

But we digress. "Satan is Real," released in 1959, finds the brothers at the height of their God-fearing powers and tells it straight: "Satan is real, working in spirit, You can see him and hear him in this world every day." From which point we're dropped into the recounting of a story in which a man visits a church service and Satan is discussed. You can see Satan: "in songs that give praise to idols" and "the destruction of homes torn apart." All of the above clearly intoned over a straight and highly effective country backing, with brotherly harmonies on each refrain of "Satan is real."

Doubtless the Dark Lord had his problems with the Louvins and their fans, and rejoiced for every listener the demon rock n' rollers stole away. But this makes Hell's Hot 100 for two reasons. Firstly, this is the musical equivalent of a racist bigot admitting Stevie Wonder is a genius or a raving homophobe throwing shapes on a dance floor to a Culture Club megamix. The leading Christian musicians of their day admit to the unquestioned existence of Lucifer and acknowledge his power. Secondly, and at this point Satan smirks a bit, time hasn't served the Satan is Real album cover very well. Despite the righteous power of the music it contains, the cover sees action online where the tacky and misguided sleeves of the gormless are also celebrated. A quick glance at the artwork shows the white-suited Louvins with outstretched arms, apparently singing. In the background a humourless Satan stands in evil readiness to preside over any errant sinner coming his way, glowering atop the raging fires of Hell. A closer look reveals Satan in this instance to be a clunkingly two-dimensional twelve foot model. It also reveals the fires of Hell to be raging forth from a massive pile of recently torched tyres (or for our US readers: tires.) Granted, the 1959 equivalent of Photoshop involved literally cutting pictures and pasting them onto a board to be photographed again, but – FFS – surely they could have, like, got a better Devil and done something to hide the treads on the tyres/tires. The Louvin Brothers were country big-leaguers at the time after all.

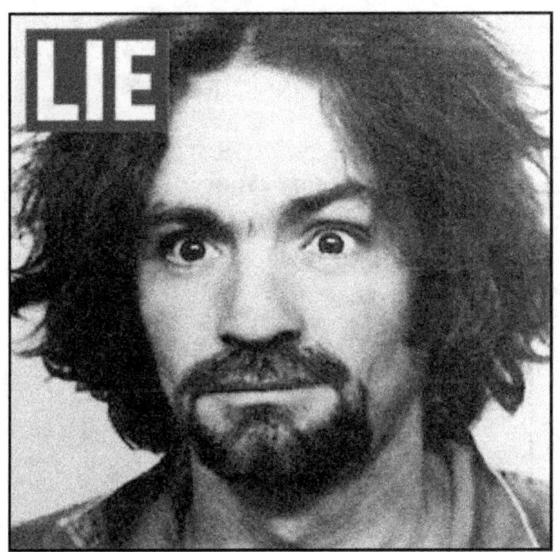

Charles Manson: Don't do Anything Illegal

Satan Sez: Seriously, this guy cracks me up.

Manson – convicted mastermind of mass murder, darkside philosopher of some note and all round cult hero for the disaffected – would just have to be there on Satan's jukebox. Where the satanic side of music is discussed Manson's output is usually somewhere in the mix and the current authors bow to Gavin Baddeley, author of Lucifer Rising (1999), for coining the epithet "the Elvis of alienation" to describe Manson. Manson's hopes of becoming a Monkee (seriously, he was up for giving it a go) were never likely to amount to anything but the demo recordings cut whilst leading his "family" of misfits and conspicuous social casualties are widely recognised to have some musical merit. The Beach Boys "Never Learn not to Love" is credited to Dennis Wilson, though it is widely recognised as a fairly blatant reworking of Manson's "Cease to Exist" and the lilting and highly listenable "Look at Your Game, Girl" was covered by Guns N' Roses (well, okay, it's Axl Rose, Dizzy Reed and a drafted in Carlos Booy on guitar, because the others in the band wanted nothing to do with it.)

Manson has some musical chops of note, end of. The best of his output is on the album Lie (aka The Love and Terror Cult) and these songs have endured in a cultish way since their original release. Manson's incarceration since 1969 has obliged him to scale down the sonic ambitions, though smuggled recordings, mainly vocal and acoustic guitar, continue to emerge. And, we have to give the guy some credit for one album, ironically titled Live at San Quentin. It's questionable to what extent Manson was ever in the service of Satan. A more pragmatic view sees him simply as the demented product of a chaotic beginning and the effects of spending half his life in prison before encountering the rag tag army who did most of the killing he apparently ordered. But, he gets lumped in with the satanic crew and doubtless the Devil is well aware of Manson's position as a poster boy, with a few accessible tunes to his name, in bringing in the hordes.

"Don't do Anything Illegal" is a catchy little gem which reveals a certain ironic humour given the percentage of Manson's life spent in jail. It also opens with a simple metaphor in the lyrics suggestive of American state oppression squashing personal freedom.

"Don't do anything illegal, Beware of the eagle, That's right in the middle of your back…"
So, the demand to stay on the right side of the law is not to be taken literally.

Manson's surreal and trippy logic often employs the same kind of trickster twists that made the likes of Muhammad Ali such potent cultural figures, and his own life and musical works present the kind of contradictions that draw in the impressionable and those seeking meaning well outside the mainstream. Lines like "I gotta see your id my friend, I got to see where you begin" are speaking directly to such people, and will continue to do so for many years.

So, however sincere Manson was in anyone's service is beside the point. His music and the man himself continue to serve the satanic because – in the best moments - they perfectly blend a darkside philosophy and direct delivery of tune and words, all carried by a charismatic star. Like the man said: "the Elvis of alienation."

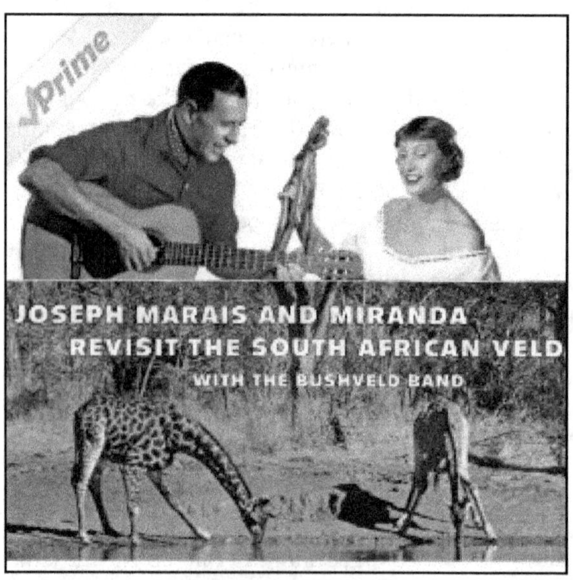

Marais and Miranda: Siembamba

Satan Sez: "A charming little South African lullaby"

We'll bow to the copious research that marks out the Ill Folks blog spot as a prime stop on the surfer's journey in search of the strangest sounds, and let them tell you about this act: "The genteel, nearly forgotten husband and wife team of Marais and Miranda [were] … Goodwill ambassadors for South Africa during a naive age, fluent in songs involving both the conquering Dutch and the pissed off Africans, Marais and Miranda toured the world. They were sort of a European version of labelmates The Weavers…'Siembamba' is sort of the South African version of "Rockabye Baby." We don't mind crooning to our kids about a baby hauled into a tree, and then falling to the ground when a limb breaks. Guaranteed, baby breaks a few limbs, too."

A fair series of points, but the actual recording is still a short, sharp, shocker. Crooned tunefully in the original Afrikaans/Dutch a live version exists in which Josef Marais' guitar gently lilts under the perfectly trilled vocals of his wife, at which point Josef arrives with soothing harmonies and gradually joins in singing the words before he takes over the lead, singing in English: "Siembamba; Mummy's baby, twist his neck and hit him on his head, throw him in the ditch and he'll be dead". It gets worse because the final line includes "just for luck she throws him in the ditch, Mummy's sweet little, sweet little b...baby". The live recording available of this includes loud laughter from the crowd and just enough hesitation on the "b" sound after "sweet little" to leave a really grim thought hanging. We've established the baby is a boy, so "bitch" which is the obvious rhyme, is a non-starter. But there's another word, beginning with B which might, like, refer to the colour of the infant so callously allowed to die. Bear in mind, this is clearly intended as a comedy song.

These were very different times, obviously, and Marais and Miranda's stock has fallen to near invisibility in the twenty first century, though one website did snag the url maraisandmiranda.com (possibly against zero competition) and it does give a short overview of this pair in their brief pomp: "Josef Marais and Miranda were balladeers. Both immigrants to the U.S., they met during WW2 while working at the Office of War Information. They pooled their musical talents, fell in love, and built a strong and dedicated marital and musical partnership. They first presented their artistry to the rather specialized audiences who attended New York folk music clubs such as the Village Vanguard. However, their popularity quickly grew, not just in the U.S. but worldwide, and resulted in a loyal following that has persisted from 1945 to the present.

"Their repertoire encompassed an eclectic selection of folk ballads, art songs, indigenous music, and original compositions, sung in both the original language and the English adaptations of Josef's arrangements. Whether they performed a song that was original or traditional, their presentation was utterly unique and their style completely their own. Their voices blended masterfully with Josef's guitar and baroque viols, while Miranda often provided rhythmic accompaniment on indigenous instruments. Together, they unerringly conveyed their joy in music and their zest for living."

All of the above is supported by whimsical, zestful and very tuneful recordings. Music enjoyed around the world, albeit, not music that has lasted to the point that their catalogue retains any great value today, despite what their online fans might claim. What leaps from the speakers now is the mirthful delight at the sheer callousness of the song and the skilful way the pair milk the glaring inconsistency between the beautiful tune, the sound of the words sung in the original language and the grisly English translation that reveals everything. It's way worse than "Rock-a-bye-Baby" because the death here is no careless accident, it's hands on, apparently pre-meditated and appears to may have a purpose other than simply killing for pleasure. Whether this purpose is practical (one less mouth to feed), or whether the audience are laughing because it's one less black (with all the uncomfortable racist implications the laughter might carry) is skilfully sidestepped because of the humour.

As an insight into the dark underbelly of the musical world before rock 'n' roll "Siembamba" is a grotesque little charmer that belongs in a grotesque collection held in the Grim one's jukebox.

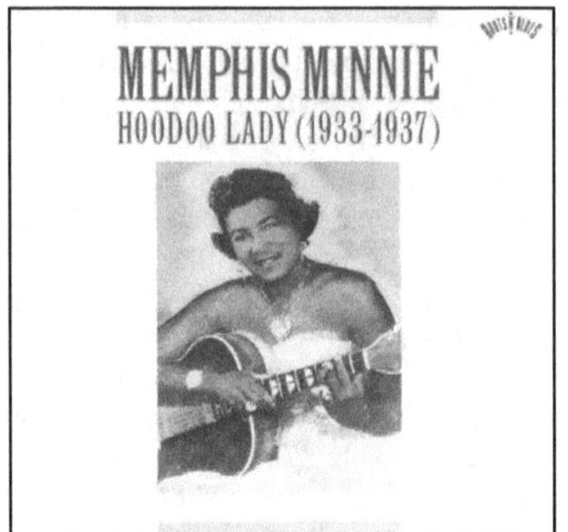

Memphis Minnie: Hoodoo Lady

Satan Sez: Be afraid, be very afraid!

Lizzie Douglas (aka Memphis Minnie) (1897-1973) was the real blues deal. Born in Louisiana and the eldest of 13 siblings, she ended up at various times playing on street corners, touring with a circus and working as a prostitute. Surviving photographs show Minnie sporting a feminine look, often well-dressed whilst cradling her guitar. Those that knew her describe an explosive performer who chewed tobacco much of the time and performed with a cup close by so she could spit into it. Minnie's proficiency in a fight, and her willingness to produce weapons, including a firearm, have also been reported. Unusually for a female artist of her generation the gospel element in her work is virtually non-existent and largely a matter of accident rather than design. Minnie was a country and blues artist, with the emphasis on blues and a catalogue of songs chronicling life's misfortunes. She was baptised late in life but, possibly, only to placate her sister.

"Hoodoo Blues" is prime period Minnie, and an agreeably dark and uncompromising take on life's evils. Minnie pleads with the Hoodoo Lady who is inflicting misery wherever she goes. Minnie is powerless before the evil woman who can "turn water into wine" and her only hope is to appeal to the unpredictable nature of the lady and ask for the most practical of favours; "Hoodoo lady, I want you to unlock my door, So I can get in and get all my clothes." Nothing is assured, there's no hint of any divine power available to stop the evil, Minnie's only real hope is (no pun intended) to get the hell out of there: "Don't put that thing on me, 'Cause I'm going back to Tennessee." So, life really is as bad as she's suggesting. This little horror story comes with a strident guitar and Minnie singing the lines with some real sense of urgency. Classic stuff!

Michael Mills: Hidden Satanic Messages in Rock Music

Satan Sez: There's no such thing as bad publicity!

There is a long and convoluted history regarding the presence of backward masks and other subliminal messages in popular music. Elsewhere in this book – like in the discussions of the theme song for the television comedy Mr Ed and the consideration of The Boo Radleys' song "Find the Answer Within" – these issues appear again. However, for a headlong hurling of yourself into the hysteria we strongly recommend helping yourself to this lengthy gem, currently resident on YouTube and generally easy to find elsewhere online. The full rant runs way over 50 minutes and dates from the eighties when Christian DJ and evangelist Michael Mills was at the height of his powers as an acknowledged expert on the subject. The entertainment value of the broadcast so long after the event revolves squarely around the assertions of what can be heard on who's record and Mills' somewhat sketchy grip on solid facts. Even if you're not that well acquainted with the music he covers two things leap out repeatedly; firstly Mills' targets are generally in the BIG league (Beatles, Zep, Queen) and secondly the "evidence" is a mixture of stuff his listeners are prepared to accept about what's on the records plus general hearsay about what it all means. If you engage with just one section of the whole shebang we strongly suggest it is the trawl of Liverpool's finest and their apparent love affair with The Lord of Darkness. The usual tropes are turfed out (secret messages on the Abbey Road cover etc.) along with some scandalously scant research (Mills is convinced "My Sweet Lord" was a Beatles' single.)

The present authors would venture to suggest the worst moments of stretching logic and asserting the false as true do terminal damage to the overall argument, but we'd also advise you give it a listen. IOHI it is bollocks, but bollocks of such engaging strangeness that it provides timeless entertainment. Then again, we're respectful of Mills' sincerity and he may convince you more than he convinced us.

The overwhelming message from Mills suggests the great and good of the music industry are in league with the Lord of Darkness to bury their best-selling output under a countless collection of tweaks and secreted satanic messages, all of which are fuelling an ongoing epidemic of varied evils. If this is the PR of Satan's enemy, he can give his own guys a few weeks off.

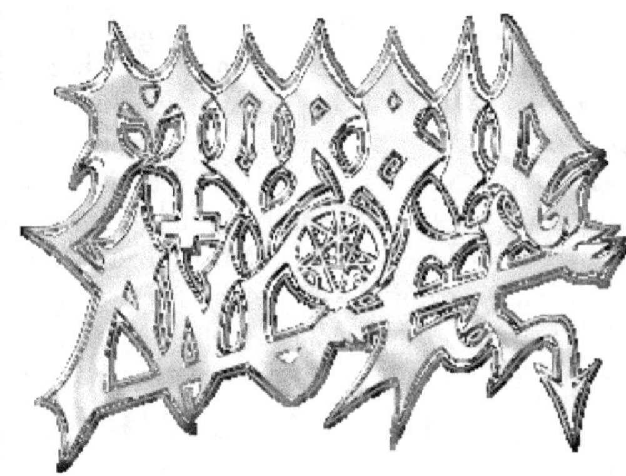

Morbid Angel: World of Shit (The Promised Land)

Satan Sez: Death metal does it for me!

Given the massive tonnage of death metal of all hues out there even Lucifer's iPod would be struggling to hold the whole lot. So, on the face of it, this catchy corker, clocking in a few seconds shy of three and a half minutes, from Covenant, the Florida based band's third full-length outing is nothing special. The big sound, solid grind, and lyrics that cover the usual death metal bases – "Smell of shit is so foul, Writhe in disgust, Earth heaves and death comes to call, All the waste - Cling to your lie, You are as sand and the wind blows" – are par for the death metal course. In fact, worse than that, this is damn near catchy and commercial, and Morbid Angel's difficult third album represents their first outing on Giant Records and their first serious stab into music palatable enough to draw some of the heavy metal crowd in their direction. They might be banging on about shit, but this is a sugared pill for sure. And, on that score it has added power, because this death metal is to the truly hardcore as a spliff is to smack. Tempting enough to draw you in, catchy enough to become part of your life and suggestive – just – of what you might gain by losing yourself completely in this world.

Which – sort of – explains why the Lord of Darkness might give it a blast now and then, especially when the days down below have been particularly demanding and he wants his sounds to reflect his mood, but not challenge him too much.

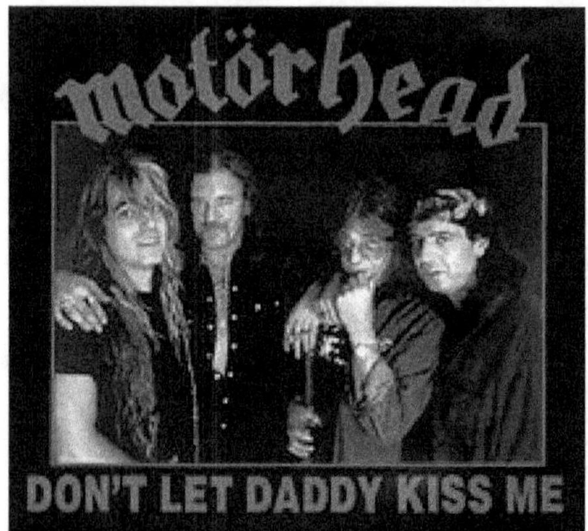

Motörhead: *Don't Let Daddy Kiss Me*

Satan Sez: I'm always there for life's calamities.

It's totally unfair to see Motörhead as satanic and also full-on ignorant to assume they're nothing but a raucous metal band. A better way to consider why this single A' side and track from the Bastards album might just see jukebox action in Hell is to locate it with Richard Dawson's "Poor Old Horse" and a few others in this book, as a stark exploration of a situation so hellish in its own right that the mere thought of the song's existence will be enough to plunge some people into a hopeless, possibly godless, despair. Recruitments to the dark side thrive in this territory. Lemmy – who wrote the song and sings lead – is one of those bluff behemoths known to stagger through their musical careers with little regard to fashion or the more delicate feelings of some listeners. "Don't Let Daddy Kiss Me" is what you think it might be, a chilling tale of abuse. A young girl lies alone in bed, her mother is nowhere around, her father comes home… Lemmy sings most of it in a thin voice, lacking any production trickery and backed by a gentle acoustic guitar. Even when the band kick in later the drums and lead guitar are more AOR than roaring Motörhead mayhem, by which point the lyrics, perfectly audible, have done their work: "And she's wide awake, scared to death, She smells his lust and she smells his sweat, Curled in a ball she holds her breath." God makes three appearances in the lyrics, but only to be highlighted for his lack of connection. The distance between the girl and God ratchets up until she is: "Praying to her God with his heart of stone."

Lemmy's voracious reading habits made him something of an authority on life's atrocities, especially those of a military nature. His collection of genuine Nazi regalia didn't make him a supporter of such ideologies, completely the opposite in fact, but the willingness to reach deep into the darkness of life and highlight the cruelty and hopelessness that drive people permanently into damaged lives is writ large over Motörhead's career. They're a band – live and on record – for those of a strong constitution, comfortable and accepting of the darkness. Encountered by those of a very suggestible and sensitive nature, their most uncompromising moments can be traumatic.

As an aside, this song could have taken on a different hue, if not a different meaning, but two former members of The Runaways - Lita Ford and Joan Jett – were amongst a small coterie of acts who turned down the chance to release it.

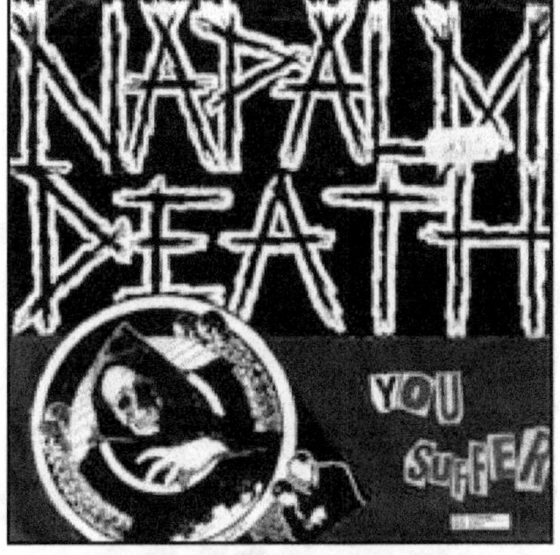

Napalm Death: You Suffer

Satan Sez: Yes!!

It is one second long, it goes "Eurrghhh!" a full thrash metal band crashes in the background and the two and a bit seconds of the official video are complete demented genius. The perfect anti-song, an out and out fuck you to anyone who thinks crafting away is the only means of making a point. Coming up to thirty years after it first saw release this is a song seldom forgotten once heard. It's primal, it packs power and you still think it's all over you well after it's finished. Classic!

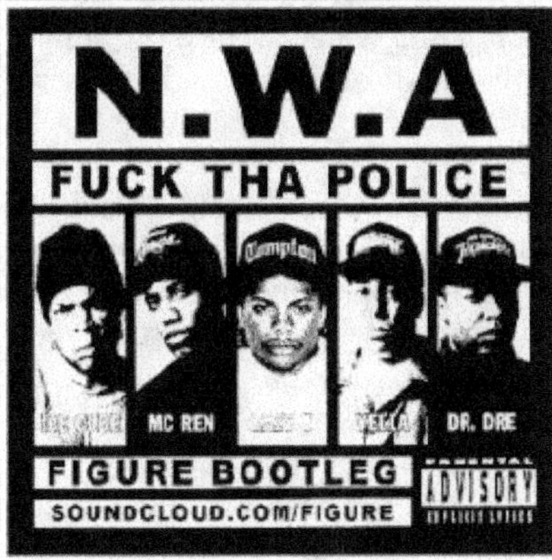

N.W.A.: Fuck the Police

Satan Sez: When routine bites hard and ambitions are low…

Gangsta rap and its offshoots probably did more for Satan's side of the musical war than God's. Apart from anything else the work that set the Gangsta/Hip-Hop agenda often shot from the hip, got in your face and beat the metaphorical shit out of you until the point was laboured to death. At least N.W.A. did all of the above with some sense of their self-worth and enough humour to make the points palatable. But this track is "fuck this shit!" angry from start to finish. It also makes the point that 1988 years after the birth of Christ, in the world's most advanced nation, there is still racism, bigotry and ignorance that leaves the forces of law and order "Thinking every nigga is dealing narcotics."

If the human race can't rise above this shit, the passing traffic in Heaven is likely to look like that in post 1986 Chernobyl. N.W.A. deliver the raps with enough skill and artistry to make sense of the mess but when we're promised "a young nigger on the warpath" is going to deliver "a bloodbath" we're listening to the real deal. This is music about hard, often hopeless, lives where dangerous behaviour makes sense. Eazy-E takes the stand to tell the court how he feels about "this bullshit." Seven years later he was dead at 31, of AIDS, his last message to fans being a confession "I did it raw [unprotected sex]" most of the time. This being a reference to sexual behaviour saw him father seven children by six mothers. N.W.A. channelled hopelessness and walked their own moral path, light years away from the religious right and their moral messages of the day.

The Straight Outta Compton album, and this track in particular continue to influence and inform much of what has followed. There is still racism, bigotry, hopelessness and – in the kind of communities that continue to produce the best of this music – there is still the feeling the police are the enemy.

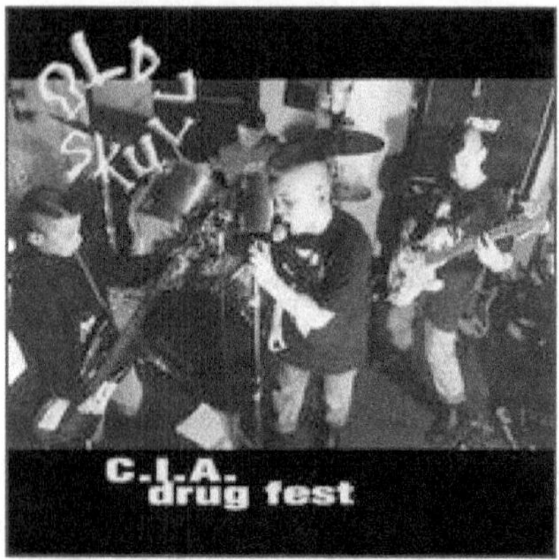

Old Skull: CIA Drug Fest

Satan Sez: Out of the mouths of babes, eh?

As a rule punk has done more for Satan than for God, though much of the indignation, ranting about hypocrisy and general anger unleashed by the music harps on some well-worn themes. Shit lives, poor housing, anger at the rich hanging on to their wealth and the lack of employment were all staples of the first major wave of British punk, which went on to inform everything that followed. All of which made for some great music.

Somehow, it's all more disturbing when the same power and focus comes from the precociously young. Which is where Old Skull score over everyone else. Latter day punks and kitted out in the kind of haircuts and uniforms that were par for the punk course they may have been. But…in recording CIA Drug Fest (the album) this band were years younger than most of the punk competition. In listening to it, for most of the duration, you wouldn't have a clue. They play hard, the drums sound like bombs detonated near to the band, the guitars set up a massive wall of noise and vocally it's full-on, unrepentant, anger at big targets. Lyrically, they know their stuff and the opening cut, and title track, from the album is as powerful as it gets with a rant about the rank hypocrisy of the CIA. When the band formed in the late eighties the mainstays, brothers J.P. (Jean-Paul) Toulon and Jamie Toulon, were ten and nine respectively. By the time this track and its parent album were unleashed in 1992 they'd acquired enough competence and power to escape some of the obvious novelty tag.

There are moments on the whole album where the band's youth shows through, either with an exposed vocal betraying the higher than usual voice of J.P. (who also drummed) or the choice of viewpoint on a song like "From a Little Kid's Point of View." And "Bill" is basically howling and banging fit to turn a teenage tantrum into an attempt at a song. That one may be a novelty, but it's fucking good one. By contrast, the title track opens the album by ripping mercilessly into an establishment target, using the basic punk weapons; raging vocal, speed, noise, anger to beat the shit out of the target, and supporting all of that with a solid grasp of what the band is on about and a sample from a broadcast news report to show they've done some research before ranting in song.

Kids so angry are hard to convert to ways of moderation, even in old age (something spared J.P. who died in 2010) and kids this angry, armed with their music, are prone to be role models to others. On balance, this infectious anger and disrespect does more for cynicism and the dark side than the godly counterpart. And it rocks.

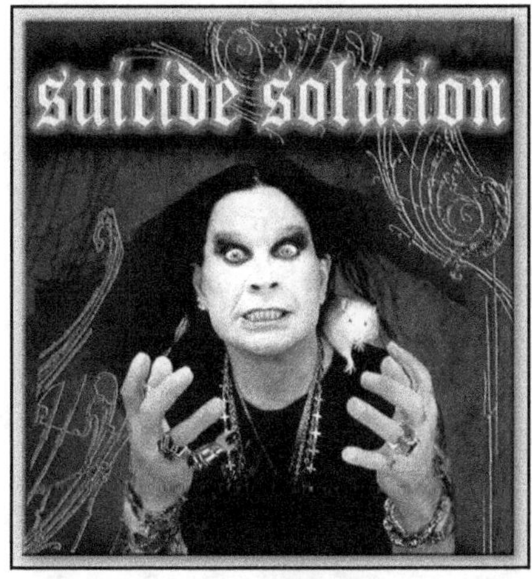

Ozzy Osbourne: *Suicide Solution*

Satan Sez: Another "satanic" classic that is nothing of the sort. Keep 'em comin'

Track five from the first solo outing by Britain's befuddled master of musical mayhem, "Suicide Solution" nestles just before the classic "Mr Crowley" on the four times platinum (in the US) selling Blizzard of Oz album. An insistent rocker, co-written with guitarist Randy Rhoads and bassist Bob Daisley, "Suicide Solution" sits on Satan's jukebox as a reminder of the handful of heavy metal recordings that have become mired in legal controversy because of their – apparent – power to unleash genuine darkness, and destructive acts. The parents of the late John McCollum, a teenager who committed suicide, apparently prompted – in part at least – from listening to the song, set out to convict the singer in a 1986 court case. With fitting theatricality the song, its meanings and the greatly differing lives of the McCollum's and Mr Osbourne were all part of a trial that was only ever likely to have one outcome (Ozzy was cleared of any involvement, voluntary or otherwise.) The minutiae of the lyrics were dissected as the plaintiffs attempted to prove the song was an incitement to destructive action. The case for the defence always had two very strong arguments. Firstly, when the song opens with: "Wine is fine, but whiskey's quicker, Suicide is slow with liqueur, Take a bottle, drown your sorrows, Then it floods away tomorrows…" it is surely exploring the deadly power of alcohol and not suggesting anyone uses a firearm (John McCollum shot himself in the head.) Secondly, there is the considerable weight of evidence in the fact this track appears on a multi-platinum selling album, most owners of which continue to enjoy healthy and sane lives.

The trial threw up a few interesting curve balls, notably the two lyricists (Osboune and Daisley) clearly having different inspirations. Ozzy apparently having his mind on the recent death through excess alcohol of AC/DC front man Bon Scott whilst Bob (who was in Ozzy's employ at this time) was more concerned that Ozzy's prodigious pouring of all manner of beverages down his already addicted throat might well mean the boozy Brummie was next in line for dead legend status (thereby rendering Daisley and the rest of the band jobless.) Don Arden, former Black Sabbath manager and Ozzy's father-in-law also weighed in with a priceless comment: "To be perfectly honest, I would be doubtful as to whether Mr. Osbourne knew the meaning of the lyrics, if there was any meaning, because his command of the English language is minimal." Arden and Ozzy had a fractious relationship on their good days, but this backhanded dig did strengthen the case for the defence by suggesting Ozzy was little more than a pantomime act making enough of the right noises to keep the credulous keen on his output.

As a bizarre sideshow to the strange career of Ozzy Osbourne this little legal interlude now makes footnote status at best (though it is worth remembering the court case arose from the death of a depressed teenager, so it isn't all laughs.) Though, there's dark, hollow, ironic chuckling to be had in Hell every time this one blasts forth from the jukebox if only because the court case, and subsequent notoriety of the song, provide another example of the forces of moral righteousness giving Hell and its associated operations a PR boost.

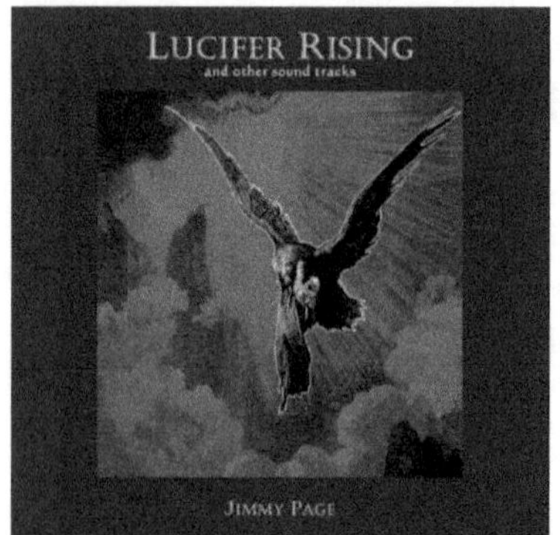

Jimmy Page: Lucifer Rising

Satan Sez: The famous NOST album.

There are one or two famous "NOST" (NOT the original soundtrack) albums out there, notably Alex North's unused and classically strident score for 2001 A Space Odyssey. This collection of sounds, from Page's album Lucifer Rising and Other Soundtracks (2012) represents the Zeppelin guitarist finally reclaiming a work many had been anticipating for years. We'll take the liberty of including the whole NOST as one work, despite there being differently named tracks, because this is one thematic work. The Lucifer Rising movie has a troubled history, which involves Anger hanging round the heart of the high-profile hippie movement in London and San Francisco, befriending the likes of Mick Jagger and reworking his movie idea completely a couple of times so it was filmed in the UK rather than the originally intended San Francisco, and so that footage of The Rolling Stones and music by Mick Jagger ended up in another movie – Invocation of my Demon Brother – rather than Lucifer Rising. But, we digress again, though this rambling lack of focus is very appropriate where Lucifer Rising is concerned.

Jimmy Page befriended Kenneth Anger in 1972 when the two were bidding for an item once owned by Aleister Crowley at a London auction and the in the general, loose, kinda way things, like, happened back then, Man! Anger ended up living in Page's basement in London and Page agreed to compose a soundtrack to Lucifer Rising. Movie funding and some different tangents for the project continued to be a problem but Page and Anger's arrangement – which had been reported in the press – rumbled on for a few years. Page composed and recorded alongside his demanding Zeppelin schedule. Zeppelin released and toured Houses of the Holy and Physical Graffiti before Anger got into a massive row with Page's other half, Charlotte, (yeah, yeah we know, but he definitely had a partner who lived in his house in London; Hammer of the Gods isn't necessarily a true story.) The resulting fall out left Anger in need of a new landlord and two very strong personalities – Page and Anger – falling out on a massive scale. Anger's furious tirade at a subsequent press conference took in more than their parting, getting deeply personal and extending itself to the claim that Page was "dried up" as a musician. So, the soundtrack was definitely off, then.

Wounds were licked on both sides. Zep's 1976 release – Presence – was an uneven affair but any band capable of unleashing an instant epic on the scale of "Achilles Last Stand" were far from finished, a fact demonstrated by Zep's subsequent touring. Anger for his part was contacted by sometime Charles Manson acolyte Bobby Beausoleil, who had time on his hands in jail. Bobby had the idea that he could recruit musicians and snag some help to score the movie. Bobby Beausoleil and Anger had already crossed paths and Bobby had been in the frame earlier to compose the soundtrack, and…seriously, the history of this movie is, ahem, complicated. But Bobby Beausoleil's soundtrack is also discussed in this book.

Finally, in 2012, the definitive version of Page's work was made officially available. If offers an eerie series of drones, lingering tones, clear influence from Page's travels in north Africa and sampled sounds, like the wind. In its most accessible moments Lucifer Rising (NOST) is an extension of those meditative moments when Led Zeppelin head off somewhere vaguely in the direction of world music, like the opening sounds on "In the Evening." It's also a clear nod to Page's affinity with some of the more atonal and experimental classical composers. It is, by common consent, accomplished and listenable, but more of a curio when heard as a separate piece of work. How this would have sounded against the film is easy to gauge by playing the movie with the recording. It is less clear whether what we now hear on the official release is what Page would eventually have signed off had Kenneth Anger and Charlotte Martin (Page's live-in lover) managed to calm down once their argument kicked off.

Lucifer Rising (NOST) certainly achieves the difficult job of visiting enough clichéd satanic landmarks for those listening out for something satanic whilst also sounding original and ambitious. So it fits on the Devil's jukebox without too much trouble. It also sits well in Page's limited but impressive little collection of film music and shows that, from the start, he was always the kind of composer interested in tones and setting a mood rather than extending his trademark riffing style into the film world. Finally it shows Page's consummate skill in making the strong elements of tension between opposing sounds the focus of a musical work rather than part of the dynamics of a rock band. So, worth waiting for then.

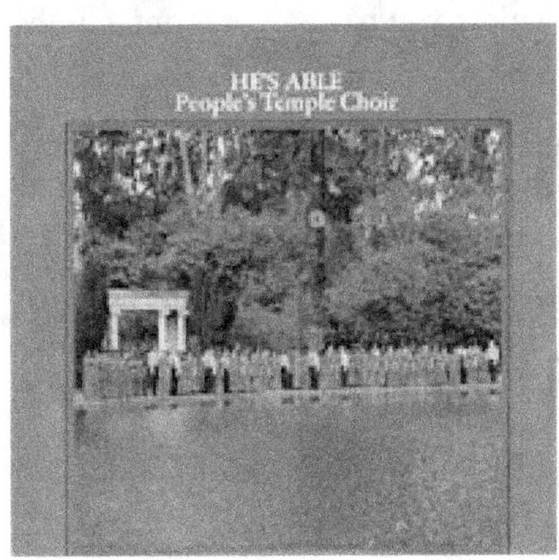

People's Temple Choir: *He's Able/ The Jonestown Massacre*

Satan Sez: Mass suicide in the hope of Heavenly resurrection.

Whether the Lord of Darkness would avail himself of the whole bootleg album on Grey Matter Records, offering up no official release date in its packaging, is debatable. *He's Able* starts out as a regular seventies gospel album, opening with a chirpy choir of children, offering up a spirited working of "Walk a Mile in My Shoes" – a much performed standard in Elvis' set at the time – and some competent if predictable musical chops. The guitars probably try too hard at times to infuse the whole show with a lurking sense of psychedelia and elsewhere the drumming is annoyingly busy, or a fraction too far ahead of the beat. The vocalists change, a few of the cuts emerge as characterful and sincere takes on seventies gospel and the high-spot in terms of hairs on the back of the net soulful connection is an agreeably understated run through the old standard "Black Baby."

But let's not kid ourselves...*nobody* bought this bizarre twofer for the first album. That simply gave the CD reissue its title and – frankly – an excuse. The final track, album length in itself, is a little over 41 minutes of live recording, and this is the sounds Satan may well be slammin' too. If you haven't sussed it yet this is the Jonestown massacre. The final sermon of the Reverend Jim Jones, recorded live in Guyana on 18 November 1978 and ending with the clearly audible screams of his followers dying after drinking Flavor Aid laced with a potent cocktail of drugs, including Cynanide. In all 918 people involved with the People's Temple died, including their charismatic, increasingly erratic, paranoid and rambling Elvis-alike leader: Jim Jones. Until 11 September 2001 this was the greatest loss of US civilian life at one place, at one time, by means other than natural disaster or war.

The convoluted story of how so many US citizens ended up in their own compound in Jonestown, Guyana, how their increasingly concerned relatives sought to extricate some of them, how Congressman Leo Ryan flew to Guyana to investigate and how his murder as he attempted to fly back with a handful of defectors promoted the mass suicide of the beleaguered group is well chronicled elsewhere. So, are the words on the "Death Tape" which forms the final track here: "Mass Suicide."

For the most part this sounds like the one-mic, low quality analogue cassette recording it is. Opening with some clearly audible frenzied staccato rantings from Jones, we get a couple of cuss words, some general shouting on the nature of love and a rousing call to arms combining a threat on anyone seeking to attack the People's Temple and an assertion: "I'll fight, I'll fight..."

The sound quality and thread of the story soon vanishes, unless you have a transcript, but the key moments in the ensuing drama do leap out. The fate of Congressman Leo Ryan is discussed, Jones stating that the plane taking Ryan and the defectors from Guyana will be downed when the pilot is shot by one of those on board. Jones' notion of "Revolutionary suicide" is the main point of debate and his voice prevails. One temple member, Christine Miller, tries to revive hope of the whole cohort fleeing to Russia; beyond American justice and influence. But, between 20 and 25 minutes another voice, Jim McElvane, persuades people differently. Citing himself as a "therapist" McElvane discusses his work with past-life regressions and assures people that everyone recalling the moment of death in the therapy he carried out, experienced it as a moment of peace. A few minutes later an unidentified man announces "The Congressman has been murdered," Jones reiterates "The Congressman's dead" and the voices opposing revolutionary suicide vanish from the debate.

Surviving witnesses stated the first to die included the youngest, poisoned by their own mothers with Flavour Aid squirted from a syringe from which the needle had been removed. As the half hour mark approaches the gaps between speeches on the tape are clearly filled by the sounds of dying. Time matters, Jones and others figuring they have around 40 minutes before they're interrupted. One unidentified woman urges everyone to "Hurry up." The tape had ran to a stop long before the majority of the deaths. But, what is recorded is enough to give a sense of the scale and nature of the tragedy that ensued. Above all else it is the chilling logic and efficiency of the mass suicide that overwhelms anyone hearing this horrific document. Jones' wisdom in the final minutes includes: "If everybody will relax. The best thing you do to relax and you will have no problems. You'll have no problems with this thing if you just relax," and "I don't care how many screams you hear, I don't care how many anguished cries, death is a million times preferable to ten more days of this life. If you knew what was ahead of you – if you knew what was ahead of you, you'd be glad to be stepping over tonight."

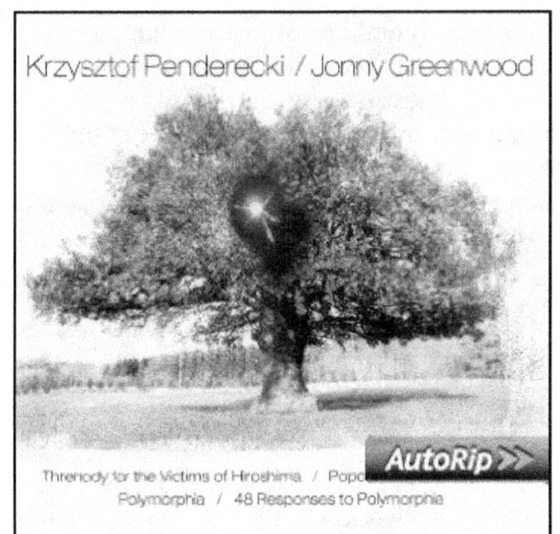

Krzysztof Penderecki: Threnody to the Victims of Hiroshima

Satan sez: Oops, humanity did it again!

Many of those claiming to be unfamiliar with the work of Krzysztof Penderecki, or his "Threnody for the Victims of Hiroshima" will recognise the sounds from the soundtrack of the movie The Shining. The classical work, composed in 1960, is an attempt to represent the experience of those suffering the bombing of Hiroshima and also mark the tragedy in such a way that people will never repeat it. The Lord of Darkness, with his familiarity with atrocities and the infliction of mass death throughout the ages, may well have a hollow chuckle at those ambitions. He may well feel more at home in the harrowing sounds than most human listeners. Technically speaking "Threnody for the Victims of Hiroshima" pulls a few compositional moves so well as to turn their collective impact into a masterpiece. The work has seen performances all over the world, becoming a staple in the repertoire of classical combos specialising in challenging works. It also gets the odd play on radio shows like Stuart Maconie's Freak Zone which otherwise focus upon the stranger end of rock and pop. So, whilst it chronicles the most destructive act of war linked to the unleashing of a single weapon, "Threnody for the Victims of Hiroshima" is also a crossover musical work of some power and merit. Considered in the grimmest possible humorous terms, it is a greatest hit in both senses of the word.

There are discussions online about the expert use of mircotonality, the avant-garde compositional practices that saw Penderecki requiring string players to improvise within a certain range of notes and the "invisible canon" of the piece. The invisible canon refers to the way the collective impact remains the point throughout, and the individual contributions, whilst personal and creative, are simply lost in the overwhelming power of the sound, rather like the destruction of stories, dreams and lives in the face of a nuclear strike. Compositional considerations aside "Threnody to the Victims of Hiroshima" screams, continuously, for over eight minutes. Close listening betrays movements, slapping sounds and individual acts in the sound. Many of these are random because the individual players are responding to direction to slap the bridge of their instrument, or tap the soundbox. All performances of the work are, therefore, different because the instrumentalists have creative control of how they respond, but all performances are also the same because every 52 string ensemble interpreting the work will, by default, begin slowly and end up sounding like an elongated howling mass with individual voices which can be heard, but which remain hopelessly trapped in the conflagration.

The contrasts are key to the way the work represents the bombing of Hiroshima. There is sense, shape and purpose to the work, even a sense of beauty. But this is a terrible beauty, admirable in what it achieves but uncomfortable in your ears, and disturbing to thoughts and imagination. The rapid and random movements in the opening sections of the piece, and the sense of individual life in the voices of the instruments is all too easy to interpret. The damaged and distressing voices that emerge towards the end before the final lingering sound are powerful and chilling at the same time.

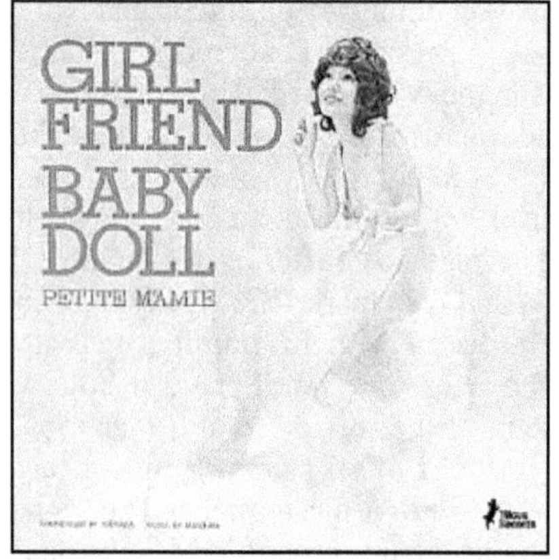

Petit M'Aimie: Make-Love

Satan sez: Make messed up lives, in a pleasurable way.

Sexuality is a strange beast when measured against the varied cultures of the world. We'll try and avoid too much wanky bollocks rambling on this entry, cos the main point is fairly simple. But we're right about sexuality, mind. Some cultures parade it, others parcel it up and sometimes the whole thing is turned into product so focussed on one country or one market that it mystifies the rest of the planet. All of which can leave the human race in a constant state of constant confusion wherein people barely understand each other, needless causing of offence and anger is rife and anyone in search of a casual shag is forced to abandon moral principles and the values they once held dear, all so's a few minutes of rapid physical action and the exchange of a few drops of vital bodily fluids can be achieved. Tickets to Hell are pre-booked in these moments, even if the passengers have their minds on other things.

Around the world self-regarding religious organisations of all denominations try and impose rules to control such behaviour, many of the rules of one lot contradict those of another, and the constant confusions and misunderstandings continue, whilst the planet goes on lusting and thrusting. Truly, in those moments Hell ain't a bad place to be. Granted, there's the considerable problem of eternal damnation and the like. But the battle of good and evil rages and some of the battle grounds take the oddest shapes.

Consider Petite M'Aime's album Girl Friend Baby Doll and, in particular the track "Make-Love." It's a Japanese take on the kind of breathy and sensual vibe that made "Je T'Aime" an international hit, but it's also a strange insight into the psyche of a nation that has turned innocent young girls (especially those still at school) and female subservience into a cultural fantasy. Girl Friend Baby Doll is what you'd imagine, two sides of the perfect imaginary Japanese girlfriend - innocent, willing, fun, giggly and respectful – set against light orchestral backings and the sweetest swirls of melody. A musical fantasy, an unthreatening view of a relationship and aural wank fodder of a very oriental persuasion. These days, granted, it exists more as a widely downloadable curio and a glimpse into a bygone age when such product made more sense in the market. But the points above, about sexuality, cultural confusion and the like, still hold sway. Something Satan can ponder as he chills to a few minutes of polite giggles and slow melodic strains.

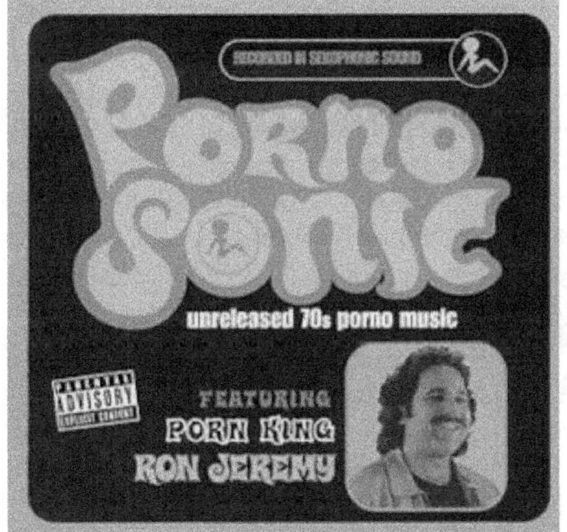

Pornosonic: Her Magic Carpet Ride

Satan sez: OOOOOOOOOHHHHhhhhhhh… yes!

Jukeboxes can provide as much after dinner cheese as a cultured individual might usefully need and this particular selection does that job to perfection. Ron Jeremy lent his name and cover image (fully clothed) to the Pornosonic compiliation which is little more than a cheap cash in stuffed with – generally unused – sound clips from the scoring of pornographic movies. That is adult/pornographic movies from back in the day when movies were a mainstay of the porn industry and they were watched on cinema screens, or mailed out as VHS tapes. Back in those days there was some (generally cack-handed) excuse for a plot and a modicum of character development (usually involving a frustrated housewife experiencing a life-changing sexual awakening after the plumber turned up to unblock the sink, or similar.) We digress…

This steamy segment in the varied slew of musical moods (some intercut with dialogue) is a standout track simply because it offers up a musical time-capsule. Slowly strummed guitar with a little echo, hand-hit drums gently tapping out a loose rhythm and a slow, slow sensual orgasm mixed tastefully back into the gently sweeping sounds. Proper porn soundtracks, the way the best of them used to be. Hell, you'd almost believe that in addition to crass exploitation by way of fleecing the lonely and vulnerable of their meagre reserves of spare cash, porn could actually celebrate sexuality in a tender and life-affirming way.

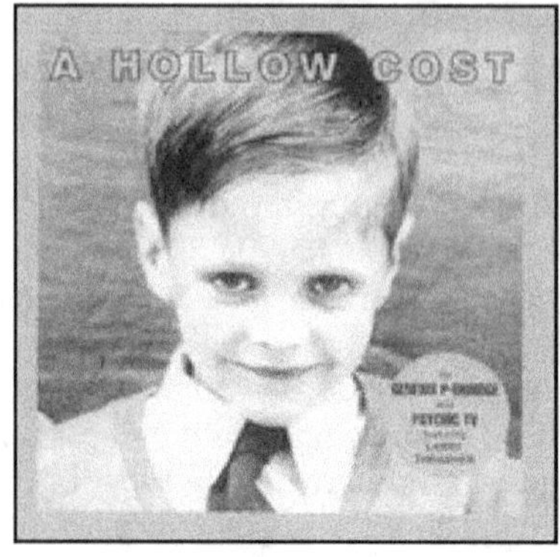

Psychic TV: A Hollow Cost

Satan sez: The only joy is violation

Another epic excursion for those moments of intense mind-fuck that mark the more demanding evening entertainments offered by the Dark Lord's jukebox. Released in 1995, this lengthy spoken word and sample piece is a rambling meditation on the meaning of life. It had been a decade and a half in development before it was unleashed on album. Shot through with a tangible cynicism and the solipsistic notion that only self-knowledge can guide the true free thinker, "A Hollow Cost" is a lengthy journey that functions as a monumental sermon fit to destroy the notion that any established system of belief is to be trusted. Considering ancient Egyptian symbolism Genesis P. Orridge intones: "regular trips to the undercurrent display confusion in precise detail; the effect is one of accuracy of purpose and description." In other words, what we learn from everyone else's truth is only fit to help us define our own journey. The work is all the more powerful because it packs a fierce intelligence behind the attitude and playful sound clips. The juxtaposing of often harrowing imagery with random sounds and electronic music adds a significant power, often at the least likely moments when the sounds are almost childish and wouldn't be out of place backing the likes of The Clangers or other children's television favourites. "A Hollow Cost" has enough sense of the experimental end of the dance scene to sound, just about, like an album aimed at a youth market, but that only leads those listeners in to an audio nightmare for which mid-nineties club culture had barely prepared them. In this work, as stated by Orridge early on in the proceedings, "the only joy is violation."

Genesis P.Orridge and his varied bandmates in the flexible line ups trading as Psychic TV and Temple ov Psychick Youth are often cited where the collisions of Satanism and popular music are discussed. In that context this is a touchstone work, and a recording that walks the walk with regard to pushing forward that niche of Satanism that overlaps with free thinking in general.

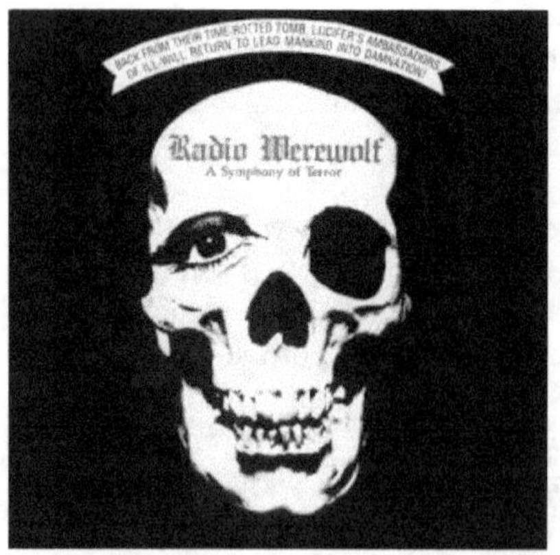

Radio Werewolf: Triumph of the Will

Satan sez: A cloven hoof tapper, with gloriously twisted lyrics.

Another of those borderline burning acts who'd argue art and expression on their side and take incoming fire from those believing them to be deranged and sick. Heard burbling in the background "Triumph of the Will" has that strident and accessible vibe of The Levellers at their best. But a closer listen to the lyrics "we came, we saw, we conqured; the triumph of the will" added to "do you remember when the dream was not yet dead" and topped with: "he promised us a kingdom that would last a thousand years" tells you everything you need to know. The song is told from the nostalgic and unapologetic position of a former Nazi still hankering after the old dreams. The onstage sight of frontman Nikolas Schreck striding around in full SS uniform as he led the singing of the song was also a (goose) step too far for many of liberal sensibilities.

The L.A. based band (1984-1993) didn't last as long as the Nazi party. Wikipedia and other general sources frequently fall back on truthful but vague overviews like: "stylistically eclectic musical collective" as a summary of what Radio Werewolf were about. Their lingering infamy now rests on two pillars. Firstly, the varied line ups and frequent forays into taboo territory soon cast the band as prime agitators. In this regard they functioned like a heat seeking missile when pin-pointing the right combination of words, images and actions to get attention. Nazi symbolism and propaganda was something of a touchstone and influence. Radio Werewolf, as in the band's name, came from their own propaganda radio station. Another song, "Strength through Joy" also reworked a Nazi slogan. The second pillar of the band's lingering cult status is more simply explained and understood. Their reputation earned them interest and the relative shortage of officially released material bred bootleg reissues. The band were, and remain, that rarity, a cult act who can deliver. The shortage of material served to provide the kind of "treat 'em mean, keep 'em keen" marketing that left people desperate for some acquaintance with the work, at which point bootleg or legit copies of records offered up catchy songs so heavy on the irony and reworking of taboo touchstones of all kinds that those encountering the stuff for the first time simply had to share it. Today, in a world of limitless downloading the same rules still apply. Once you twig you're in the hands of demented genius mavericks who are both celebrating and satirising in the same moment, you've "got" Radio Werewolf.

How much of this they meant when they first released it decades ago is now – largely – beside the point. This is music for sharing, at which point the wilful depravity remains infectious.

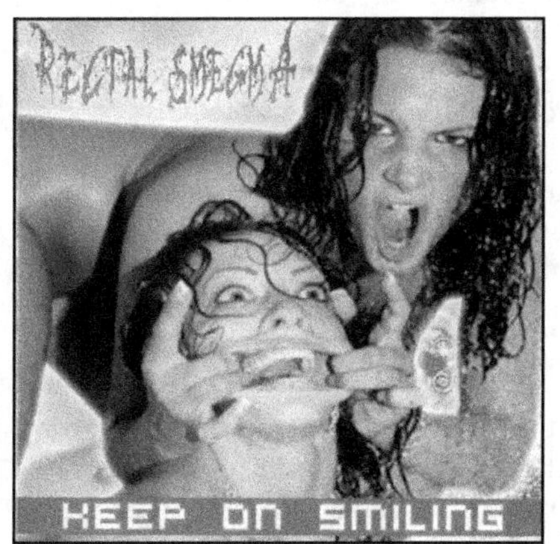

Rectal Smegma: *Menstruation Cocktail*

Satan sez: My names are legion.

Warning: Adult Content. Or, to be specific, we're going to get all arty bollocks/word wanky about little more than a single minute of disturbing noise. It's doubtful if Rectal Smega (the band not the unpleasant discharge) ever expected this.

If the Lord of Darkness worries like any owner of a large operation about issues like footfall, customer uptake of the standard offer and the means by which repeat business can be confidently generated (we seriously doubt he does but – in business parlance – work with us on this one, eh?) then, he has a few very consoling thoughts on which he can fall back. Firstly, the regular uprisings of fundamentalist belief, widespread fear of evils barely known etc. is always a means of making the extreme end of rock music a default home for all kinds of demonology.

Whether true evil lurks in the countless welter of goregrind atrocities, endless rehashes of the basic satanic themes and ceaseless reinvention of dark moody band photographs isn't really the point. Those not learning from history are doomed to repeat mistakes and an historian might usefully draw parallels between political miscalculations and the relationship of the "moral majority" with extreme musical messages of all kinds. A common experience of hard line military invasions with – apparently – simple aims has been to drive the local population so invaded into more complex forms of resistance and mire the invading forces in unwinnable conflicts in which telling friends and enemies apart is sometimes only possible when the person you are watching suddenly opens fire. Historians cite the likes of the Tet Offensive (wherein the North Vietnamese forces struck effectively at the South Vietmanese/US forces with surprise attacks, making light of the superior forces in the south by striking with precision and decisive action.) Combatants from Northern Ireland to Iraq and Afghanistan are also familiar with the balance of power outlined above.

Rant, sort of, over, but let's talk music. In particular let's talk everything from the habits of white audiences a century ago in the US to consign early blues to the "race music" market, by way of the various crusades against rock n roll, via the Parents Music Resource Centre right up to date.

Morally righteous people have always feared the apparent power of the wrong sounds and messages to bring widespread depravity. The fear has led to everything from organised campaigns to rants in bedrooms aimed at slacker kids slumped and cocooned in headphones. And, like the "Mission accomplished" message of George W Bush in 2003 there is usually a gap in reality between the words, and reality on the ground. Within this gap, a surgical revolutionary strike, by way of creating music, can easily occur.

Frankly, we could have culled any one of countless cuts from Bandcamp, any number of other online homes of extreme sounds or any one of equally innumerable missives on cheaply produced compilation CDs. Extreme metal in its many gross-out forms rubs shoulders in these places with any number of rap and hip-hop offshoots, industrial noise and whatever else a mind can conjure up as an audio shock tactic. Rectal Smegma sear your eardrums with less than a minute and half of insanely rapid ranting and riffs, you can't make out a word, but what they're singing, and what you imagine they're singing are probably fairly close.

For as long as impressionable sorts are told to avoid this stuff, and those doing the telling offer up an apparently simple message about its inherent evils and the desperate fates awaiting all those who enter this forbidden zone, there will be bands like Rectal Smegma and banging tunes for the Devil's jukebox.

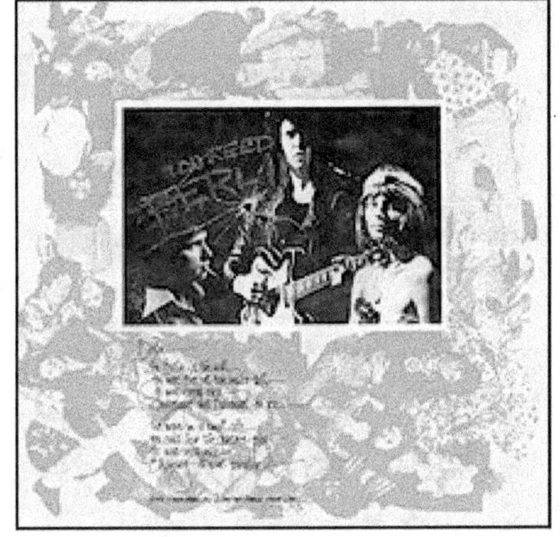

Lou Reed: The Kids

Satan sez: Listening pleasure, and pain.

Lou Reed's Berlin (1973) is the most ambitious and thematically linked work produced by the artist. Released to mixed reviews, and subsequently hailed as an artistic success, Berlin is one of those divisive albums which – when played – may motivate your friends to leave the room. It's also infamous amongst its peers as one of those annoying classic rock releases that was always too long for one side of a C90 tape back in the day (although in this category it rubs shoulders with the likes of Astral Weeks, so that's the best company to keep.) The thematic strength and slow-build of the story make the complete album a shoo-in for Satan's iPod. But, this song, partly because of a certain infamy above and beyond its meaning within the story told on the album, is the choice for the jukebox.

Keeping this simple, Reed's runaway success with his Transformer album and "Walk on the Wild Side" single allowed him and producer Bob Ezrin to push the envelope on budget, artistic ambition and exactly who to call when the follow up was being recorded. The end result, Berlin, is a true concept album, also conceived as a stage show, following the doomed lives of a tragic couple, Jim and Caroline. Plot wise their extremely troubled lives, already infected with drugs and depression, get progressively worse over the two sides of vinyl, leading to Caroline's children being taken away, an event which causes Jim to comment on the state of their lives in the song "The Kids." With very mixed critical responses and poorer than hoped for sales Berlin didn't do sufficient business in 1973 to convince people the projected stage show was a good idea. Though Reed did finally get round to it in the twenty first century.

"The Kids" is infamous for both its mordant and lengthy exploration of a domestic tragedy and for the sounds that occur just over five minutes into the proceedings. The song is sung from the perspective of Jim, explaining: ""They're taking her children away / Because of the things that they heard she had done / The black Air Force sergeant was not the first one / And all of the drugs she took, every one, every one." So, Caroline's addiction has led to prostitution and this is common knowledge to the point her children are removed from their home. All of which occurs late into the album, after lengthy dirge like songs and orchestral passages, along with the expert playing of a stellar crew including Steve Winwood and Jack Bruce, so Reed's ravaging of any optimism you might take to this album is almost complete by the time "The Kids" is five minutes old. At which point he delivers a sucker punch as two young boys scream, as in really scream, for their "Mommy."

The commonly believed tale behind the convincing and harrowing sounds that mark out "The

Kids" as the emotional low point of the set is that producer Bob Ezrin told his sons, David (then 5) and Joshua (1), their mother was dead. The rumour went unchallenged and widely retold for many years before Ezrin revealed that the cruellest thing he did was to tell them it was bedtime. Either way, these are his children, genuinely disturbed enough to make the sounds of pain, and those sounds are fed firmly into a conceptual work so unrepentantly grim that it continues to clear rooms when its disciples decide to inflict it on their friends. Doubtless, it draws the assembled demons and demonic types closer when Satan pushes the buttons to bring it onto his personal jukebox.

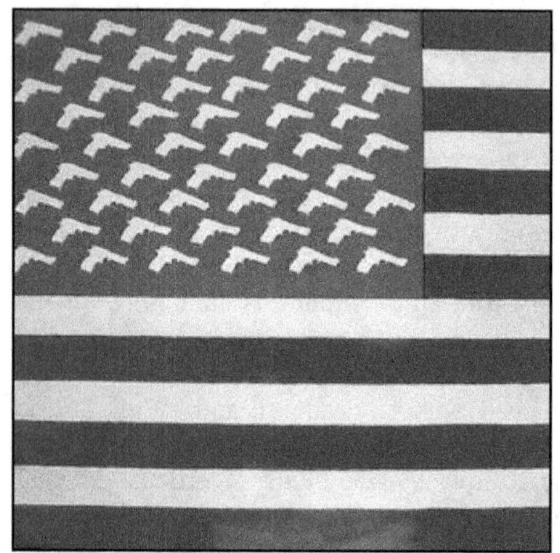

Ambrose Reynolds: He's Dead Alright

Satan sez: From the album Greatest Hits. These are my kind of hits!

Reynolds' moments of high profile revolve around his presence in the Liverpool indie scene of the eighties, including being a founding member of Frankie Goes to Hollywood and his time as a member of the band Pink Industry. The "Music…isms" blog on the "incestuous" nature of the various bands at the time charts the crossing of paths between Reynolds and situationist stunt-mongers, like Bill Drummond (later of the KLF). The varied sounds and styles, and the collision between local bands and insanely ambitious ideas made this scene one of the most productive and far reaching in UK music history. It spawned lasting and bankable bands, like Echo and the Bunnymen. But, it also kept John Peel in strange and challenging sounds for years and led to some unique and highly sought after music. One of the simpler concepts and more successful artistic ventures in this regard is Ambrose Reynolds' album Greatest Hits (1983). The whole concept of the collection plays on the punning possibilities of the word "hits." In the context of this collection hits are assassinations, the key samples in the various tracks are original news recordings of assassinations, or the fallout from assassinations, and the musical creativity revolves around tape loops and melody built around these recordings. Crudely, the album apes the styles of what passed at the time for the experimental end of dance, though there's not much evidence Ambrose Reynolds' Greatest Hits provided any dance hits that saw turntable action across the country. The collection remains a vinyl only release. Since its first issue in the early eighties nobody has seen fit to reissue it on CD. At present the authors of this book have struggled to find any of the obvious weird, wonderful and out there music blog sites offering this collection as a downloadable mp3. But the track above – which is one of the standouts – does appear on YouTube.

With looping bass guitar groaning away and some insistent dance rhythms thrown in, "He's Dead Alright" is catchy and agreeably disturbing. The track chugs forward at a steady pace as the in-the-moment commentary on the assassination of JFK is looped to tell a story. It's enough of a story to allow the track to function like any other dance/pop track and the phrases made up on the spot are given enough emphasis to provide some character. This isn't by any means the most inventive or experimental music on the album. The story here – of JFK's assassination – is the best known of all the events providing source material for Greatest Hits, so this, arguably, is the greatest hit on Greatest Hits. Elsewhere the assassinations of Martin Luther King and Robert Kennedy, along with Richard Nixon commenting on students shot by the National Guard at Kent State University make for the subject matter of tracks on Greatest Hits.

In the case of "Get the Gun," the track dealing with the death of Robert Kenney, we are in the same strange twilight world of audio entertainment as the authentic Jonestown massacre/ mass suicide tape. We are, quite literally, listening to the sounds associated with genuine deaths. However, for dramatic impact and the kind of perverse listening pleasure offered by Satan's jukebox "He's Dead Alright" probably shades it as the prime choice. The events are unfolding, the phrases used to convey the tragedy show both the gravity of the situation and the fact that no pre-prepared script is available and Reynolds loops: "The chief executive of the United States has expired" and "He's dead alright" like a grisly chorus likely to make sense in some demented dancehall. It's uneasy listening partly because it works as well as any other experimental dance track of its era, and has an insistent catchiness, if not exactly any notable charm. The fact that the worst moments in human history make sense in musical mash ups is something to celebrate when Satan sits down to listen to this one.

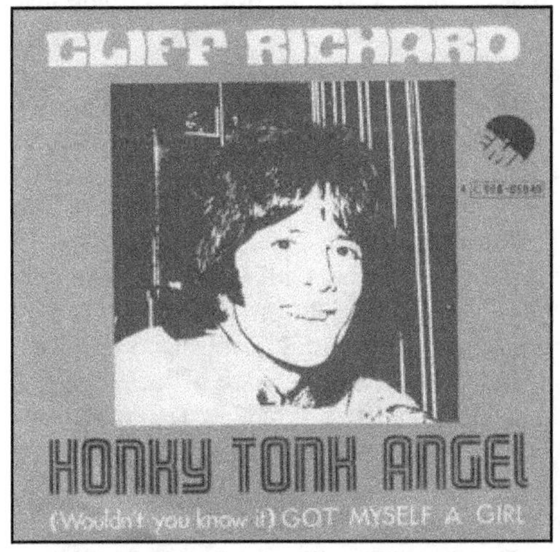

Cliff Richard: *Honky Tonk Angel*

Satan sez: Fackin' get in there my son!! (and he sounds like Ray Winstone when he's saying it)

OF COURSE he'd have Sir Cliff in there. Keep your friends close and your enemies closer, right? In any case, you'll find heavy metal hard men unwinding to minimalist classical music and near-catatonic folkies who slam to goregrind. That is often the way things go. But there's more. If Heaven rejoices more over a repenting sinner...you get the drift, and when a high profile adherent of all that's righteous stumbles and falls that's a satanic celebration right there. Presumably those sporting a cloven hoof give each other a high-two at such moments. Incidentally, regarding Sir Cliff's stumbling etc. We're concentrating on the music, for all details of progress in any other, alleged, matters contact South Yorkshire Police, not the publishers of this book, okay?

Cliff's chart achievements in the UK dwarf most other pretenders, though the tonnage of chart weeks still leaves him fairly short in the overall records sold/exactly where your biggest sellers sit in the all-time lists stakes. From the late fifties to the mid-seventies he regularly racked up chart hits, scored a slew of #1 singles and could be relied on to clock up hits year on year. Though, by the mid-seventies the wheels were clearly coming off to some degree. The chart performances were slowly but surely dipping and the big hits were reliant on some additional factor, like being a Eurovision entry. Britain's most enduring pop star couldn't muster a top ten hit in 1974. The signs of desperation were there in the recorded output. "(You Keep me) Hangin' On" – his sole chart entry in 1974 – Cliffified a stone gone soul beauty from the USA as he went in search of a mature audience. The big hopes for 1975 were pinned on a country tune.

"Honky Tonk Angel" is a slowly unfurling tale in classic country (little guy with the big dilemma) tradition as a man pours out his heart to his distant and unresponsive woman (we'll assume his wife.) He loves her, wants to work at it but, if it all does go to shit; "there's a honky tonk angel who'll take me back in." Either way, he'll get laid, but he'd sooner it was with the woman currently playing hard to get. Good chorus, emotional tale (even if neither of the girls gets a word in) and the kind of semi-tearjerker an emotive and expressive singer could get inside and turn to gold.

To put this in context, country music in the mid-seventies could fill Wembley Arena (the biggest of the "big shed" venues in the UK at the time) but the biggest dents in the charts came with the very mainstream likes of Jim Reeves. In this reality the UK market was open for equally pale home grown talent and Cliff's country single came two years after Des O' Connor produced Sing a Favourite Country Tune and two years before Vera Lynn's infamous In Nashville album. British national institutions – popular music variety – could make a stab at country when everything else was going down the tubes.

But the devout Cliff, and a few of those around him, had majorly missed the ball when they saw "Honky Tonk Angel" as the solution to scoring a hit for an artist mired in mid-career mediocrity. Frankly, the white bread country that formed the staple British diet at the time may have been a major part of the problem. Phrases used in lyrics simply got lost on audiences in Britain, which missed many of the nuances of country. "Honky Tonk Angel" made it all the way to pressed records in shops and a television appearance promoting the single before Cliff was truly aware that the gist of the song involves the narrator saying openly he'll go back to his favourite prostitute ("honky tonk angel") if the wife is offering him none of it. Cliff confessed his ignorance and withdrew the record, because it didn't square with his Christian beliefs or – frankly – the sentiments providing a comfort zone to many of his most loyal fans. He completely avoided UK singles chart action in 1975 as a result, though a significant revival of his fortunes was soon to occur.

His relationship with the song didn't end there. It was revived and performed to massive audiences on his 50th anniversary tour in 2008, Cliff apparently having forgotten why he withdrew it in the first place. EMI Records, for whom he earned a veritable fortune starting in 1958 parted company with Cliff just before the end of the twentieth century, though they continue to shift his back catalogue where – once they'd parted with Cliff - "Honky Tonk Angel" soon appeared as a bonus cut on I'm Nearly Famous (reissued in 2001) and The Singles Collection (EMI 2002.)

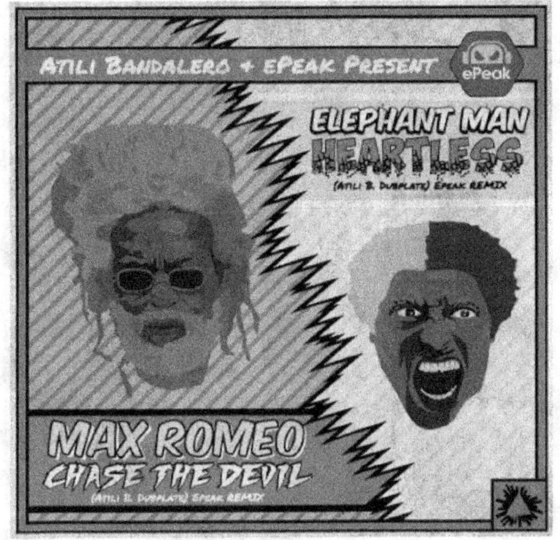

Max Romeo and the Upsetters: Chase the Devil

Satan sez: Oh yeah, you and which stoner army?

Prime period reggae gold written by Lee Perry and Max Romeo and probably best known from the liberal use of a chunk the song in "Out of Space" by The Prodigy. "Chase the Devil" sits proudly on the magnificent War Ina Babylon album and holds its own against some acknowledged classics. Taken literally this is Romeo chanting away with passion about ridding the world of Satan's evils by donning an "iron shirt" and chasing him into the cosmos. It's a party favourite on the Devil's jukebox for a few reasons. Firstly, it's slamming reggae with one of the top performers from the most celebrated era of the music at the top of his game. Forget the lyrics for a second, this is a banging tune. But, beyond that, this must be amusing to the Devil in the way playing football with toddlers is amusing to any athletically challenged adult.

Is Romeo serious? "Satan is an evilous man" just about makes sense, but it does reduce the Devil to being a human being, which – kind of – misses the bit about satanic lore and the greater powers on offer to the grim one. After spotting his foe Romeo appears to be fixing for a one-to-one scrap and his greatest threat involves chasing Satan "to outer space, to find another race." Seriously, how scary is that? The other race might, like, be more corruptible and generally evil than humanity. So, this might be a bonus. In any case, don't God, and the Devil, already know what's happening off the Earth?

Romeo has explained the whole lyric metaphorically, as a battle between negative thoughts and the inner strength of humanity. But most people encountering his original, or The Prodigy's prodigious lifting of its catchy chorus, won't be aware of that. So the chirpy battle described is likely to continue to have a cheery feel and comic book reality in the minds of many listeners. And, if casual reggae fans know anything about Max Romeo, they surely know "Wet Dream" the steamy sexual joke so explicit it was widely banned by radio. "Wet Dream" confesses that "every night" the singer has a wet dream. It goes on to suggest that the nearest available woman will do to satisfy his needs "You in your small corner, I stand in mine/ Throw all the punch you want to, I can take them all/ Lie down girl let me push it up, push it up…give the fanny to me." It's a bouncy and infectious number, but not one that impresses all listeners, especially all female listeners.

So, when Satan hears Max Romeo fixing to chase him beyond the solar system he's probably busier skanking to a classic riddim' than giving a shit about the threat Max is posing. Deep down, he knows the man who made "Wet Dream" may well have done him a few favours along the way.

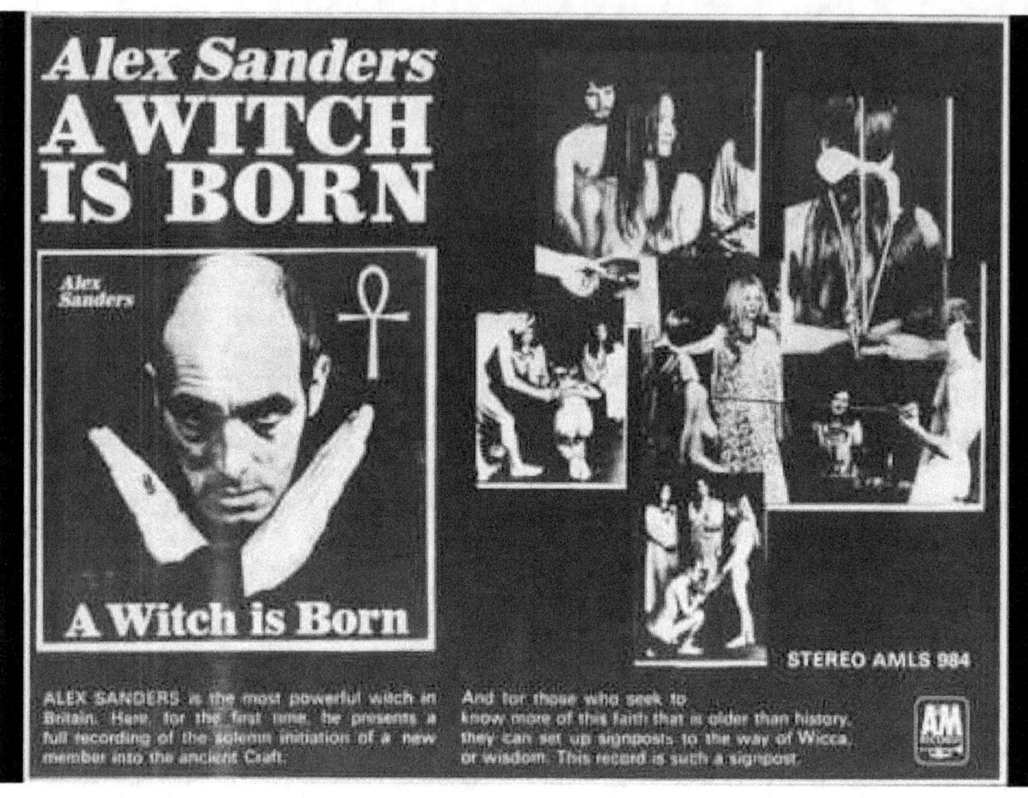

Alex Sanders: The Initiation

Satan sez: Ah, the rite stuff, love it!

Sanders (1926-1988) was one of the best known and most celebrated witches of his generation. A detailed Wikipedia page notes an associate stating Sanders never courted fame, but found himself unable to avoid it. He certainly had a choice about this work – released around the same time as the first Black Sabbath album and bought by those with a serious interest, and some of those for whom the Sabs and their ilk were their main point of contact with all things occult. *A Witch is Born* presents three tracks and three samples of witching lore. The main piece of business – "The Initiation" – features almost 25 minutes of ceremonial rite, serious ritualistic business carried out with due reverence and notable English accents. Janet Owen becomes a witch (and finally gets to speak around the 18 minute mark) as a detailed ceremony is reverently enacted with a permanent backing track of classical music. For the most part it's all well-modulated English voices, intoning rites and Wiccan lore, over classical favourites more familiar to modern ears as the bedrock of mass appeal classical stations the world over. The collision makes for surreal listening. The serious point of the recording is to present Wiccan rites as they take place and Stuart Farrar provides commentary on the main ritual as High Priest Sanders leads the rite that makes Janet Owen a witch.

Low key CD reissues have become available; reproducing the grainy black and white photographs, dark cover and copious sleeve-notes of the original album. In a world of extreme dark magic/magick of all forms *A Witch is Born* now presents a slightly staid, and very English take on the whole business and – like the Aliester Crowley recordings also chronicled in this book – does have a certain approachable charm.

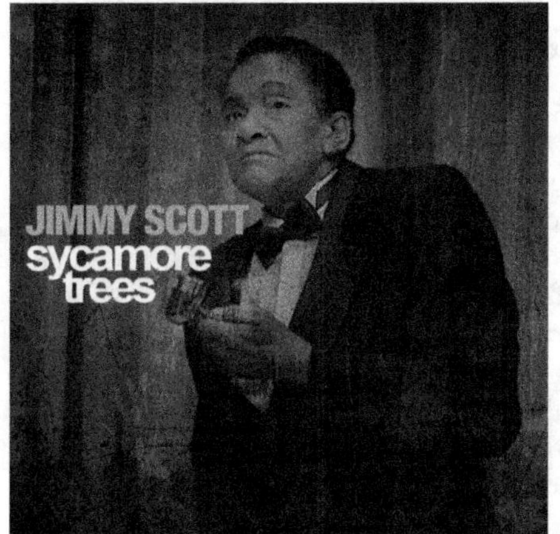

Jimmy Scott: Sycamore Trees

Satan sez: This one always raises the hairs on the back of my cloven hoof.

Scott (1925-2014) enjoyed a lengthy jazz singing career with stellar early success, including work with legends like Lionel Hampton, followed by a long period of low-profile as his fortunes declined. His final years were marked by a comeback and some incredible late period work as a range of imaginative producers and musicians worked with him to produce some spell-binding and memorable sounds. "Sycamore Trees" is best known for its use in a scene of eerie revelation from Twin Peaks, and was concocted for that purpose with lyrics by David Lynch and music by Angelo Badelamenti. It is available on the film soundtrack Fire Walk With Me.

"Sycamore Trees" bears a passing resemblance to the blues standard Strange Fruit, and – like that song – uses long syllables, a soaring voice and minimal, mordant, backing to evoke a sense of lingering pain and darkness. Strange Fruit is specifically about lynching of black people but "Sycamore Trees" pins nothing down. The singer is taken for a walk under "The dark trees that blow, baby" but he is taken for a walk by someone who is both there, and not there: "And I'll see you in the branches that blow/ In the breeze." In the context of the twilight zone around Twin Peaks it all makes perfect sense (or as much sense as David Lynch will ever allow it to make.) Shorn of the context "Sycamore Trees" is a brooding and slightly malevolent excursion, all the more disturbing because Scott's impassioned vocal conveys a real sense of unease and his voice remains a true androgynous wonder, slightly roughened with age, but strong and steady through the longest notes.

Selecting Scott to deliver this marginally demented marvel was a typical Lynch master stroke. "Little" Jimmy Scott (as he originally was billed) had Kallmann's syndrome, a rare genetic condition that stunts growth and holds back or prevents puberty. He didn't reach five feet in height until his late thirties and only ever stood five feet seven. His high and, basically, undeveloped voice gave his work a feminine quality and he mastered its use to the point his best work allowed him to soar vocally over the sound of a band. For all its arty and surreal pretensions Twin Peaks with its cast of eccentrics behind the façade of a popular resort town had a freak show quality. Scott's musical contribution fitted the mood and plot to perfection. "Sycamore Trees" stands out as a song capable of changing the temperature in a room and invading your thoughts to drag your attention away, without you quite knowing what's going on. It's uneasy listening of the finest quality and a simple tune that stands repeated hearing. For those moments when the Dark Lord wants to forgot his wealth and enjoy the tasteful, this is essential listening.

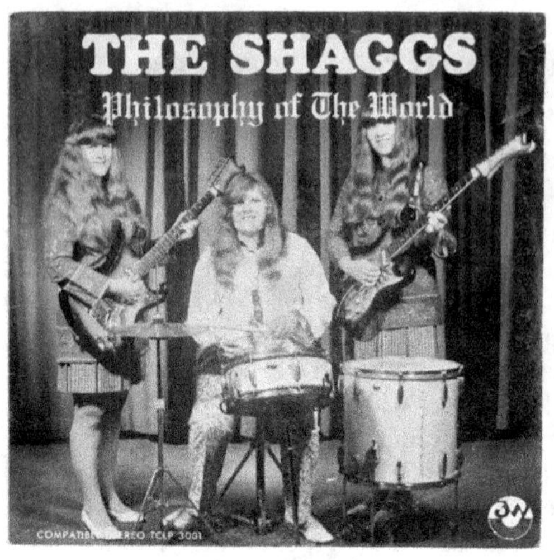

The Shaggs: Philosophy of the World

Satan sez: Torture gets results!

The story of The Shaggs, the three Wiggin sisters coerced by their father into forming a band, is somewhat convoluted, a tad tragic and a rite of passage to those intent on investigating outsider music. To all intents and purposes The Shaggs became a band the day in the sixties their father, Austin, came home and announced his mother had read his palm and the results suggested the sisters were about to form a massively successful girl group. This was hugely odd for two reasons: 1 – the Wiggin sisters hadn't hitherto been allowed out to social events or exposed to much music. 2 – They hadn't any history as musicians. Never-the-less an intense five years of learning their craft in isolation followed, giving rise to an approach to composition and performance within which traditional notions of the way standard pop group instrumentation worked were never likely to intrude. Unwordly and seriously unready the band began recording their own compositions and playing gigs they still recall hating, before a sudden heart attack claimed their father at the age of 47 and The Shaggs' disbandment followed shortly after, much to the relief of the trio.

When – many years later – their recorded works began to gather a cult following nobody was more amazed than The Shaggs. To put this in context Kurt Cobain, listing his 50 favourite albums, put The Shaggs' Philosophy of the World album at #5 (ahead of Never Mind the Bollocks.)

Shaggs' music typically features the girls singing in unison, the lead guitar playing the same melody as the vocals and the drums galloping along in an attempt to embellish the lead lines. Accompaniment doesn't exist in any formal sense as everyone crowds the centre ground, singing the same note, except when one or two voices go fleetingly flat. It's idiot savant genius, complicated by the fact it sounds like work produced in pressure cooker circumstances by confused girls who haven't a clue but want desperately to please. This much has been confirmed in subsequent interviews. And, in any case, on certain band compositions the story of trying and hitting a brick wall is obvious in the lyrics. "Philosophy of the World" (title track of the album) opens with: "Oh, the rich people want what the poor people's got/ And the poor people want what the rich people's got/ And the skinny people want what the fat people's got…" It concludes with a line that also forms a refrain in the song: "You can never please anybody in this world."

The belated recognition of the band has put their work in circulation. It also led to a reformation and some live work. But the band never forgot the pressure and discomfort that poured itself into their original recordings. The ethical problem that lingers is that those citing them now as genuine originals, possessed of a strange and differently-abled talent, do have a point. The Shaggs' minimal canon sounds unique, mystically strange and compelling. It exudes a power light years away from almost anything else released as pop music because it's divorced totally from notions of pop as a sexual statement, a means of earning serious money or – indeed – any of the other traditional uses of pop songs. The Shaggs are chart music in some other-worldly hell we struggle to imagine. All of which presents The Shaggs as important in the way laboratory animals may be important. This music, and in particular songs like "Philosophy of the World" are genuinely the sounds of people in pain. Mental pain rather than physical and generally a pain that doesn't equate to the kind of anguish you would find channelled into blues music or other cathartic genres. But pain for sure. The Shaggs' story has a happier ending (though not for their dad) than the stories of a few other outsider musicians whose suffering has been part of their appeal. But it's still far from comfortable. And, therefore, it may well be the case that Satan betrays a sly grin as he thinks of Austin Wiggin's insane vision, and the way it finally became a reality.

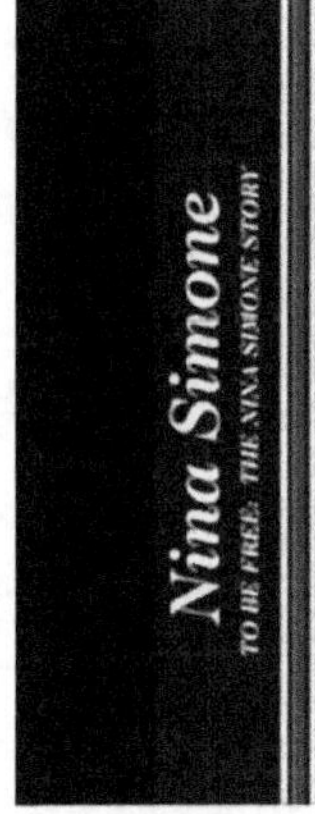

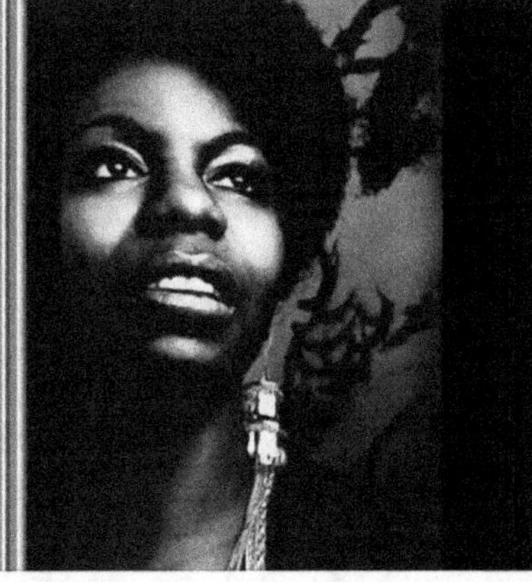

Nina Simone: Pirate Jenny

Satan sez: C'mon people, I'm a man of wealth at taste.

"Pirate Jenny" comes from The Threepenny Opera, the same production that unleashed "Mack the Knife" on humanity. Listening to Jenny, a maid working in "crummy old hotel," we slowly navigate a revenge fantasy in which all the contempt and disregard she suffers is channelled into a new reality in which pirates, rather than the cavalry, ride to her rescue. It's a fantasy, but Simone owns the song to the point it's totally believable. A pirate ship comes into the harbour, levels every building in town bar the hotel, and leaves the pirates to round up the townspeople and present them to Jenny:

By noontime the dock
Is a-swarmin' with men
Comin' out from the ghostly freighter
They move in the shadows
Where no one can see
And they're chainin' up people

And they're bringin' em to me
Askin' me,
"Kill them now, or later?"

Jenny takes the Columbine option, ordering the deaths of everyone before sailing away with the pirates. Okay, Columbine didn't end exactly like that, but you get our drift.

Simone's definitive take on the song owns it in a way the original dramatic setting – devised by dramatist Bertolt Brecht and composer Kurt Weill - doesn't begin to predict. Recorded live, Simone performed the song at a time when people still insisted on referring to the current world heavyweight champion as Cassius Clay (NOT Muhammad Ali.) When Simone cut her live version Martin Luther King's "I have a dream" speech was fresh in minds, and represented a massive threat to many people. So, Simone's song, by default, appears to channel a deep-seated anger about racial inequality, and present mass murder as an acceptable solution to the problem. It's an unrepentant recognition that humanity – even intelligent thoughtful humanity - can be bestial, and problems may be beyond solving. (Pirate) Jenny has a dream, but it's more fuck you than any journey to the Promised Land. Hell, Jenny would sooner hang out with pirates than white folks. All of the above makes sense because Simone's performance rises and falls with the dramatic moments and gets so eerily intimate that we share her anger and vision of mass murder, with herself as judge and jury. It's a sublime performance from Simone's masterful In Concert set recorded in 1964 and a demonstration of her artistry at its most potent. It's also unremittingly dark and a worthy addition to the Devil's Jukebox.

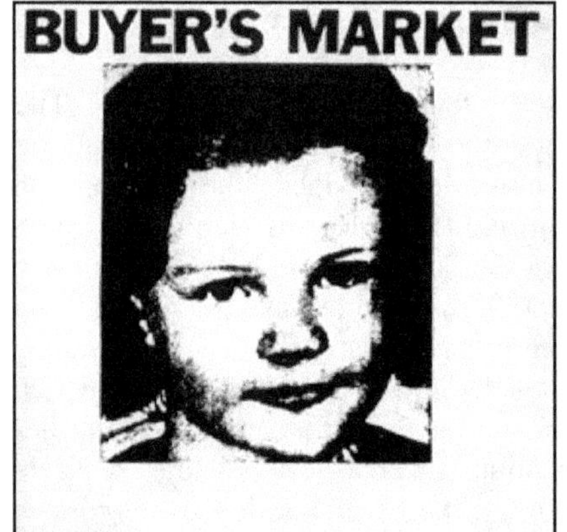

Peter Sotos: Buyer's Market

Satan sez: Not exactly a golden hour.

Even by the standards of extreme, and extremely evil, recorded works this one is up there with the most unrepentant audio ever offered for anyone's listening "pleasure." This blended collage of audio recordings explores sex crimes from the varied angles of those involved – criminals, victims, close family of those concerned and law enforcement officers – rotating the different recordings to achieve a momentum of short and long clips, and some sense of balance as we move from personal insights to fly-on-the-wall presence in those moments when abuse is disclosed. Sex and sexual sadism has been a lifelong interest of Chicago- born Sotos. His career has seen prolific authorship of books and consistent controversy. In a general sympathetic consideration of Sotos' work Michael Lujan invited readers to meet a: "renaissance sadist who explores his thoroughly socially-unsanctioned lusts via the medium of the written word."

So this sound collage is a detour on a journey where the written word has paved most of the way. As an exploration in the variety of evil and damage attaching itself to sex crimes Buyer's Market is both insightful and comprehensive. And, in that context, it charts a godless and highly depressing landscape where damage limitation and the ability to survive are the only victories on offer. It's also a highly disturbing listen simply because the editing skills, pacing and variety of material give the collage the feel of a good and arty work for radio. In this context the fact you are listening to a mother recounting the discovery of her barely breathing and horrendously abused child, or a prostitute calmly and coldly explaining how sexual abuse gave her the distance on sex that allows her to like the money and dislike her clients, means that the consummate skills of production simply keep the seemingly endless parade of evil both lively and compelling long past the point when your senses would generally be reeling at the onslaught.

Few works of creative sound editing dive so deeply into darkness or hit as hard so consistently. Sotos overturns notions of what is listenable, what constitutes art and what is acceptable. He constantly challenges you to tear yourself away as he simultaneously reminds you that you are hearing real people, recounting real events. The dynamic between curiosity (or worse) on the part of the listener which keeps drawing you in, and the pain and horror so often found in the clips is, largely, the point. Many listeners find themselves questioning the motives that concocted over an hour of this. Others might reflect on the fact that such a ceaseless and disturbing audio assault is less harrowing by a large margin than the actual experiences recounted by the victims paraded here.

It is questionable where this work actually belongs, who would want to own it and for what purpose. XXX Maniac are amongst a handful of extreme bands who have sampled sections for use in their own works (in this case "Skeleton Toucher" on their grimly titled album Harvesting the Cunt Nectar.) But if any one jukebox, anytime, anywhere were prepared to countenance this work rubbing shoulders with other sounds, then that jukebox would surely be in Hell.

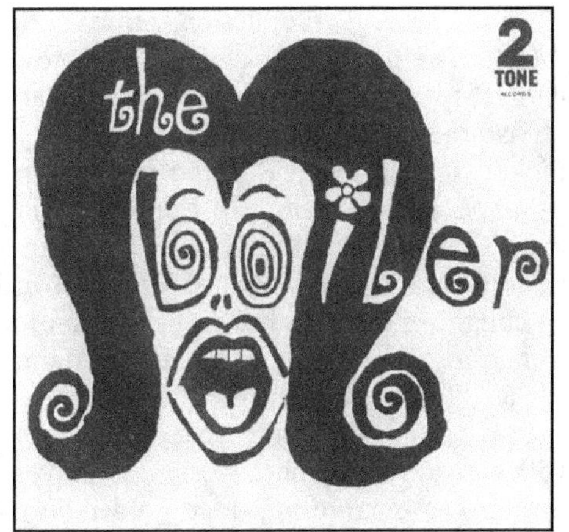

The Special AKA featuring Rhoda Dakar: The Boiler

Satan sez: Feel bad radio fodder of the most riveting kind.

A chugging piece of ska with Rhoda rapping over the top this is a track of two halves. The jaunty opening segment has our heroine discussing her unexpected good luck when a "hunk" steps in to pay for her shopping. She's self-depreciating and marvels at her luck when he asks her out, seeing herself as an "old boiler." It goes well, for a short time. Her bloke is "a real hard man" but he's soft on her. The end might be predictable but the way it's handled is full-on and realistic to a harrowing degree. The hunk wants paying back sexually, she points out "it's a bit soon innit" but he manipulates her and they end up alone with "no one about." The violence is one thing, but about the only break from the full horror in the final minute is that the hunk only tries to rape her. The assumption you might just draw from the lengthy and full throated screams, which might as well have come from a horror movie, or worse, is that the screaming just about headed off the rape, but our "boiler" still feels as bad about her life as it is possible to feel after the experience. The backing music subtly changes but stays firmly in the slow chugging mode, with an occasional melodic flourish suggesting fifties dark noir, driving us forward to the final horrors with the same force as a grisly movie getting to its hellish conclusion.

This 1982 recording is feel bad radio fodder of the most riveting kind, so much so that it's fallen off the playlists wherever audience numbers and the ability to attract advertising determine the decisions. But it's still a selection wherever listeners want those unforgettable, one-off records that push the possibilities of what a song can do. Wherever they want those sounds and words that touch raw nerves and change the entire atmosphere in the room so much that, once heard, they won't be quickly forgotten. So, it makes Satan's jukebox with ease.

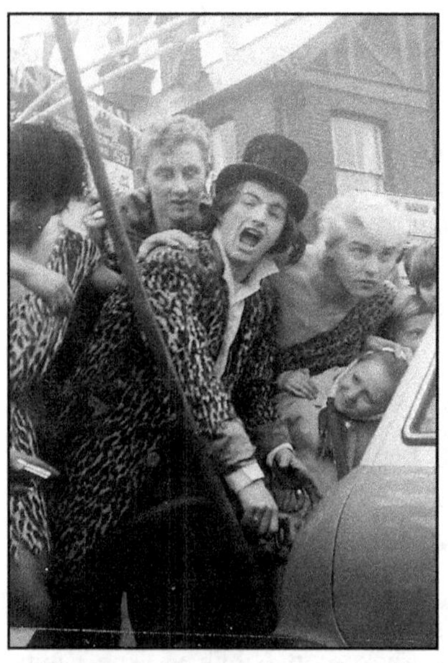

Screaming Lord Sutch: 'Til the Following Night (aka "Till the Following Night"), (aka "My Big Black Coffin")

Satan sez: Cod almightly

Sutch at his scary best from his 1961 debut single, "'Til the Following Night" offers up two demented genius types for the price of 7" of vinyl because the cacophony of horror noises and general production duties are handled by Joe Meek. The online Book of Bands notes: "it sounds considerably more malevolent and mean spirited than 'Monster Mash,' the novelty record by Bobby 'Boris' Pickett in late 1962." Indeed it does, in fact the lengthy – 40 seconds – section of ripping coffin lid, screams, moans, rattled chains and a distant tack piano is sampling gold for those in search of little known audio gems. Once the cod rock n' roll number starts chugging along we're in grisly comic book territory. Sutch was more a conveyor of a song than a great singer but he surges along with a story of emerging from his coffin after dark, tells us: "I got two horns on my head and a twinkle in my eye," and discusses his furry feet whilst presenting the hours of darkness in a graveyard as little more than a glee filled rock n' roll party. Sutch's best work was clever enough to avoid outstaying its welcome and this grim corker is more mix-tape gold than a work worthy of endless repeats, but it's fun, as good a laugh as any low-rent rock n' roll should be and all the better because you know that one half of the major talents on show here

(Meek) went on to make some of the most demented and deranged pop music imaginable before ensuring long-term notoriety by murdering his landlady and offing himself in the same fun filled afternoon on the Holloway Road. The other talent (Sutch) went on to form the Monster Raving Loony Party, an outfit so wilfully off-the-wall they have, over the years, advocated turning excess butter produced in the EEC into an artificial slope for skiers to practice on, removing Britain from the EEC and joining it to the Dutchy of Cornwall to benefit from tax breaks and ensuring all X-Ray machines are manned by a skeleton staff (Boom Boom.)

So, we're into childish knockabout fun/guilty pleasure land here with regard to why Satan may slam to this particular sound, but no well stocked jukebox is complete without a few of those records.

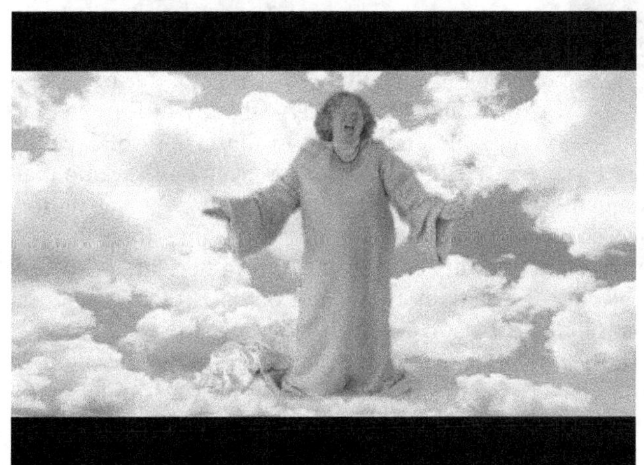

Jan Terri: Ave Maria

Satan sez: Arf Arf Maria!!

Jan Terri's home produced hokum has garnered a fairly sizeable following online. The extent to which the appreciation is ironic is hard to tell when most of the critical comments applied to her output amount to posts underneath her YouTube videos. Middle-aged and matronly, it has to be said that Terri's work packs a major charm on two fronts. Firstly, she's fearless in venturing everywhere in her search to walk the rock star walk as well as talking the talk. The flying V guitar strangled in classic fashion (albeit in front of a fountain and shot fairly cheaply) in the video for "Skyrockets" is a top Terri moment, so too her courage in attempting songs so definitively covered by others that any reworking is dangerous. Terri's take on "I Honestly Love You" is faster and way less intimate than the version that added a new dimension to Olivia Newton John's career in the mid-seventies, but it claims the song for Jan and her ilk. Terri's second major strength is her ability to exist in a world beyond parody and provide the kind of instant thrills beloved of the click-bait crowd.

On both fronts this shambolic demolition of Schubert is online gold, even if its various downloads have yet to trouble a chart anywhere. It's cod-dance, karaoke light, fleetingly flat at the highest vocal points and the kind of cobbled together calamity that – once heard – stalks the nightmares of any music lover so violated. Of course, all of the above is an opinion and we respect the right of Terri's devoted followers to claim this as a sincere masterpiece. But, as guilty pleasure/fun and the kind of irreverent reading of a reverent work that, at least slightly, tarnishes the power of the original, this one has a place in Hell's Hot 100.

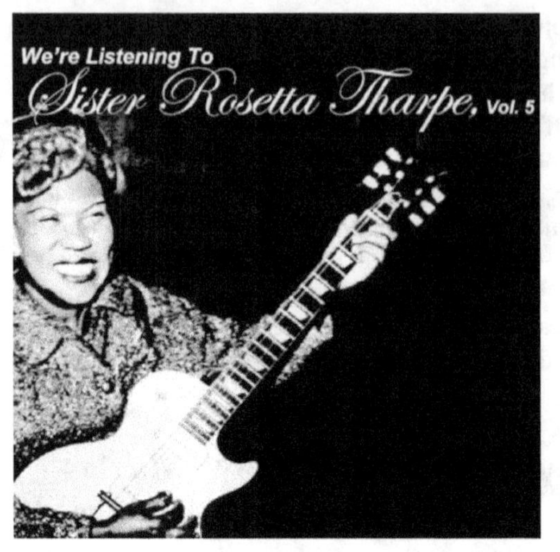

Sister Rosetta Tharp: The Devil has Thrown him Down

Satan sez: Yeah! So, what's your point?

Satan might well start with a smirk at the thought that the gospel singing Tharp (1915-1973) would be turning in her grave at the thought of her inclusion, and the appearance of this song, in Hell's Hot 100. Tharp suffered misunderstanding and some outright prejudice during her career, not least when her gospel audience started to desert her as she made R&B records in the fifties. It wasn't until late in her career, and – ironically – mainly in Europe that Tharp began to get true recognition for everything she contributed to the history of rock n' roll. In the USA pre and post war it didn't help her need to get records played on the radio that she was both female and black. Her frequently incendiary guitar style was an influence on the likes of Chuck Berry and her influence on Elvis has also become known since their deaths. But first and foremost Tharp was a gospel artist and this banging tune, with her guitar picking driving a strong story, makes the jukebox for the same reason The Louvin Brothers make it. This is a recognition from a righteous minded artist of the overwhelming power at Satan's disposal when the unwary slip up. "The Devil has Thrown him Down" is a simple enough idea, time and again people are within touching distance of salvation but the Devil intervenes and they are lost. This even applies to those close enough to see Christ in the flesh. In this reality salvation is a slim hope and temptation a constant threat, and many are thrown down by the Devil. Sister Rosetta brings the menace alive with a rapid and unsettling picking style that sets up a steady and uneasy ripple on the guitar, over which the lyrics are delivered with authority and a sense of the fire and brimstone preaching she knew from regular church attendance.

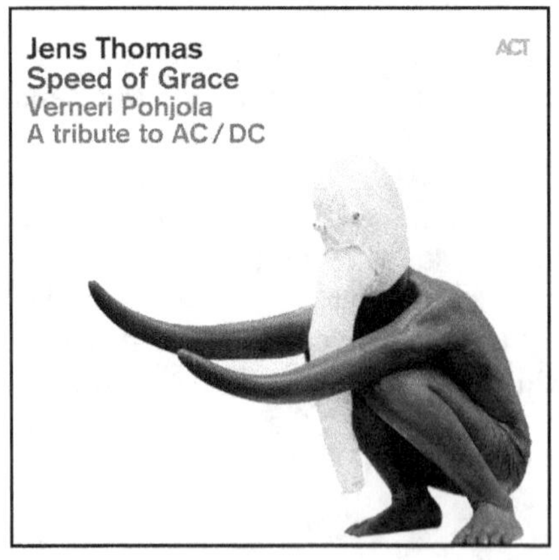

Jens Thomas and Verneri Pohjola: Highway to Hell

Satan sez: Just like me, you think you know something then it morphs into a new form right in front of you!

Yes indeed, this is the AC/DC stormer, a rite of passage to teenagers of several generations and one of the simplest and most effective hard rock songs ever written. It's also (just about) recognisable as that animal, certainly by the time Thomas breaths, sighs and intimately intones the words millions already recognise. But the only other sounds on offer are those of his expertly played jazz piano and Pohjola's sparing and sympathetic trumpet lines. Thomas takes the basic chords of the original, and the simple melody, using them to guide him as he embellishes a little, hammers the deep notes and keeps the light top-end trills to an effective minimum. At those moments when the original calls for Angus Young to scream out of the mix Phjola is there with flurries of simple jazz patterns played with a soulful grace.

The point is to find the minimal and mature beauty in AC/DC's unrepentant anthem and reinvent the song as a recognition of the inevitable rather than a fuck you gesture to the so called moral majority. The pair playing this version are old enough and smart enough to be overwhelmed by musical choices, but they choose to make this ground their own.

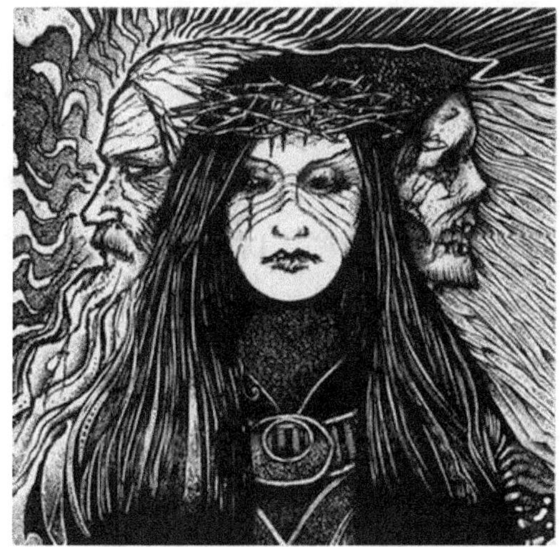

Jex Thoth: Stone Evil

Satan sez: "As a Beautiful Princess crosses a Bridge under which Four Great Trolls are performing Doom Metal…"(well, actually, Julian Cope said that, but Satan doubtless agrees.)

Jex Thoth (like early Alice Cooper the name refers to both a five piece band and their lead singer, we'll file them under T for Thoth) have sold a few records, and generated a tonnage of words amongst those who've heard the sounds. Kim Grim, discussing the act in a blog about "Women of Occult Rock" notes: "Jex Thoth is one of doom's most enigmatic and entrancing high priestesses…[the 2008 album Jex Thoth is] all woozy, meandering, thudding doom and swaggering desert rock, augmented and propelled into the outer limits by Jex's inimitable smoky, soaring wail."

"Stone Evil" is the closing cut on this collection, a fitting vocal finale for an album also ripe with portentous doom 'n' dirge noodlings of a decidedly dark hue. Lyrically it speaks with a sparing starkness that matches the best of the music: "Wounds like barren trees/ Dripping with disease/ Blank soul decimate/ Fire without flame." The involvement of Julian Cope in the band's burgeoning fan base says much about the dark psych/ acid rock swathes that bathe their music in an otherworldly eruption of moods and ideas. He also nails their sound and vibe: "Rural as fuck, and Heathen as a Cunt and thrice as mysterious, Jex Thoth's is a strange ministry. I imagine this quintet's audience dwelling in scattered & out-of-the-way homesteads, rarely coming together as a community, and so obliging this itinerant quintet to spread their barbarian information out to their congregation by any means necessary; for their music contains few highs or lows of the Urban variety, and replaces obvious hooks with insidious melodies that emerge then take over our melting plastic minds."

The self-titled album mines this mash up to the extent that the only useful comparisons are bands that crossed boundaries with ease. Cope cites Van der Graaf Generator and Crown of Creation period Jefferson Airplane. We'd suggest some affinity with the proggier end of Nordic black metal might help. For a few seconds Jex Thoth might evoke early Black Sabbath; a few seconds later acid folk erupts. "Stone Evil" slides through some styles; an acoustic intro morphs into dark thrash riffs, a blast of acid rock guitar follows and Jex (singer) arrives to soar above the seething firmament much – indeed – "as a Beautiful Princess crosses a Bridge under which Four Great Trolls are performing Doom Metal…" Given the minimal chances of this collision of royalty and mythic beings actually happening in Hell, or your neighbourhood, the only acceptable alternative is to acquire your own personal jukebox and load up at least one Jex Thoth track.

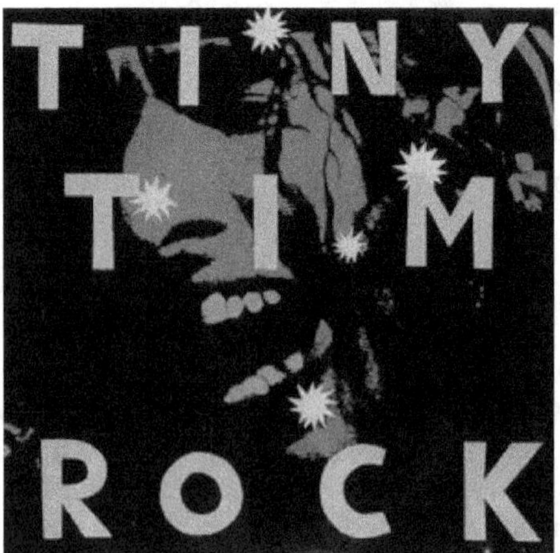

Tiny Tim: Eve of Destruction

Satan sez: C'mon man; it's genius.

Tiny Tim (1932-1996) was an oversized high-voiced eccentric who briefly breezed in from his own planet to achieve a modicum of high-profile success. His reworking of the pop standard and twenties film song "Tiptoe Through the Tulips" was a genuine hit around the world and the Richard Perry produced God Bless Tiny Tim is an object lesson in how to tease a varied and surprising full-length album out of a performer with minimal notions of how the hard-edged, commercial, end of the music business actually functions.

Tim was always more a force of nature than a standard creative talent and his ideas on all manner of things – from marriage to the correct toilet habits of decent people – were, ahem, individual. This uncompromising streak, along with the bizarre and strangely hypnotic sounds he made gave Tim a fan base including arch Satanists Anton La Vey and Boyd Rice, the first a major influence on satanic thought, the second a cutting edge musician who joins the avant-garde only on his more accessible outings. So, Satan slams to Tim, then?

Well, probably to this tune anyway. This late period (1993) epic is an apocalyptic wonder that channels the Book of Revelation through an unholy mash of prog rock flourishes, standard pop tricks and moments when any nearby sound is pumped into the mix to sustain the 23 minute plus demolition of a sixties slice of pop psychedelia. It works, magnificently, because Tim ignores Barry Maguire's designer hippie take on the P F Sloan written song and opts instead to ride the rollicking waves of sound much in the manner of an eyeballs-out demented preacher haranguing a crowd who lack any conception of what is about to happen.

Tim's force of nature capabilities do the rest as the song sets out to beat the listener into believing the end is about unfold itself. There are moments of demonic laughter, inappropriately pretty keyboard flourishes and an air of mayhem and confusion in the more focussed moments, all of which contribute to a confusion within which Tim's regular appearances intoning the chorus provide the clearest explanation of what is happening. Bear in mind the Barry McGuire hit is a radio friendly three minutes and 38 seconds, Tim's take clocks in over twenty minutes longer, without too many additional words. So the original words are expanded to mind numbing overkill and aided a little by spoken word interludes and random yodels. This is the kind of outing that defies any linking with musical genres and stands alone as a work both "insane" and "unholy." Which is where it hits the spot on Satan's jukebox. Frankly, by the time you've clocked that this, ermm, song is proving that the end times are beginning by channelling the sheer force of the apocalypse into your ears it may well be too late for you to sincerely repent. Any attempt you make will only be scuppered by the constant distractions exploding in your ears as Tim delivers another bizarre vocal turn.

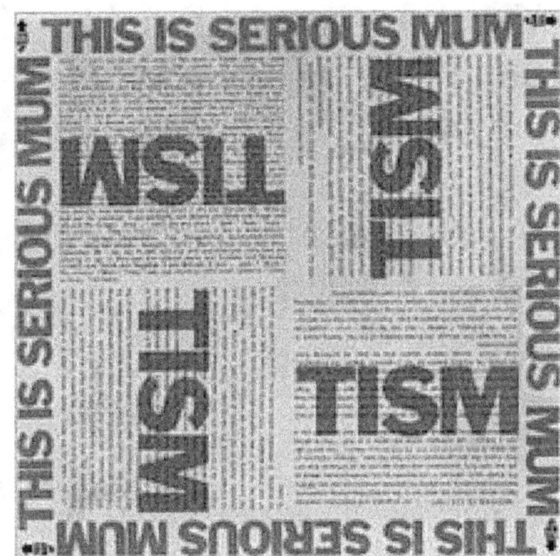

TISM: Defecate on my Face

Satan sez: Oh shit! Forgot this was on the jukebox.

TISM (which stands for "this is serious man") burned brightly from 1982 to 2004 and brought musical muscle and a certain smirking malevolence to Australian audiences during their glory years. At times too clever-clever for their own good TISM have – never-the-less – carved a career of consummate audio carnage, colliding deft musical chops with stomach churning ideas, of which "Defecate on my Face" is a prime example. For Satan's jukebox, we'd venture it's this combination that does the trick. The whole strength of mirth-monsters like these guys is their ability to take the piss so completely because they clearly love the thing they mock so mightily. Because of this much of the fun is infectious. Providing you find the notion of a face full of fresh shit at least hypothetically funny, of course. With the infectious fun comes a contempt for the staid, official and highly moral, so this shit (sorry!) is the dark side with a smirk.

For anyone willing to venture further into exploring the trajectories taken by TISM reading their history online is something of a hoot in itself. Having branded their first gig such a failure it forced their disbandment, every subsequent group activity is labelled a "re-union." This includes their nudging an album into the Australian top ten and various viral successes with songs over the years. Officially TISM are an anonymous band; a wheeze that has allowed various members to hide behind gleefully outrageous disguises and names such as: "Ron Hitler-Barassi, Eugene de la Hot-Croix Bun, Tokin' Blackman and Les Miserables." In reality a number of online sources name the various members and cite their sources of evidence in doing so, revealing the band to have its roots in serious musicianship and professions like school teaching (which was rumoured to be the case from the start given the clear intelligence behind what they were doing.) Some corking titles sugar the TISM pills and their lengthy career has thrown up albums including: *Great Truckin' Songs of the Renaissance* (1988) and the awesomely punning *Machiavelli and the Four Seasons* (1995) which soared all the way to #8 in the Australian chart. The compilation *Machines Against the Rage* probably deserves a mention too, though for sheer infamy their EP "Australia the Lucky Cunt" still shades it. The one banging tune we'd speculatively suggest makes Satan's hot 100 is the highly danceable "Defecate…"

Packing a Heaven 17 stylee muscular groove and an insistent chorus, this fist pumping fun is so damn clamorous and catchy it makes the whole turd to tongue malarkey sound – like – tasty, which is doubtless the way the Prince of Darkness would want you to see it.

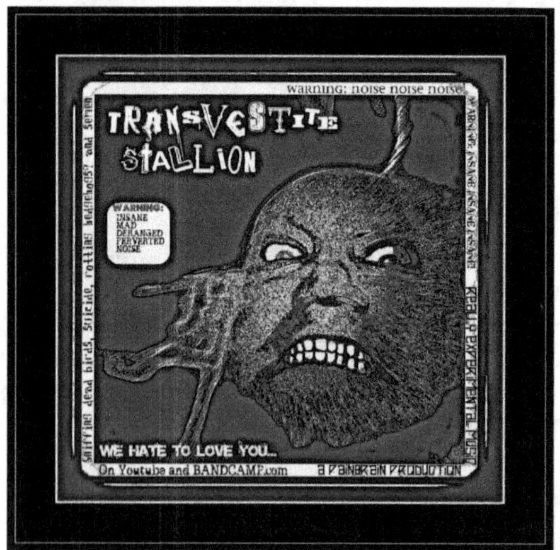

TRANSVESTITEstallion: Sniffing Dead Birds, Suicide, Rotting Hedgehogs and Semen (dada poetry and noise)

Satan sez: And now we rise, and we are everywhere.

According to TRANSVESTITEstallion's Bandcamp profile: "we are quite experimental...
atona outsider, Noise anti-music, glitch electro, art, dada, Poetry, random Musique Concrete, Neo Krautrock. electronica and sometimes beats :)" The present authors would suggest the graphic ":)" at the end of the wordage is as important as any of words. We'd also want to provide a reality check, of sorts. When Jacob Aranza wrote the second of his two books warning the world about backward masking, and the plethora of satanic sounds available in 1985 he could offer up generalities like: "Most of Prince's music is sexual. He seems to be obsessed with a warped sense of morality."* Back then there was clearly a view amongst the righteous and "right" in political terms that this fetid tide could be turned with a combination of clear argument and re-programming of the slavering hordes who bought the wrong music.

Fast forward 30 years and Bandcamp are providing a home to the likes of TRANVESTITEstallion. "Sniffing Dead Birds…(dada poetry and noise)", is what you might imagine. Warped mind-fuck spoken word cut-ups, random bleeps and echoes and a deranged story hanging somewhere out of reach: "Sam sucked on a hedgehog with spiny teeth." Let's leave aside what – if anything – TRANSVESTITEstallion mean by all this and lay back with Lucifer as he settles down with these sounds. Compared to the minor moral panic about

Prince, Bandcamp and its social networking sidekicks is an explosion of rampant endangerment likely to require way more than a well-crafted argument to spike its power. In this world TRANSVESTITEstallion are ravaging the righteous thinkers in ways Jacob Aranza and his followers never began to anticipate.

You can head to Bandcamp in search of the most innocent and pure outpourings of sincere hearts, click on a wholesome tag and find yourself staring at this stuff in seconds. Granted, the present authors were actively seeking filth and fury when they stumbled upon TRANSVESTITEstallion (as a result of following the tag: "semen" if you must know.) But "Sniffing Dead Birds, Suicide, Rotting Hedgehogs and Semen (dada poetry and noise)" is also tagged with "birds" and – therefore – lies one click away from new age and nirvanic noises like "Forest Sounds with Relaxation Music." Add to this that TRANVESTITEstallion are, like, OFFERING THIS ONE FOR FREE DOWNLOAD and you understand why sound hounds are saturated with possibilities, and why every person seeking to stem this tide is, metaphorically speaking, sticking a finger in a leaking dam. The notion that the world will ever again agree on one musical message, style or moral position is fanciful, and every creed or group that suggests otherwise might want to spend an afternoon locked in a room listening to the complete catalogue of TRANSVESTITEstallion.

*Jacob Aranza: More Rock & Country Backward Masking Unmasked (Huntington House, 1985) p.109

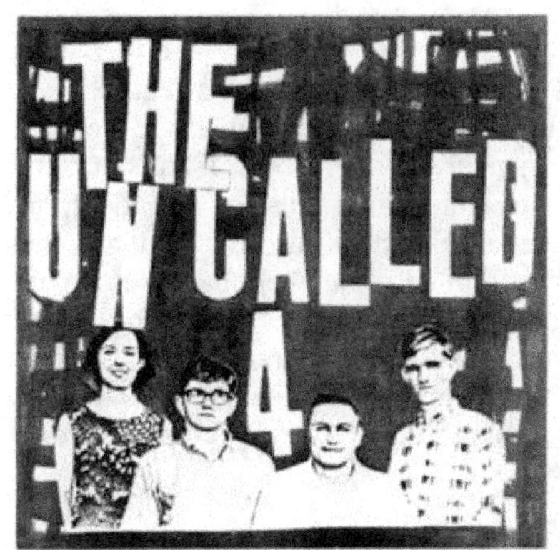

The Uncalled 4: *Grind Her Up*

Satan sez: Murder can be fun.

In a slew of salacious low-fi trash rock this gruesome little gem has earned a certain cult following. Its cheery two minute 20 second missive delivers audible vocals that still retain a sense of glorious hysteria, an insistent and improbably simple riff and a killer lyric that does little to conceal its delight as Ed Gein's capers (murder and cannibalism) are covered in a classic punk-pop fashion. The whole piece is perfectly pitched over the short duration to get just enough variety out of the assorted atrocities "Grind her up…put her heart in the refrigerator if you want to save it for later, the neighbours dropped by but they couldn't know what Ed was heatin' up on the stove." Apart from anything else, there's lyrical genius in rhyming "girls your mother hated" with "eviscerated."

There were loads of Gein jokes in honour of Winconsin's worst son, ordering a "Gein beer" meant all body and no head (heh heh), since when Gein's crimes have prompted a range of rock n roll responses, including the band Ed Gein's Car. But if you want just one fun reminder of the guy who inspired movies like *Psycho*, *The Texas Chainsaw Massacre* and *The Silence of the Lambs*, this is Satan's must slam to song.

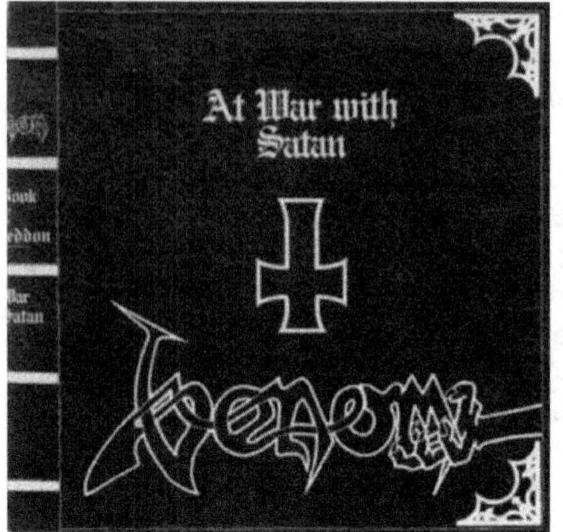

Venom: At War With Satan

Satan sez: One side of the original vinyl, one Hell of a headbanger.

That "difficult" third album turned into Venom's definitive statement. Extreme metal mavericks from the north east of England, the band never made the mega league in sales terms. But the Dark Lord loves 'em and all their endeavours, especially the opening cut and title track from the At War With Satan (1984) album. This monstrous epic sprawls over the whole vinyl of side one and ranks as one of the definitive black metal statements. Online you'll find swathes of discussion about where black metal stops, death metal starts etc. You'll also find much consideration of whether the lack of monster sales for Venom is down to their rigid adherence to the dark side with its resulting rejection of their music by radio stations and record shops. Another school of thought, supported by former Black Flag frontman Henry Rollins, suggests they simply couldn't play or perform to the same standards as a band like Metallica and invented black metal by default because they substituted speed for skill.

We'll ignore the endless going round in circles and get stuck into their finest cut. Ripping along for damn near twenty minutes "At War with Satan" is both the centrepiece of Venom's best known album and a distillation of what the band have always done best. It's a story, told to perfection, dragging the dark side into view, playing with satanic imagery and ideas, and never afraid to let a roaring scream or rapid flurry of guitar tell part of the tale. Venom – then and now – are a power trio with the strength of the best limited in numbers bands. It's about timing, stops and starts, building and riding a riff and unleashing the power of the limited dynamics to perfection. The drums drive the whole show and take over sporadically, the guitar speaks and the bass is the glue. Venom cited Rush as an (obvious) influence but came together in the era when punk challenged every metal band with regard to speed and the level of attack in their guitar sound.

"At War With Satan" takes on all of the challenges and comes back as its own beast, complete with Conrad "Chronos" Lant's clear north eastern accent in the vocals. At War With Satan (album) is a concept piece about a war between Heaven and Hell; with the lot from the lower floor taking the spoils in the end. Lyrically, it's up with the best of the bestial, an early flurry: "Satanic majesty sits proud, the joyous drones of celebration enact scenes of blasphemy, lust and destruction. / Raping the holy trinity the Sabbath chimes the tunes of bless and sanity, the Heavens in their last throes of death." From which point the shit really kicks off: "Advance great legions strong /Crush the gates and enter free /Our lord of Hell must take God's throne… Come on!!"

The storm of the struggle is acted out in every metal cliché known to man, unleashed rapidly, thrown from the speakers and from one point in the stereo mix to another. The end sees the triumph of the underdog: "Martyrs pray disaster for the land of hate and scorn/The Angels curse the day the Antichrist was ever born…" At which point the whole show kicks off again, and begins to fade out.

For 1984, with MTV exploding, the vacuous end of hair metal starting its climb to world domination, a polarised Britain split between Thatcher's economic miracle (big hair, shoulder pads, big pay and city jobs) and the communities built on making things (ignored, depressed, pissed off and jobless) Venom were a true blast of disaffection and determination. Elsewhere the opposition to the monetarist mainstream values looked like the fey and articulate Morrissey or worthies like Billy Bragg. But Venom had an agenda a mile wide and a hotline to Hell, all driven with a ferocity that assumed metal was a weapon, not a musical genre. That coupled with the notion they were partial to a pint and never likely to forget the more mundane hell of the jobless and depressed north east gave the band a sense of reality. Like most of Satan's musical slaves, it was the combination of a monumental message and a mundane sense that this lot were role models that put the lasting satanic power into every groove.

Rant (almost) over! Venom aren't, and never were, about being the most musically ambitious. This is music that makes sense and works decades after it was first unleashed. Even their harshest critics can't take away the number of times this trio, and this album in particular, are cited in the discussion of the development of dark metal into its countless current forms.

This monster still rocks, especially when the Lord of Darkness punches the right buttons on his jukebox.

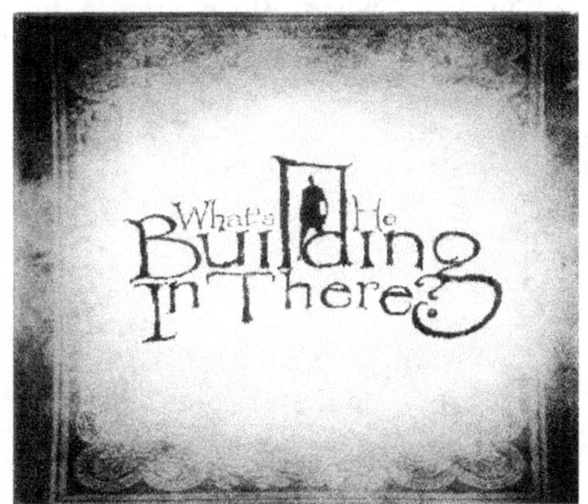

Tom Waits: What's he Building?

Satan sez: Wouldn't you like to know?

Known to many as "What's he Building in There?" this cut from 1999's Mule Variations album is Waits at his most enigmatic and teasing. The singer/ main character watches the goings on at a neighbour's house and wonders "what the hell is he building in there?" The song is obviously addressed to the listener, Waits drops in a fleeting "you see" early into the proceedings so we're all in on the conversation and the questioning. He throws in more open ended conundrums as we go: "what about all those packages?" Musically the sounds of static on a radio as it is tuned, and random noises intrude as a stumbling alternative to percussion and backing instruments, all negotiating a disturbing balance between discordant and perfectly matched, making for a very uneasy but compelling listen. Waits rambles but the more he questions, the less he knows: "I swear to

God I heard someone moaning low... and I keep seeing the blue light of a T.V. show..."

As an insight into paranoia and distrust amongst modern Americans "What's he Building?" is a comfort to Satan and his minions. The whole point here is the lack of any answer. Maybe the singer is paranoid, maybe (as some who seek meanings in songs have suggested) the whole lyric is inspired by the story of the Unabomber. But in every suburban home there may lurk a scheme fuelled by some variant of satanic evil. Enjoy!

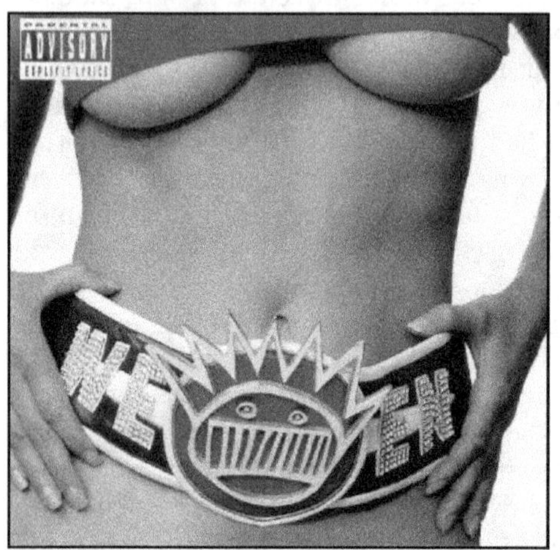

Ween: *The HIV Song*

Satan sez: Kiddie-friendly toe tapping darkness.

Hank Shteamer's book length study of Ween and their work – Chocolate and Cheese – has a lot to say about little more than two minutes of knock about fun, including: "Despite its extreme simplicity and brief length, it's nevertheless one of Ween's most memorable compositions...due to its maniacal central conceit: the juxtaposition of the words 'AIDS' and 'HIV' with whimsical carnival music." That is, pretty much, what you get. A lightweight kinder music melody, the hint of a decent Ween riff creeping in towards the end and spot-colour vocal interjections alternating "AIDS" and "HIV." The vocals are so far forward in the mix that there's no mistaking what they're on about. From which point on the song has lived a charmed and ambiguous life. Released in 1994 when Ween were a hot international act, "The HIV Song" is, if anything, more powerful to generations who know little of the act that spawned it.

It's perfect jukebox material much in the manner of – say – The Doors' "The End" because it can start in the background, the person putting the music on knows what is coming, others in the room may not. Dedicated Doors' fans have enjoyed moments when their big song is playing in the background and they cease talking at the right time, leaving the music to fill the gap and their friends to say, incredulously: "Did he just say: 'Mother, I want to fuck you?'" Well, yeah, he did, and Ween did just chortle "AIDS" and "HIV" to a musical backing you'd more readily expect to soundtrack some colourful children's characters bouncing up and down in a dayglo landscape. There are mash ups of a similar style online, the present authors suggest you visit YouTube and investigate the collision between Thomas the Tank Engine and Limp Bizkit. So, for the feel good vibe with the dubious comedy edge that'd play happily on the Devil's Jukebox, it's got to be Ween.

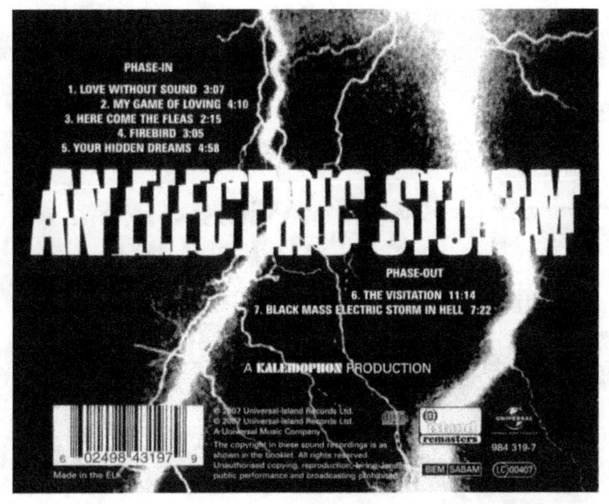

White Noise: Black Mass: An Electric Storm in Hell

Satan sez: Loops, strange percussion, bouncing from speaker to speaker and calling it all a black mass. Honestly darling, that's soo-o-o-o 1969. Hang on, this was done in 1969!

One of the most influential electronic albums of all – Electric Storm (1969) - offers up some satanic fayre of the highest order. White Noise balance on the borderline between proper band and experimental laboratory. Basically, their use of the a brand of electronic instrumentation which would look prehistoric by present standards produced such cutting edge material that the world and his bedroom confined dog has been in awe of the results ever since. At the time White Noise were only a band by default, they had a contract with Island Records and released this, but didn't behave the way bands/groups of the time behaved. In reality the membership included Delia Derbyshire, influential maverick now celebrated for her sterling work with the BBC Radiophonic Workshop. Most bands in 1969 were blokes, with instruments (not electronic gizmos and tape recorders), who, like, got out and gigged.

In later years White Noise's way of working became the standard approach for all manner of experimental noiseniks, many of whom perform occasionally, if at all, on bills in venues like art centres. By contrast, David Vorhaus - who has been in White Noise since 1968 - and his current partner in operations – Mark Jenkins – have been fairly busy and reliable giggers. We digress…

"Black Mass: An Electric Storm in Hell" makes the Devil's grade because it combines the awesome double whammy of genuine mind-fuckery and impressive musical accomplishment, and it does so by being innovative. Sales wise, the parent album did little at the time, but currently sits well beyond 100,000 sales. You can usefully assume a fair tonnage of sales to obsessive types who'd follow several sessions hunched with headphones listening to this stuff with a lifelong quest to acquire noise making machinery and pour their own darkest demons into slabs of psychotic sound. "Black Mass…" offers up a deep dark chant, doom laden electronic chords and then a circular, almost jazzy percussion track before screams and increasingly sharp shards of electronic sound assault your ears and the whole concoction starts ricocheting from speaker to speaker. It builds for nigh on seven minutes before slowly fading. The perfect end to an album that offered one of the strangest sound journeys of its time. As with much of the music on Satan's jukebox you can discuss exactly how satanic this might be.

What's not up for debate is that this example opened the floodgates for a veritable army, including some conspicuous loners of a very dark and deranged nature, and it made these people believe (big time) in their right to get scary and satanic with their musical toys. So, "Black Mass..." was well titled, because it unleashed an electric storm. The current storm gods may well be found on Bandcamp, residing under names like TRANSVESTITEStallion.

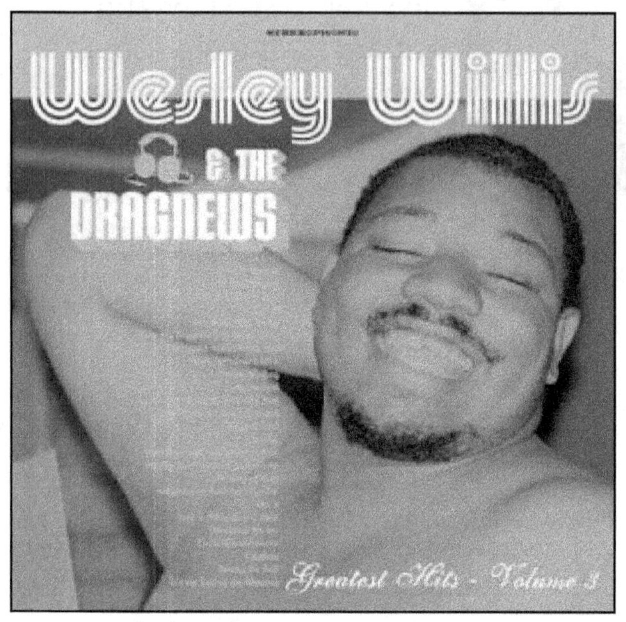

Wesley Willis: *Suck a Pit Bull's Dick*

Satan sez: C'mon gang, we're going for another Hellride.

Willis (1963-2003) had learning difficulties, suffered serious and lasting mental health problems and had a low-profile career as one of outsider music's most reliable and prolific heroes. His death in 2003 came as sites like YouTube were finally making stars of the most unlikely local heroes. Whether such a development in his life would have been a good or bad thing for Willis is debateable. Early in his performing life Willis fronted the Wesley Willis Fiasco, an aptly named outfit with a changing line up who struggled along in a punk rock style as their leader ranted and defined a style that earned the name of "Savant-garde." With the break-up of the band Willis went into solo work, performing alone with a keyboard in front of small crowds roaring him on to ever-increasing gross outs. Officially he cut over 50 albums, usually offering a generous 20 or more tracks. In reality much of this work is an ongoing variation on favoured subject matter; bus routes, fast food, demons, sexual deviance and the need to "rock." Similarly, Willis' songwriting often amounts to a favoured rhythm track, standard chords and allowing himself the space to rant over the backing noises. Willis' own take on his mental problems involved seeing these "Hellrides," a term he coined, as quite literal. He could encounter demons on Chicago buses and his favoured means of battling their threat was to produce a free-form stream of lyrical gross out in the hope of driving them away. "Suck a Pit Bull's Dick" is such a creation, but it has many close relatives in his prodigious output. Progress in Willis' career is marked as much by the subtle changes in sound, caused by his obsessive trading of Technics keyboards for newer and more capable models, as it is by any change in style or content.

For most listeners Willis is rock-n-roll rubbernecking of the highest order, we are in close proximity to the wreckage of the man's mind throughout most of his recorded output. Many of those most motivated to share their love would claim to be curious but the tension in listening to the man revolves around whether we laugh with or at him, or – indeed – what response, exactly, is appropriate. Willis loved to perform and the crowds kept coming, usually roaring in encouragement at the gross out rants and Willis' capacity to work himself up to an emotional peak on stage. Today his output continues to find new fans. If you're a newbie to any of the above we'd highly recommend you start with one of the Greatest Hits compilations to get a real measure of Wesley.

Wesley is mixing it with Satan because Wesley said so, repeatedly. This shit was real to him and that's how he wanted us to take it. So he's on the jukebox.

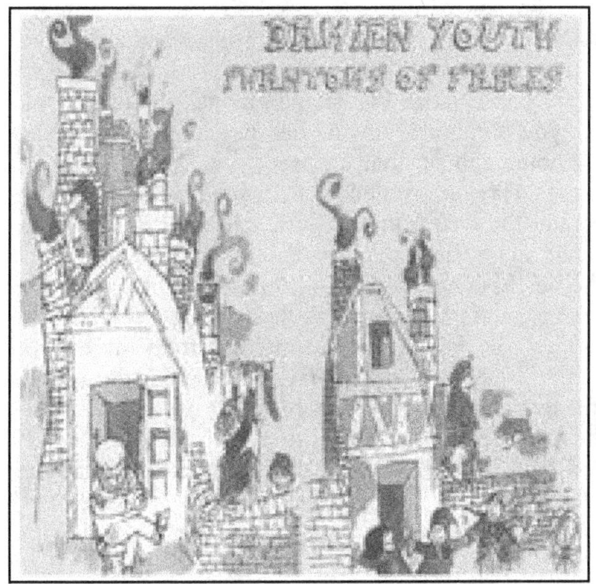

Damien Youth: Charles Earnst

Satan sez: A cool bedtime story.

Damien Youth has been releasing material since the late eighties, originally on cassette only releases and – since the nineties – on CD. His work remains low key to the point of invisible in major market places like Amazon and Bandcamp with much of his available output simply not figuring in the listings. Touchstone artists for Youth are the likes of Robyn Hitchcock (for the dark acid folk tinges and resonance between his voice and the lower notes of the acoustic guitar), Syd Barrett (for the casual eccentricity and lunatic qualities of the lyrics) and acts like Television Personalities (for the sense of using music to break down barriers.) At times Beck might be a yardstick, but Youth's low-key recordings frequently lack the more expensive flourishes of Beck's output and concentrate on building stories rather than soundscapes.

Youth's main style is a cynically twisted dimension of acid folk with an accomplished lyricism in his words. The words are the first entry point to a dark and deeply cynical world, Youth often apparently inhabiting a character but daring you to decide how much of what you hear is his own opinion or experience. Straight faced descriptions of increasingly surreal and demented vignettes give many of his songs an instantly memorable and long-lingering resonance. At his most accessible, on tunes like "Hermaphrodite Jesus," Youth is playing with a dark strain of irony that is smirkingly, if not laugh out loud, funny and he's up there with the likes of Die Antwoord in re-arranging familiar ideas to question what they ever meant in the first place. Like Warren Zevon on songs like "Excitable Boy" Youth sings it straight and tells it crazy, letting the real darkness infect you rather than assault you. A long car journey and a Damien Youth album is a recipe for a slow but steady change in your view of the world.

There's real intelligence at work here, and sometimes the target is a specific swipe at religion. "Bible Hymn" – for example – reworks the grisliest scenes from the Old Testament to sound like a news report from the scene of some current atrocity, all of which leaves the question of how kind and just the God of the Old Testament might be. But Youth's humour is strong and "Bible Hymn" ends when his mobile phone interrupts the song and Youth swears as he answers it.

All of the above is by way of introducing the kind of artist who is likely to be a favourite amongst the Dark Lord and his demonic hordes. "Charles Earnst" fits in with Youth's catalogue but it's on the extreme end, funny only in that you have a confident and able artist, apparently unworried about commercial success, playing with a really disturbing reality. A terminal loner addresses his spoken word piece to Charles Earnst and gradually unfolds a tale of psychotic logic. Telling Earnst: "I owe you one human head" because he has ripped this head from a dried human body, carried it home and gradually dissected it, creating a grisly plaything for increasingly macabre adventures. Having invaded Earnst's brain pan; the "empty theatre of your dreams," the narrator separates the face from the skull and gradually turns the whole thing into a play object so mundane he and a friend play football in the front yard – this is the US so the head is thrown – and the neighbours don't begin to notice anything wrong. The sound effects slowly build and images of authority intrude as the playing with the head goes on even when a "record of Jesus songs" is playing. Later some ash from the head is ground into a carpet on which a preacher subsequently stands. By which point the grudge against society of the narrator, the horrible details he reveals about his early life and his belief that "the living are a minority amongst the dead here" all make sense. At the end of a horribly gripping five minutes of expertly delivered monologue you can assume that once the narrator has access to firearms and someone in the area has pissed him off mightily his name will become known more widely.

Which is, sort of, the point where Damien Youth is concerned. His material is the kind of darkness that surrounds us in the most mundane moments of life and his genius is to make this believable to the point we get it, even if only for the time it takes to listen to one of his tracks.

Chris Rea: The Road to Hell

Satan sez:!!

Nah, only kidding.

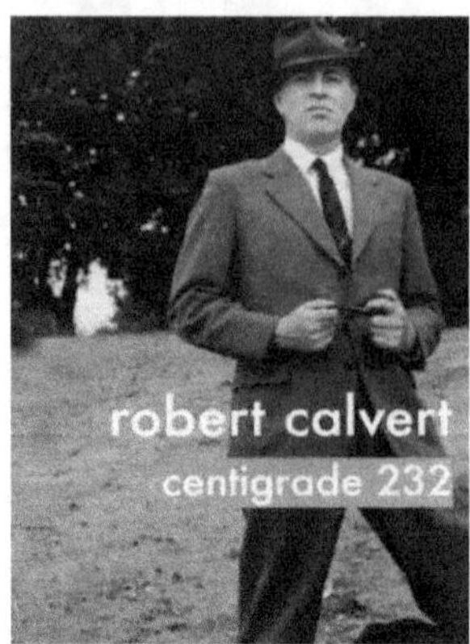

Robert Newton Calvert: Born 9 March 1945, Died 14 August 1988 after suffering a heart attack. Contributed poetry, lyrics and vocals to legendary space rock band Hawkwind intermittently on five of their most critically acclaimed albums, including Space Ritual (1973), Quark, Strangeness & Charm (1977) and Hawklords (1978). He also recorded a number of solo albums in the mid 1970s. CENTIGRADE 232 was Robert Cal vert's first collection of poems.

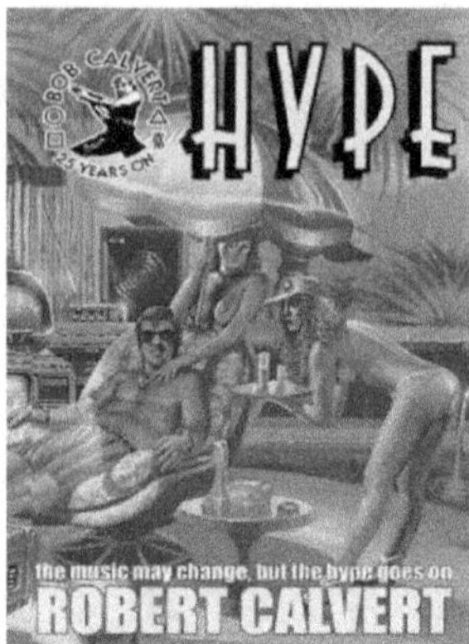

Hype 'And now, for all you speed ing street smarties out there, the one you've all been waiting for, the one that'll pierce your laid back ears, decoke your sinuses, cut clean thru the schlock rock, MOR/crossover, techno flash mind mush. It's the new Number One with a bullet … with a bullet … It's Tom, Supernova, Mahler with a pan galac tic biggie …' And the Hype goes on. And on. Hype, an amphetamine hit of a story by Hawkwind collaborator Robert Calvert. Who's been there and made it back again. The debriefing session starts here.

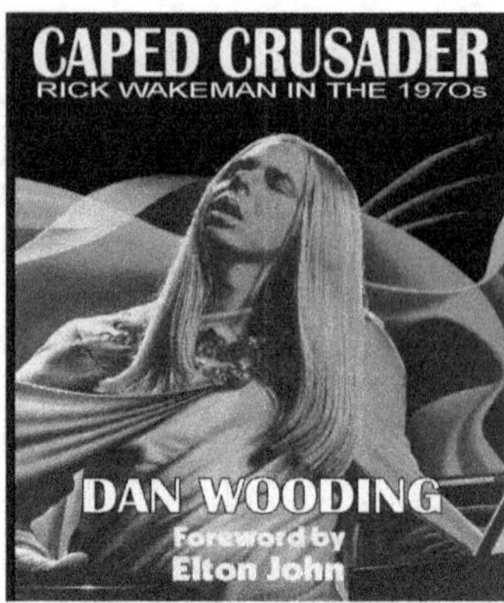

Rick Wakeman is the world's most unusual rock star, a genius who has pushed back the barriers of electronic rock. He has had some of the world's top orchestras perform his music, has owned eight Rolls Royces at one time, and has broken all the rules of com posing and horrified his tutors at the Royal College of Music. Yet he has delighted his millions of fans. This frank book, authorised by Wakeman himself, tells the moving tale of his larger than life career.

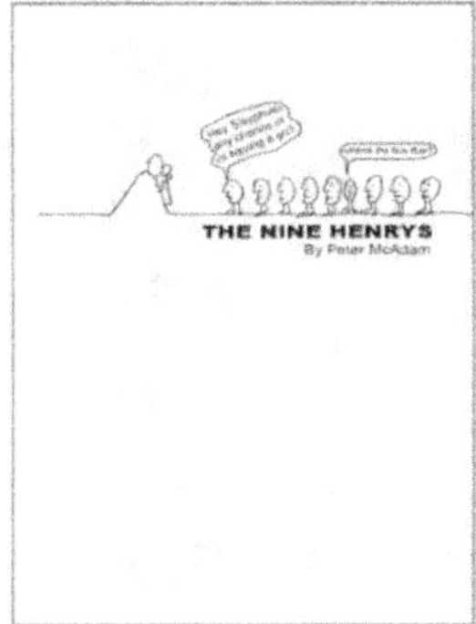

There are nine Henrys, purported to be the world's first cloned cartoon character. They live in a strange lo fi domestic surrealist world peopled by talking rock buns and elephants on wobbly stilts.

They mooch around in their minimalist universe suffering from an existential crisis with some genetically modified humour thrown in.

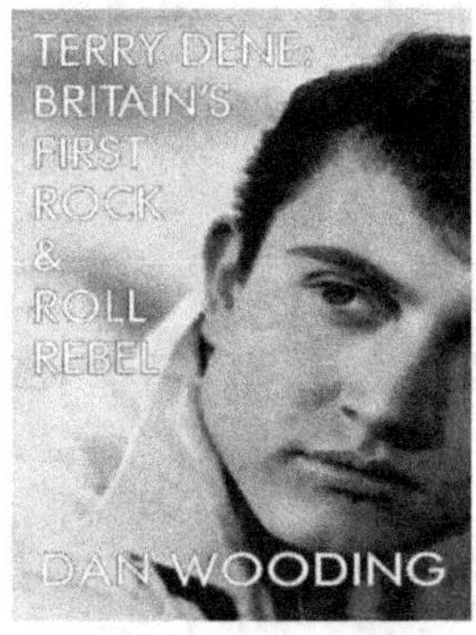

Marty Wilde on Terry Dene: "Whatever happened to Terry becomes a great deal more comprehensible as you read of the callous way in which he was treated by people who should have known better many of whom, frankly, will never know better of the sad little shadows of the past who eased themselves into Terry's life, took everything they could get and, when it seemed that all was lost, quietly left him … Dan Wooding's book tells it all."

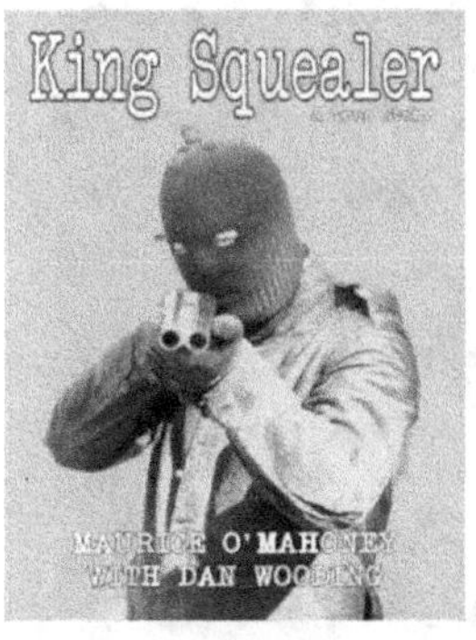

Rick Wakeman: "There have always been certain 'careers' that have fascinated the public, newspapers, and the media in general. Such include musicians, actors, sportsmen, police, and not surprisingly, the people who give the police their employment: The criminal. For the man in the street, all these careers have one thing in common: they are seemingly beyond both his reach and, in many cases, understanding and as such, his only association can be through the media of newspapers or television. The police, however, will always require the services of the grass, the squealer, the snitch, (call him what you will), in order to assist in their investigations and arrests; and amazingly, this is the area that seldom gets written about."

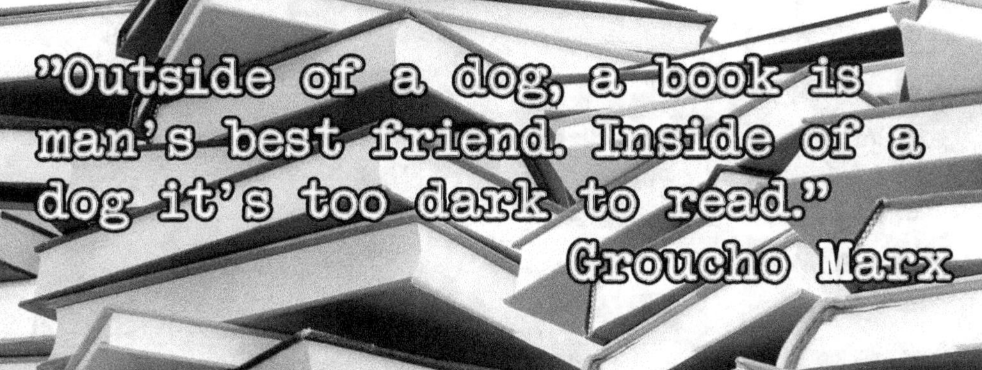

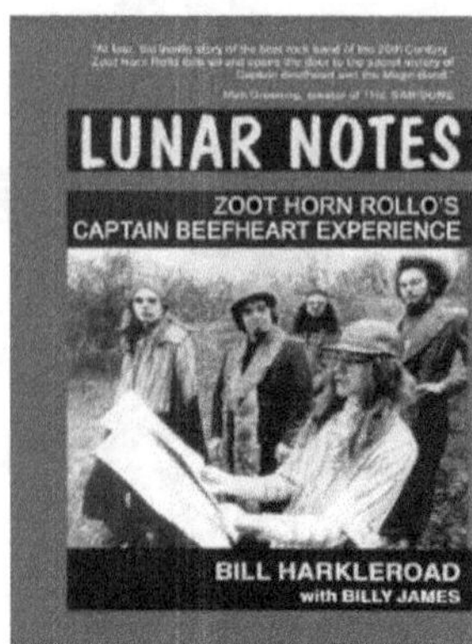

Bill Harkleroad joined Captain Beef heart's Magic Band at a time when they were changing from a straight ahead blues band into something completely dif ferent. Through the vision of Don Van Vliet (Captain Beefheart) they created a new form of music which many at the time considered atonal and difficult, but which over the years has continued to exert a powerful influence. Beefheart re christened Harkleroad as Zoot Horn Rollo, and they embarked on recording one of the classic rock albums of all time Trout Mask Replica - a work of unequalled daring and inventiveness.

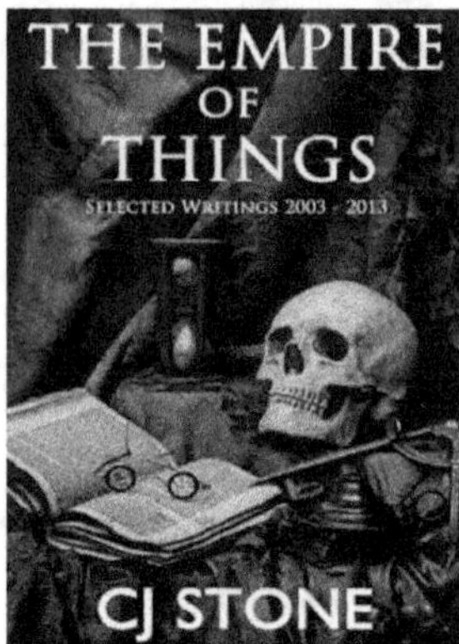

Politics, paganism and .... Vlad the Impaler. Selected stories from CJ Stone from 2003 to the present. Meet Ivor Coles, a British Tommy killed in action in September 1915, lost, and then found again. Visit Mothers Club in Erdington, the best psyche delic music club in the UK in the '60s. Celebrate Robin Hood's Day and find out what a huckle duckle is. Travel to Stonehenge at the Summer Solstice and carouse with the hippies. Find out what a Ranter is, and why CJ Stone thinks that he's one. Take LSD with Dr Lilly, the psychedelic scientist. Meet a headless soldier or the ghost of Elvis Presley in Gabalfa, Cardiff. Journey to Whitstable, to New York, to Malta and to Transylvania, and to many other places, real and imagined, polit ical and spiritual, transcendent and mundane. As The Independent says, Chris is "The best guide to the underground since Charon ferried dead souls across the Styx."

This is is the first in the highly acclaimed vampire novels of the late Mick Farren. Victor Renquist, a surprisingly urbane and likable leader of a colony of vampires which has existed for centuries in New York is faced with both admin istrative and emotional prob lems. And when you are a vampire, administration is not a thing which one takes lightly.

"The person, be it gentleman or lady, who has not pleasure in a good novel, must be intolerably stupid."

Jane Austen

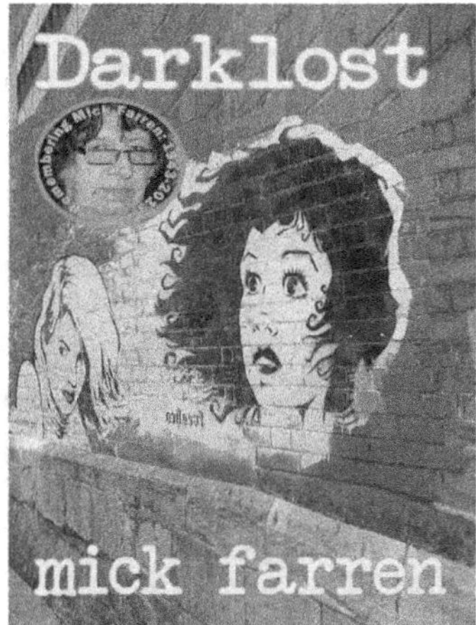

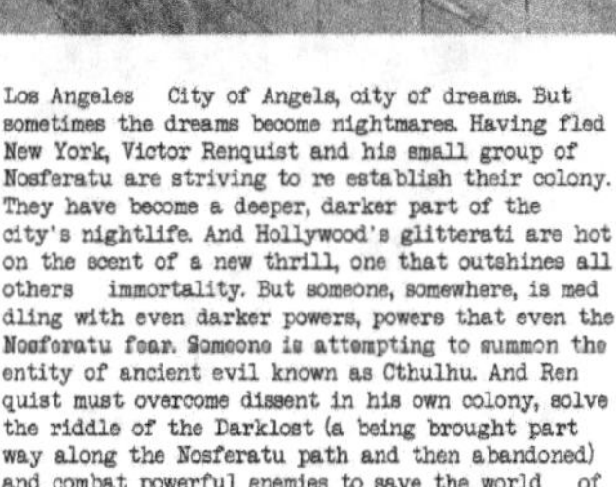

Los Angeles   City of Angels, city of dreams. But sometimes the dreams become nightmares. Having fled New York, Victor Renquist and his small group of Nosferatu are striving to re establish their colony. They have become a deeper, darker part of the city's nightlife. And Hollywood's glitterati are hot on the scent of a new thrill, one that outshines all others   immortality. But someone, somewhere, is med dling with even darker powers, powers that even the Nosferatu fear. Someone is attempting to summon the entity of ancient evil known as Cthulhu. And Ren quist must overcome dissent in his own colony, solve the riddle of the Darklost (a being brought part way along the Nosferatu path and then abandoned) and combat powerful enemies to save the world   of humans!

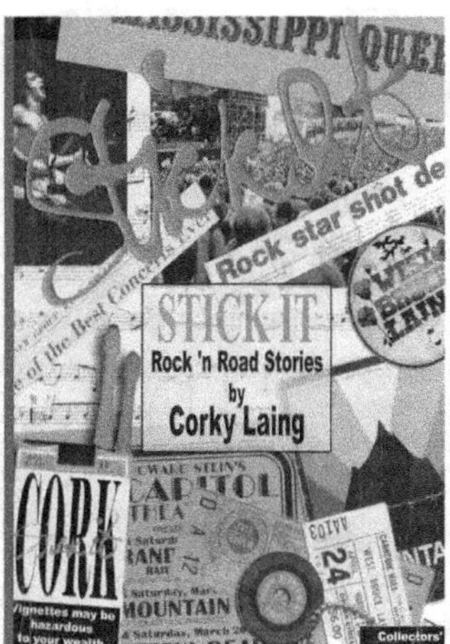

Canadian born Corky Laing is probably best known as the drummer with Mountain. Corky joined the band shortly after Mountain played at the famous Woodstock Festival, although he did receive a gold disc for sales of the soundtrack album after over dubbing drums on Ten Years After's performance. Whilst with Mountain Corky Laing recorded three studio albums with them before the band split. Follow ing the split Corky, along with Mountain gui tarist Leslie West, formed a rock three piece with former Cream bassist Jack Bruce. West, Bruce and Laing recorded two studio albums and a live album before West and Laing re formed Mountain, along with Felix Pappalardi. Since 1974 Corky and Leslie have led Mountain through various line ups and recordings, and continue to record and perform today at numer ous concerts across the world. In addition to his work with Mountain, Corky Laing has recorded one solo album and formed the band Cork with former Spin Doctors guitarist Eric Shenkman, and recorded a further two studio albums with the band, which has also featured former Jimi Hendrix bassist Noel Redding. The stories are told in an incredibly frank, engaging and amusing manner, and will appeal also to those people who may not necessarily be fans of

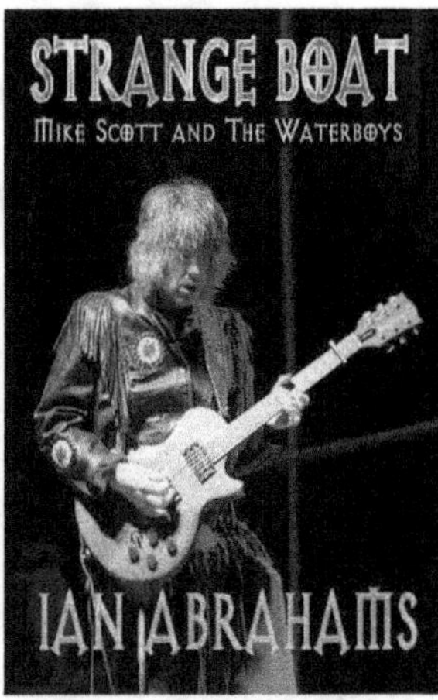

To me there's no difference between Mike Scott and The Waterboys; they both mean the same thing. They mean myself and whoever are my current travel ling musical companions." Mike Scott Strange Boat charts the twisting and meandering journey of Mike Scott, describing the literary and spiritual references that inform his songwriting and explor ing the multitude of locations and cultures in which The Waterboys have assembled and reflected in their recordings. From his early forays into the music scene in Scotland at the end of the 1970s, to his creation of a 'Big Music' that peaked with the hit single 'The Whole of the Moon' and onto the Irish adventure which spawned the classic Fisher man's Blues, his constantly restless creativity has led him through a myriad of changes. With his revolving cast of troubadours at his side, he's created some of the most era defining records of the 1980s, reeled and jigged across the Celtic heartlands, reinvented himself as an electric rocker in New York, and sought out personal renewal in the spiritual calm of Findhorn's Scot tish highland retreat. Mike Scott's life has been a tale of continual musical exploration entwined with an ever evolving spirituality. "An intriguing portrait of a modern musician" (Record Collector).

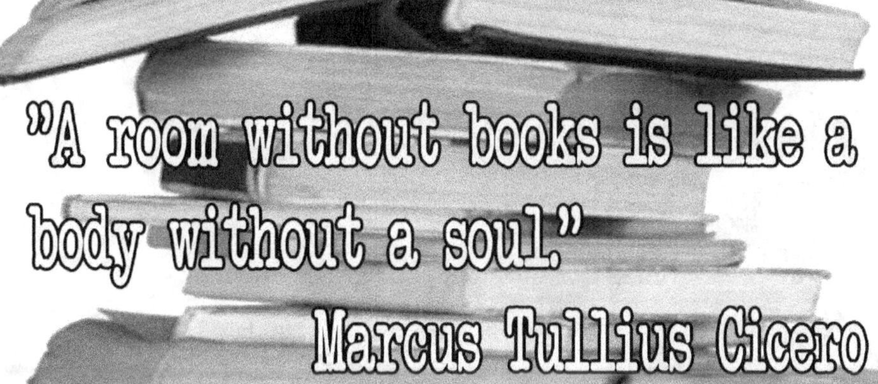

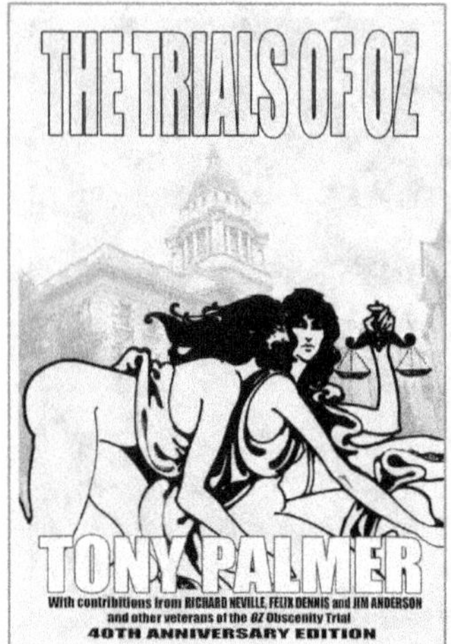

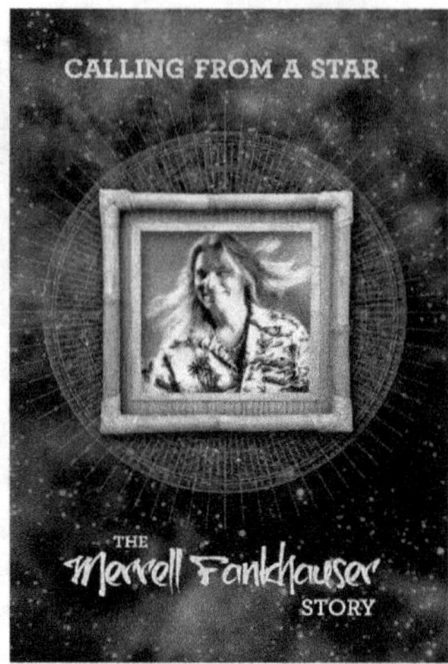

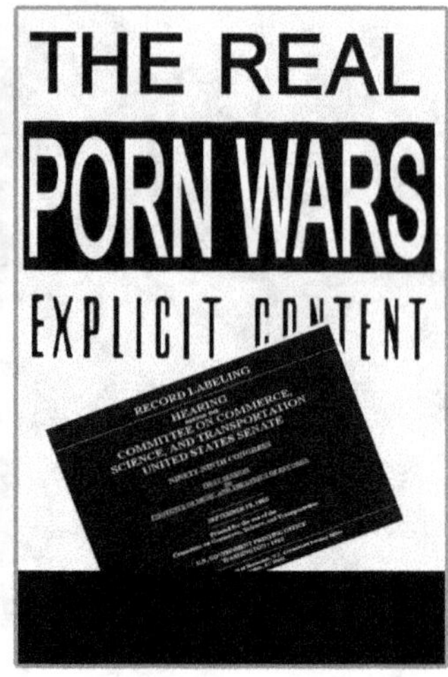

The OZ trial was the longest obscenity trial in history. It was also one of the worst reported. With minor exceptions, the Press chose to rewrite what had occurred, presumably to fit in with what seemed to them the acceptable prejudices of the times. Perhaps this was inevitable. The proceedings dragged on for nearly six weeks in the hot summer of 1971 when there were, no doubt, a great many other events more worthy of attention. Against the background of murder in Ulster, for example, the OZ affair probably fades into its proper insignifi cance. Even so, after the trial, when some newspapers realised that maybe something important had hap pened, it became more and more apparent that what was essential was for anyone who wished to be able to read what had actually been said. Trial and judgment by a badly informed press became the order of the day. This 40th Anniversary edition includes new material by all three of the original defendants, the prosecuting barrister, one of the OZ schoolkids, and even the daughters of the judge. There are also many illustrations including unseen material from Feliz Dennis' own collection...

Merrell Fankhauser has led one of the most diverse and interesting careers in music. He was born in Louisville, Kentucky, and moved to California when he was 13 years old. Merrell went on to become one of the innovators of surf music and psychedelic folk rock. His travels from Hollywood to his 15 year jungle experience on the island of Maui have been documented in numerous music books and magazines in the United States and Europe. Merrell has gained legendary international status throughout the field of rock music; his credits include over 250 songs published and released. He is a multi talented singer/songwriter and unique guitar player whose sound has delighted listeners for over 35 years. This extraordi nary book tells a unique story of one of the founding fathers of surf rock, who went on to play in a succession of progressive and psychedelic bands and to meet some of the greatest names in the business, including Captain Beefheart, Randy California, The Beach Boys, Jan and Dean... and there is even a run in with the notorious Manson family.

On September 19, 1985, Frank Zappa testified before the United States Senate Commerce, Technology, and Transportation committee, attacking the Parents Music Resource Center or PMRC, a music organization co founded by Tipper Gore, wife of then senator Al Gore. The PMRC consisted of many wives of politi cians, including the wives of five members of the committee, and was founded to address the issue of song lyrics with sexual or satanic content. Zappa saw their activities as on a path towards censor ship,and called their proposal for voluntary labelling of records with explicit content "extor tion" of the music industry. This is what happened.

"Good friends, good books, and a sleepy conscience: this is the ideal life."

Mark Twain

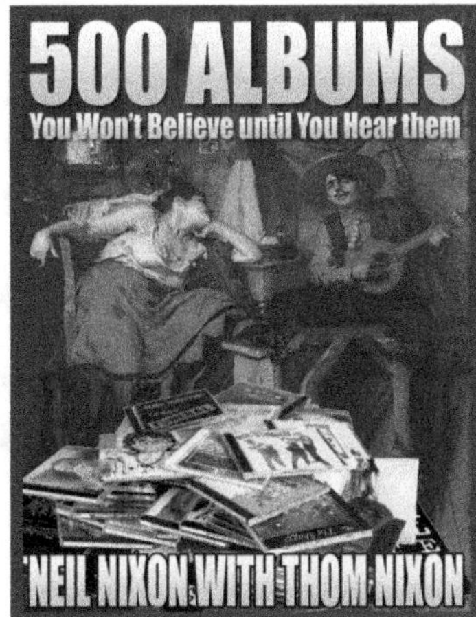

An erudite catalogue of some of the most peculiar records ever made. We have lined up, described and put into context 500 "albums" in the expectation that those of you who can't help yourselves when it comes to finding and collecting music will benefit from these efforts in two ways. Firstly, you'll know you are not alone. Secondly, we hope that some of the work covering the following pages leads you to new discoveries, and makes your life slightly better as a result.

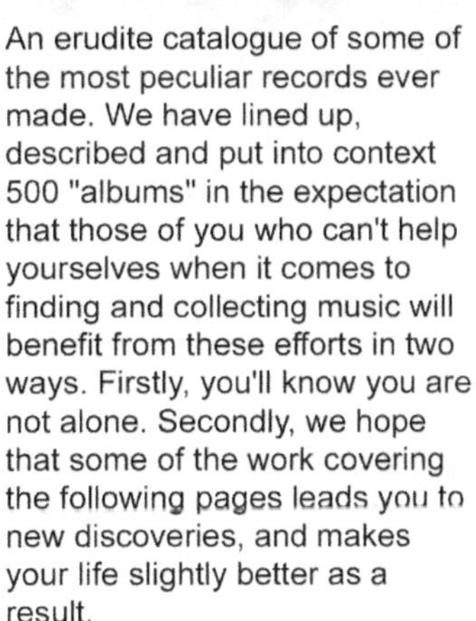

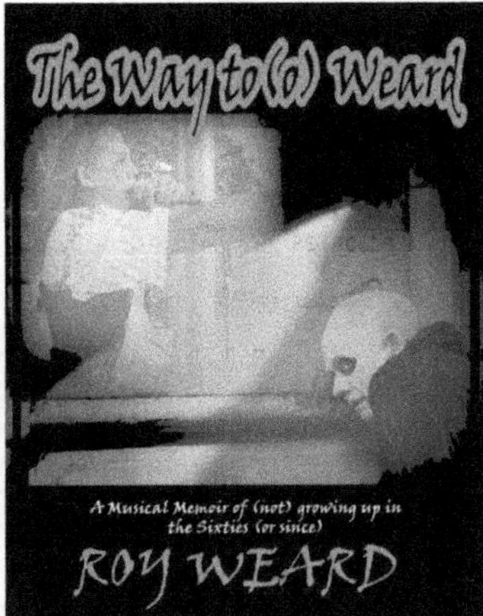

Roy Weard was born in Barking, then a part of Essex, in 1948. He spent most of the mid-sixties through to the mid seventies involved first in folk music and then in the psychedelic hippie scene. He toured with many bands in various capacities from T-Shirt seller to sound engineer, production manager and tour manager. He was involved in several bands of his own, played at many of the iconic free festivals, made three full length albums and two singles, wrote for music magazines, computer magazines and produced copious MySpace blogs. He has lived all over London, spent four years in Hamburg, Germany and finally settled in Brighton where he now resides. He still sings in a rock and roll band, promotes gigs, does a weekly radio show and steadfastly refuses to act his age. This is his story.

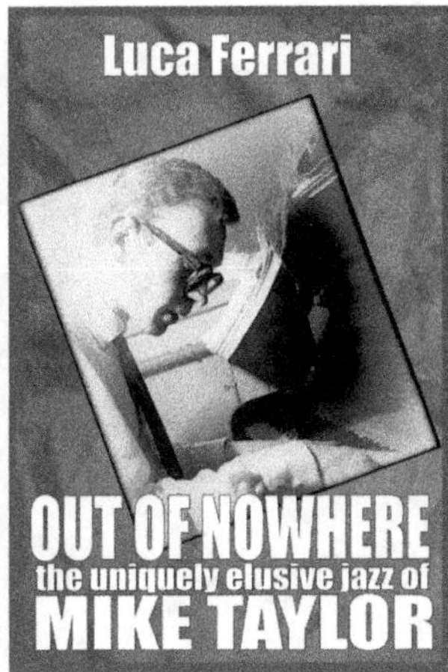

Michael Ronald Taylor (1938 - 1969) was a British jazz composer, pianist and co-songwriter for the band Cream.

Mike Taylor drowned in the River Thames near Leigh-on-Sea, Essex in January 1969, following years of heavy drug use (principally hashish and LSD). He had been homeless for three years, and his death was almost entirely unremarked. This is the first biography written about him.

www.ingramcontent.com/pod-product-compliance
Lightning Source LLC
LaVergne TN
LVHW020052110826
845155LV00021B/69

* 9 7 8 1 9 0 8 7 2 8 5 6 2 *